Praise for George Feifer's previous books:

Moscow Farewell

Moscow Farewell ought to be—and I don't doubt it will be—widely read.
—*New York Times Book Review*

Profoundly compelling.
—*Los Angeles Times*

Feifer's penetrating observations seem to catch the soul of the
Soviet citizen, recording for the West something of the taste of the country
and its people... his narrative style digs like a sharp spade.
—*London Tribune*

Feifer is possibly unique in that he has written a book with
several layers of brilliance. He is that rare being, a passionate and com-
passionately critical observer whose eye and pen run true together.
—*Daily Mail*

Justice in Moscow

The most interesting, perceptive and refreshing book by an
American on life in the Soviet Union since *Time Out of Mind.*
—*Newsweek*

This is an entrancing book.... What it gives is a vivid picture
of courts at work, and therefore, since it is very good reporting,
as sharp a picture of life and people.
—*The Economist*

A truly important work.
—*The Saturday Review*

The most vivid reportage in years.
—*New Statesman*

Message from Moscow

One of the best books about the Soviet Union to be written for
many years. . . . "Observer," as he calls himself, has high sensitivity,
intelligence, humor; he has the talents of a good novelist.
—*New York Review of Books*

Extraordinary. . . . What the book discusses is not the little bit of
Russia that the Russians let most foreigners see . . . [but] the vast
secret life and land kept secret from most foreign eyes.
—*St. Louis Post-Dispatch*

The most perceptive impression we have had through Western eyes for
decades of the feel of life and its changing style in Moscow and Leningrad.
—*The Guardian* (London)

The Girl from Petrovka

One of the memorable heroines of modern fiction . . . .
the only good American novel about modern Russian life.
—*The New Yorker*

Red Files
Secrets from the Russian Archives

George Feifer

NEW YORK

Library of Congress Cataloging-in-Publication Data
Feifer, George
Red files : secrets from the Russian archives / George Feifer.
p. cm.
Includes index.
ISBN 1-57500-081-4 (hard)
1. Communism—Soviet Union—History. 2. Cold War.
3. Soviet Union—Politics and government. I. Title.
HX313.5.F45 1999
320.947—dc21   99-41487
CIP

Photo credits on page 217.

TV Books, L.L.C.
1916 Broadway, Ninth Floor
New York, NY 10019
www.tvbooks.com

Interior design by Rachel Reiss
Manufactured in the United States of America

Contents

*For the generous **Barbara***
with admiration and love

I

Cold War Russia

The Cold War is a manifestation of the epochal clash between Communism and capitalism, two utterly opposed social foundations that are totally different at their core, therefore in everything essential about their practice. Scientific Marxism-Leninism explains why there can be no reconciliation between the two, and why socialism will triumph.

—The incessantly repeated Party line

Eager Soviet political instructor: "What's the difference between capitalism and Communism?"

Bored student: "That's easy, Comrade. Capitalism is the exploitation of man by man."

"Very good, Son, go on!"

"Yes, and socialism is . . . just the opposite."

—Classic gag of the Soviet 1960s and 1970s

UNTIL RECENTLY, NOT ONLY FOREIGNERS but also Russians lacked a clear idea of what had really been happening in crucial facets of Soviet life. The "Red Files" documentary series expanded our knowledge of four of its darker aspects. In the end those areas, like so many others in the socialist Motherland, were about battles: the East-West battles in space, propaganda, sports, and espionage-intelligence. Although Russians knew more about the propaganda they heard and the sports they watched than about their spy and space programs, secrets abounded everywhere in national life. Their uncovering, although so far less than total, was among the goals of the documentaries.

What all Russians *did* know was that life was difficult for them throughout the period examined by the four programs—but not uniformly so. They endured their grueling, hugely taxing Cold War in two distinct periods. The first began within days of Germany's defeat in 1945, its declaration coming the following year when Winston Churchill coined "iron curtain" for the repugnant barrier that had fallen between East and West. Behind it, he warned, central and eastern Europe were subject "not only to Soviet influence but to a very high . . . measure of control from Moscow."

The free world knew little about life behind the curtain during that first stretch of the forty-five-year struggle, but what it did know kept it throbbing with anxiety. While the Western allies rushed to demobilize after World War II, the Soviet Union maintained a swollen army. Several years later, in 1949, it exploded its first atomic bomb. (Espionage by American volunteers, about which the following chapter will reveal unsettling new information, speeded its design and manufacture.) A successful hydrogen bomb followed four years later, just after the first period's end. Westerners in general and Americans in particular were unashamedly frightened.

Few suspected the other side's fear was much greater. Russians knew far more about battle horrors than did blessedly protected, never-invaded Americans. Immeasurable Nazi savagery had just given them a monstrous lesson, as if they needed another one, about war's slaughter and devastation—more of which now appeared imminent. For they couldn't forget, even if their media hadn't reminded them daily, that the United States had a stockpile of atomic weapons and had actually used two, at Hiroshima and Nagasaki. President Harry Truman's grim warning about the new Soviet A-bomb made no mention of the danger the Soviet people saw in the American arsenal. ("I want to talk to you today about what our country is up against," the president addressed the people in September, 1949. "All the things we believe in are in great danger. This danger has been created by the rulers of the Soviet Union.") That was beyond our interest, or perhaps comprehension, yet it was the Russian fear of the American weapon, and of the West in general, that stiffened Stalin's determination to maintain his very powerful conventional military forces after the war. Generally speaking, Americans forgot their own military prowess while waxing anxious at the Soviet armored divisions.

In the late 1940s, the Pentagon began encircling the Soviet Union with air bases for possible—many Russians thought probable—launching of catastrophic bombing strikes against its cities. Each American speech urging that course, every call to nuke the nefarious Communist enemy, made Russian blood run cold, even without the Soviet media's presentation of those battle whoops as evidence of capitalist leaders' ultimate intent. What clearer proof could there be of the ruthless hostility of America's establishment, the warmongering clique of financial-industrial oligarchs who really ran things? The "let's-get-the-Red-bastards" noises continued well after the two superpowers had reached a kind of unspoken agreement about preventing their hostility from erupting into real war. Rehearsing for a television program in 1984, President Reagan quipped that he was pleased to tell his fellow Americans he'd "just signed legislation that will outlaw Russia forever. We begin bombing in five minutes."

The explanation that such appeals for obliterating the enemy were mere jests hardly assuaged the Russian fear. People who kidded about death to a country that had recently suffered some twenty million fatalities (long the conventional figure, although Mikhail Gorbachev claimed the real toll reached twenty-seven million) in the war against Hitler represented a frightening danger not only to Soviet life but also to all humanity.

Dismayed by that attitude and further tensed and muddled by their nation's relentless propaganda, the weary, wary Soviet people perceived the rich and mighty West as determined to snuff out their attempts to build a better life for themselves. They saw imperialist America, the West's belligerent leader, as capable of anything to destroy the social and economic system that was destined, they believed, to replace its own.

In their sealed world into which only "useful" information was admitted, Russians would have been deranged *not* to feel fear, all the more because it lay so deep in the national consciousness. The dangers were not only external. They'd known for centuries that their country was difficult to govern, partly because a stubborn strain of anarchy lay in their bones. The frailty of their instinct for social and political order inclined them to see the huge Soviet territorial expanse as a weakness, not the threat Westerners perceived. All those vast, empty spaces to defend—and with too few means. That heightened the anxiety brewing beneath the surface of their stern state controls: a sense that anything disastrous could happen in their notoriously isolated sixth of the earth's surface. That was all the more true because disastrous things indeed kept happening.

Maybe the inherent Russian resistance to voluntary organization derived from those geographical impediments—the far-flung, "roadless" landmass— to building a modern society. Anyway, too much remained beyond the state's power to cope—even in the late 1940s, under Joseph Stalin, when outsiders saw that power as absolute. That was why the Politburo masters slept badly during both Cold War periods, despite their huge totalitarian apparatus, zealously maintained by the outwardly all-powerful secret services. Mighty but insecure rulers who feared for their position despite command of vast police and military forces were almost the Russian norm. The nation's history had repeatedly confirmed that breakdown was always possible in the sprawling, often "ungovernable" country that lacked the glue of innate social cohesiveness for sustaining order, not to mention the necessary self-discipline and sense of civic responsibility. Russians accepted that structure sometimes had to be imposed on them because they were so little given to creating it themselves.

But harsh rule from above tended to introduce its own anxieties—as under the ferocious Stalin. After World War II, the country's every man, woman, and child felt immense pride in having defeated the Third Reich. (That was another feature common to both Cold War periods. The Soviet people took it on faith that *their* sacrifices had done the impossible on the battlefields and, as we'll see in the chapter entitled "The Soviet Propaganda Machine," they were largely correct.) Although there was also much enthusiasm for rebuilding the war-ravaged country and for building Socialism, another part of the psyche, compartmentalized in a way by no means unique to Russians, felt dread. To one or another degree, Stalin's murderous brutality gripped everyone, even though few knew more than scant details about it.

Their inner trepidation clutched at them despite the seeming paradox that other people—or the same panicky ones at other moments—revered their Supreme Leader and Teacher, Hope of Mankind. Although difficult for outsiders to imagine, many Russians sustained their veneration for the Great Dictator even while the secret police were targeting their neighbors and colleagues, even though they themselves went to sleep every evening dreading a midnight knock on their door. Still, idealism and loyalty surpassed almost everyone's fear.

Whether Stalin was clinically deranged or "merely" barbarously cunning and cruel, he brought huge upheaval. In fact, some scholars call his reign a revolution from above or a war against the country and the original Bolshevik Party. State personnel were shot in droves, never mind that many had only recently been awarded their positions. Their places were taken by eager new cadres, chiefly hastily educated workers and peasants. While opening up opportunities, that policy also expanded the fear. Its scope was illustrated by the fate of Mikhail Tukhachevsky, the country's ablest, most esteemed military leader.

Tukhachevsky was among the country's five field marshals. Stalin's purges physically eliminated three in a snap of his blunt fingers. Fourteen of sixteen army generals—all devoted patriots, but quickly condemned and executed on preposterous charges—swelled the ranks of the victims. All full admirals and most members of the Supreme War Council were also shot, and political leaders fared no better. Some 70 percent of the Communist Party's Central Committee members and candidates in 1934 were ousted or killed, even though Stalin himself had chosen many of them. Of the 1,827 delegates to the seventeenth Party Congress that year, a skeleton cadre of 35 would attend the eighteenth, five years later.

Those numbers—a little hint of a murderous rampage that still taxes the imagination—are easily documented. Less so are the mood and habits they generated.

Soviet military academies proudly displayed portraits of the acutely foresighted Tukhachevsky, who was reequipping the Soviet armed forces with modern machinery and strategies. (Among other things, the innovative chief of staff supported early research in Soviet rocketry, which is discussed in Chapter IV, "The Secret Soviet Moon Mission.") But when he was arrested in May 1937—the worst of the purge years, when he happened to be in his strategic and organizational prime—all traces of his presence were instantly expunged, beginning with the portraits that had proudly hung on foyer walls. Rectangles of less faded paint in their places announced the terrifying news. Instructors and students trembled, but did not mention their missing hero: not a whisper, even to friends. Anxious as they were to learn why their inspiring commander had fallen, they averted their eyes from the specter of his sudden elimination, like characters in a surrealist play. Such did the terror applied at the top mangle even the state's most accomplished and loyal servants.

Some of its facets were relaxed during World War II, when the morale of the country seemingly doomed to defeat was fed a supplement of traditional Mother Russia patriotism. But terror returned at the war's end, and although it never became as appalling as in the 1930s, it lasted until Joseph Stalin died in 1953. After that, the grisly scenes in the military academies and other Soviet institutions were not repeated. Marked changes in Soviet society made the second, much longer Cold War period qualitatively different.

With that incessantly dominant struggle of intimidation and nerves still sundering the planet and channeling minds, most of the West feared the Soviet Union as before, still seeing it as relentlessly dismal and profoundly threatening. Actually, however, the dictatorship reformed itself after Stalin's departure. Political, legal, and temperamental changes made life significantly better and freer, although still within rigid limits set from above.

Denunciations for "counterrevolutionary activity," that easy means of ingratiating oneself and/or eliminating enemies, lost their deadly power. Dread of the dead-of-night arrests and executions for no reason—or perhaps that *was* Stalin's reason, since it swelled his terror—subsided and expired as those methods were renounced. Even the KGB, which had shot so many innocents in cold blood and still appeared omnipotent to most Westerners, usually played by the rules. Repugnant to begin with, those rules were broken for loathsome imprisonment and torture, but in rare cases only. The outright killing of an opponent of Soviet rule was even rarer—especially in contrast to the mass liquidations in certain of our Central and South American "partners" during the same late Cold War time. (If the Soviet Union of the mid-1950s through the 1980s had murdered even a small fraction of the innocent men and women eliminated by "friendly" governments in Argentina, Honduras, Guatemala, and other countries, our national scream would have rent the universe.) General Pinochet's Chile, for example, was of course no threat to us, but the point here is that our view was distorted by focusing on the far fewer Soviet violations of human rights while four thousand Chileans disappeared and ten times that number were tortured.

In the second Cold War period, the lethal Stalinist suspicions were gone. Stifling as the networks of controls remained—the censorship, propaganda, prohibitions, and countless restraints, from soul-choking to pathetically stupid—they were the products of recognizably normal behavior, as opposed to homicidal paranoia's thrashings. The rulers no long "made war on their own people," as some analysts characterize the 1930s; they only tried to control them, avoiding violence if they could. In an old story that echoed throughout the gulag's vast landmass, a veteran prisoner asks a recent arrival for what he was sentenced to his twenty-five years. "For nothing," comes the fatalistic reply. "Bullshit, pal. For nothing, you get *ten* years." That people were no longer killed or imprisoned for nothing sums up the post-Stalinist period's cardinal political and emotional reforms.

Of course, dissidents were persecuted, sometimes odiously. But they were a few handfuls of the Soviet millions, even if the American media focused on them as if moving their curiosity elsewhere would have required impossible energy. Besides, those heroes, martyrs, and oddballs had done something not merely prohibited but also conspicuously daring and dangerous. By definition, dissidents openly *dissented,* criticizing the regime's methods and, in some cases, challenging its legitimacy. But the 99-plus percent who did no such thing, even those who were becoming inwardly contemptuous of Soviet rule, rarely tiptoed around in fear of police repression.

By the 1970s, you still had to give rankling lip service to socialist dogma, but if you weren't willing to sacrifice your conscience to your ambition, you didn't *have* to join the scoundrels who, for example, got juicy perks for broadcasting propaganda. You could keep your mouth shut, as all good people did. The rule was that if you did that, you could believe what you wanted and feel quite secure. Now you could also read some of the prohibited material you wanted to—if you took the considerable pains to obtain the precious manuscripts produced by underground typewriters of *samizdat* ("self-publishing") or the books smuggled in from abroad, and then kept the illicit or criminal pages under your pillow. During breaks in jamming foreign short-wave radio stations, you could hear more of what you wanted. You could certainly think what you wanted and even occasionally voice it, if you chose your listeners carefully. Generally speaking, possession of contraband "anti-Soviet" literature would be used against you only if you were already in trouble for a public display of resistance to the established order. It was something like not wearing a seat belt: you got nailed—in the Soviet case, nailed shockingly hard—only if you were stopped for an overt violation.

This is not to suggest that there was a shortage of exceptions or that the colossal Soviet bureaucracy made no mistakes or offered no opportunities for sadists. It's also not to imply that all fear disappeared. Maya Plisetskaya, the Bolshoi Theater's leading ballerina in the 1970s, gave me a lesson about that during the course of my interviews with her for an article. She was not very cleverly watched, sometimes by "friends" who "just happened" to pop into her dressing room and relatively grand apartment when I was there. (What it had taken on both our parts to permit her to invite me to dinner at home!) Nevertheless, Plisetskaya took advantage of a visit to the bathroom by one such watcher to denounce the government, whose latest abomination was including her in a group of prominent Soviet Jews who publicly protested Israeli behavior. The "sons of bitches" had done that without consulting or even informing her.

Plisetskaya had seen her name signed to the typical statement of supposed moral outrage in that very morning's *Pravda*. Her actual feelings were roughly opposite, and she became furious as she described what she considered, quite rightly, the *real* outrage. While she shrieked, I tried to understand how she could have been so callously used in light of what Graham Greene had called "the untorturable" caste of Soviet citizens, meaning those whose worldwide reputations protected them against the usual humiliations. "But Maya Mikhailovna," I ventured. "I thought you were a member of a small group who had nothing to fear."

"Simpleton! I'm sick to death of foreigners' naïveté!" Then she modulated her snarl because our KGB sentinel was returning from the bathroom. "There's no such 'caste' in this country. Brezhnev fears Podgorny and Podgorny fears Brezhnev; and they both fear Kosygin." Those were the current Politburo chiefs.

Our dinner resumed. The rare luxury of fresh vegetables in winter further testified to the world's premier ballerina's place among the country's super rich and famous. But it was clearer than ever that she had fewer rights than infants born that day in London, where I was living.

I KNEW FEW PEOPLE AS ANGRY AS THE impulsive Plisetskaya at being a serf. For most, other aspects of Soviet life served to help acceptance of life's seemingly fated boundaries. For one thing, the majority still believed that as a whole, life was better in the Soviet Union than in other countries. (Everything that follows about hardships would seem to contradict such beliefs, but they held them nevertheless, for reasons that will emerge in later pages.) For another, the majority were enriched by the "human dimension," specifically the closeness, tenderness, and sense of sharing that often accompany struggle.

Those feelings were not always limited to friends and family members. During the course of my Russian stays, I once spent an evening with the editor of *Literary Gazette*, a particularly objectionable newspaper because its considerably greater subtlety than most gave many of its intellectual and high-intelligentsia readers the illusion that now, at last, they were getting the whole truth. In purely personal terms, however, the cleverly manipulative editor was a warm, gracious, charming spinner of *connections* between us. When we left our restaurant at a late hour and strolled down a nearly empty street, he put his arm in mine as if we were old friends, two small fry whose souls understood each other and had to band together in a difficult world. Russian hardships—starting not with the KGB but with the continental emptiness and cold—may have been what prompted most people to reach for each other when they walked in pairs or threes. The comfort of physical contact was almost always sought, and spiritual varieties often went with it.

Contrast that with the editors of the London publications for which I wrote when I returned from my Moscow trips. Those incomparably more broadly educated and honest English gentlemen wouldn't dream of taking my arm, let alone talking "deep" with me about private matters. Whenever I was living in Russia, their newspapers and magazines, on the rare occasions when I was lucky or crafty enough to obtain a copy, seemed to beam down from some higher civilization on another planet. Amid the crude warping of Soviet publications, British periodicals were a beacon of toleration for opposing views and respect for readers who would make up their own minds about difficult issues. They seemed the very voice of reason, testimony to one of the most precious human achievements—and yet, as I said, the editors themselves tended to be distant in comparison to their Russian counterparts. Maybe it was only the Russian darkness that heightened the glow of personal closeness; but there it was, making the days more endurable and, sometimes, more satisfying.

Not that my days or nights were full of *only* good feelings. One often felt the opposite kind of glow, a kind of black despair. Russians, with their hard lives and stunted political development, sometimes seemed ready to tear out each other's throats over minor matters. Besides, personal warmth had been shown to be no guarantee against atrocities, as in the case of Nazi killers who lavishly loved their children and pets. Still, a certain intimate toleration of weakness and eccentricity warmed the cold Soviet air, as if we were in all this—the human condition—together. What weight this should be given in political and social analysis is unclear, but it did make some of daily life more attractive than in the equivalent circles in the West, despite a consciousness of the KGB presence.

A NETWORK OF INFORMANTS MADE IT necessary to watch your words with people whom you couldn't utterly trust. (I learned not to introduce one Russian friend to another, since both would inevitably assume the *other* one must be a snitch; otherwise, why would he risk consorting with a foreigner?) The KGB watched the vast majority of the people largely in collective ways, partly through the personnel departments of factories and offices, partly by stationing officers in civilian dress on downtown streets of the major cities. It took a far keener individual interest in people with heightened profiles, including most foreigners. Special attention went to those who exhibited traits—including attachment to Russia—that might open them to exploitation. A middle-aged woman on a tour from England in the mid-1970s was placed in that category after she, surprisingly, set up an easel in Red Square and began painting St. Basil's cathedral. While the happy tourist wielded her affectionate brush, a charming Russian man with excellent English approached. One thing led to another (that often happened very quickly in Russia, even when not on orders), and the two soon found themselves in the woman's nearby hotel room. Soon after that, she was confronted with glossies of herself coupling with the Russian, while a less attractive colleague oozed fraudulent sympathy. He assured his weeping mark that her husband never need see the photographs if only she'd help the Russia she loved defend itself against its evil enemies. "We'd never ask you to do anything active. Just to let us know when warlike measures are being taken against *us*."

I suppose it was inevitable that the KGB would try to enlist me, too. I had a relatively wide circle of Russian friends and obviously liked them more openly than most visitors did; I even liked some aspects of their life, despite everything. Of course, that was also reason to mistrust me: the security cadres had a horror of Americans presuming they could move around more or less freely. Anyway, I provided the opening for the KGB's hardest recruitment effort when I foolishly called on the editor of a major magazine that had published an article about my supposed sinister anti-Soviet activities during previous visits, an article that really amounted to resentment over my knowing too many Russians and tending to talk too openly with them. Astounded at first that I had actually appeared in his office to complain about the phony "exposé," the editor regained his composure and asked for time to investigate, promising to get back to me. I was surprised when he did—until I understood why. His call was an invitation to a lavish lunch in a good (by Soviet standards) restaurant, where he proposed we talk things out. Once at the prover-bial groaning table, however, he began toasting *Mir i Druzhba* ("Peace and Friendship"). It wasn't long before the interest of one of my fellow diners, all of whom I'd assumed were from the magazine, became clear. Over the fol-lowing years, the KGB toad kept inviting and inviting me to dinners in private rooms equipped with recording equipment that even he acknowledged during one of our last disgusting meetings. While I tried to fake my composure by choking down some food, he kept enlightening me about my moral duty to fight evil by helping expose the tricks of *Mir i Druzhba*'s imperialist enemies.

Why didn't I tell the ugly bastard to go screw himself? Because he had something on me: my wish not to be expelled from the country and barred from returning. That predicament gave me a particle of on-the-skin insight into the behavior of many Soviet citizens when they had business with the KGB—such as the watchdog at Maya Plisetskaya's apartment. That essentially pleasant journalist would have much preferred to have refused his assign-ment if he could have avoided penalties. But he had a good job, with legiti-mate access to foreigners, and through them a chance to acquire the English suits he fancied (which were enough to make him a personality amid the So-viet rumple). That was probably what the KGB had on *him*. It had something on everyone when it needed it.

How much you cooperated, how far you bent, depended on your tempera-ment and circumstances. But no one apart from the sublimely virtuous and/or marvelously brave escaped without making *some* compromise. The American commentators who denounced the Soviet citizenry for bowing to that pressure had a lot in common with, or were actually the same people as, those who, with no personal knowledge of war's suffering, urged the United States to take on the Soviet Union. Distance makes knowledge of how to behave in onerous sit-uations much easier to acquire. From the inside, no one who dealt with the Soviet dictatorship in one way or another emerged with clean hands.

Still, the kind of pressure felt by the brilliant Plisetskaya and even by tar-geted foreign visitors was an exception to the rule that Soviet people who rep-resented little opportunity for intelligence gains weren't molested. It wasn't that such exceptions were rare. It can't be repeated too often that the KGB could cast its nets anywhere, choosing and plucking whom it wanted. Still, that didn't preoccupy the majority during the course of their daily lives. A sense of oppression—of the burdens of hard times and the emergency meas-ures needed to alleviate them—always lurked in the mind; but hard times were nothing new to Russia, and they seemed to come more from the severe climate and the legacy of living on a geographical and intellectual periphery than from the KGB. A nasty beast lay out there in the ominous background, and the Committee of State Security bragged that it never slept, but you were okay if you didn't disturb it.

WHAT *DID* PREOCCUPY THE VAST MAJORITY OF Soviet people—even in the country-side, where they had so little to buy, sell, or swap—was finding a splash of something colorful, virtually anything, to relieve the boundless surface gloom. That yearning, on top of the shortages, shoddiness, and privations, created a huge black market—which generated another kind of fear, distinctly less acute but also much more pervasive.

The "second economy," as the immense aggregation of unauthorized and forbidden transactions came to be called, grew and grew in scope and impor-tance. It necessarily prompted a huge departure from the codes of proper so-cialist behavior, with accompanying ridicule of the Soviet consumer economy and cynicism about the future. It also caused outright lawlessness, since most of the items for illegal sale or trade had been filched from the legitimate econ-omy's factories, farms, warehouses, offices, trucks, and official cars (from the latter two, chiefly in the form of siphoned gasoline). By the 1960s, few people considered swiping from the state to be real stealing. After all, everyone did it—and didn't the plants, depots, railroad cars, and storage facilities belong to The People anyway?

The wheeling and dealing became so widespread that it remained under-ground only to the extent that it had to be kept quiet. Powerful pressure built up to violate goody-goody Communism's stultifying laws and lessons. Unless you wanted to dine on inferior macaroni or runty potatoes, a great deal of what you did—what you *had* to do to escape the depressing diet and garb of the incessantly praised but eternally deprived masses—was immoral by Com-munist standards, if not actually criminal to one degree or another. If you fan-cied a more or less good chicken for Sunday dinner, you often had to resort to some form of illicit barter or bribery, or of unlawful machinations to ob-tain extra cash for the luxury. The daily nitty-gritty of consumer satisfaction made you tremble more than you wanted to, even if you were blessed to have an American passport in your pocket.

Still, you and your Russian friends were safe from grave retribution unless you involved yourself in something like distributing copies of dissidents' works or otherwise supporting them, most hazardously by providing "anti-Soviet slander" (read: accurate and damning information) to foreign journal-ists. The sprinkling of Russian idealists and misfits who fought the regime in those ways, single-handedly or in secret alliances, risked everything. Everyone else had only to be very prudent not to step over the critical line of making public any opposition to the precepts or practices decreed by the Communist rulers. And, of course, to keep careful tabs on their pets.

When the very clever parrot of a Moscow intellectual escapes through an open window one terrible day, its frenzied owner scours the city in vain, then dashes to KGB headquarters.

"But why are you reporting this?" asks a busy officer.

"Because in case the little devil shows up, I want you to know I don't share his political opinions."

The death of Moscow Zoo's beloved elephant propels its keepers to a famous biology institute. How long, they ask, will a replacement take to produce? *Two years?* But that's too long, we need a new main attraction in a hurry!" Another institute's genetic engineers promise to cut the wait to two months, but that's also too long, so the keepers turn to the KGB. "Come back next week," headquarters reassures. Seven days later, the keepers are indeed there, and are led to a basement, where a whimpering rabbit is surrounded by two guards. "Just don't hit me again. Yes, I *am* an elephant!"

The far looser control—still repulsive to Westerners, but no longer mad or murderous—greatly enriched the treasury of such jokes. A few brave souls had told them even under Stalin. In one, the Great Dictator commands the printing of yet another postage stamp to honor himself—and turns furious when he hears the stamps aren't sticking, despite his orders to use the best materials. An immediate investigation is ordered. A quivering commissar soon reports to his terrible boss: "Comrade Stalin, Sir, the stamps are excellent and so is the glue. It's the damn people; they're spitting on the wrong side."

But if whispered jokes were acts of reckless courage before 1953, they later sprouted much more abundantly than, say, collectivized agriculture's forever feeble crops. Hardly an hour of dinner parties in the cities—usually informal gatherings for gorging and schmoozing, often in the cramped kitchen— passed without the telling of a dozen gags.

Together with the mass of *anekdoti*, as they're called, the disappearance of terror enabled great diversity to bloom. Naturally, the Soviet people had always been diverse, even in the grip of Stalinism. However, large numbers were too frightened to stick out in any way or to say anything faintly controversial, even to their children. If the old saying "Wise men stifle their wisecracks" ever fully applied, it was then. But with that fear largely gone, all sorts of characters emerged. Perhaps because most Russians are less conformist and inhibited than Westerners in their personal lives, as opposed to their political ones, many of those "types" seemed quintessential: more quixotically idealistic, hopelessly nerdy, old-world gracious, or crudely Rambo, as the case may be, than their counterparts elsewhere.

That aspect of the Soviet scene startled me during my first visit in 1959. My "discovery" continued during a year of graduate study at Moscow State University, which followed in the early 1960s. Why was I, a supposedly budding Soviet specialist, surprised to find such a variety of personalities in the tumble of daily life? To hear such a tangle of thoughts, dreams, passions, and complaints that had nothing whatever to do with Communism? And the steady stream of those deprecating jokes?

A local Party official questions a grizzled old-timer. "Say, brother, what will you do when Communism finally comes and you can have anything you want?"

"I'm going to get myself an airplane," comes the unhesitating reply.

"A what? What would a geezer like you do with an airplane?"

"Fly to America for some potatoes."

That kind of levity surprised me, too. My academic training, long on the ins and outs of the Communist system and much too short on the human dimension, had done little to dispel the pervading American image of Russians as robotlike drudges dedicated to achieving higher output at their lathes in order to fulfill the Five-Year Plan for the Motherland. Among the Russians I knew, the truth gradually struck me as being nearly the opposite.

By the 1970s, the majority came closer to goof-offs than heroes of socialist labor. Getting the job done for its own sake, as opposed to fulfilling some personal call if and when it came, was relatively rare. When you came to think of it, why would Russians need so many rules and restrictions if they had a normal (in Westerners' measurement) store of *self*-discipline? Without an internal drive to achieve, as opposed to half-heartedly meeting targets set by the state, most Russians did what they could to goldbrick and duck away to their private interests. An eye-opening number were willing to drop everything for a day of feasting, fishing, or picking mushrooms. In short, the attitude toward the job was usually cavalier, if not derisive. And nothing could have been more wrong than puritan America's conviction that the Soviet Union was much *more* puritan because all those robots weren't interested in anything except further beefing up their state's power—or, if they *were* interested, were too regimented to do much about it, à la George Orwell's *1984*.

Vanya's not working in the fields but lolling in the hay loft while Manya, the buxom milkmaid, is sneaking milk from their collective farm's best cow.

"Hey, Manya, come on up here."

"No I won't. I know what you want."

"But why not? We'll have a good time, you and me."

"Fresh, I said *no*."

"But Manichka, we'll . . . "

"Stop," she sighs, now climbing the ladder. "You talked me into it, you bastard."

Russians liked that story for reflecting the truth about the general ease and quickness of sexual relations that lay beneath the propaganda and required chastity in public. But aren't I exaggerating the looseness of personal conduct? Wasn't I mistaken about the variety of types? What about the seas of glum faces that washed the proletarian cities? What about the awful Soviet artificiality at diplomatic and other official meetings? Yes, Russians were often stiffer than plywood, and miserably tedious too, in formal situations. Nearly all donned their public facades of rigid political correctness together with their Sunday best. Besides, they could indeed appear forbiddingly colorless and conformist in crowds, especially when they plodded through the slush in their setting of such urban monotony that one craved some decadent neon. But when you got to know a member of those "faceless masses," he or she was likely to seem larger than life, and more spontaneous in personal behavior than their Western counterparts.

The bleached-blonde hussy in the Moscow restaurant seemed the very picture of her type. So did the studious young physicist, the go-getting young Communist, and the rabid soccer fan. Some K.G.B. underlings, like the bastard assigned to me, leered and barked like thugs—and turned even more menacing when they tried to pass themselves off as your good friends, concerned only to advance your best interests. Other officers were highly intelligent and relatively well informed about the world through their access to otherwise banned information. Some, like their predecessors in the tsarist secret police, wanted to diminish dissent by *easing* restrictions.

If you had too little time to meet such types and appreciate their dissimilitude, an hour in a People's Court would have given you an idea of the variety of characters, in both senses. Communism claimed to eliminate all basic conflicts, but one courtroom is hearing a dispute between two former friends accusing each other of plagiarism. Across the corridor, a gynecologist is being tried for allegedly taking lewd advantage of his female patients; farther down, couples are being divorced, most with hardly a frown. (The real trauma will come during separate procedures for dividing their shriveled allotments of living space, often by dropping a curtain between them in the sorry rooms where they must remain.) In another courtroom, an obviously needy worker in a wheelchair is claiming compensation from his factory, represented by three of Soviet society's fat cats: relatively well suited managers and lawyers. And on the second floor, siblings are angrily suing each other about their inheritance from a recently deceased public figure—a Communist Party elder, no less. (Inheritance taxes were very low.) The conflicts in claims, outlooks, stories, schemes, and temperaments represent almost the full span of human personalities and interests.

During those later Cold War decades, Soviet military prowess was greater than before, even without the mighty exaggerations by the CIA and other interested parties including, of course, the Kremlin itself. Partly because of that, partly because the overwhelming portrayal of Russians was woefully one-dimensional, America's fear hardly declined. At each return from a visit to Moscow, even those during which I'd run up against some of the ugliest aspects of Soviet rule, I wondered whether a touch of paranoia wasn't also affecting us good guys. (I didn't know then that we stored no less than twelve thousand nuclear weapons in twenty-three foreign countries and five American territories, a fact just revealed in declassified Pentagon documents.) My point, at the risk of laboring it, is that Russia after 1953 was a very different country internally than it had been under Stalin: far more diversified, often messy and chaotic.

That was true even though, or perhaps just because, it had become highly conservative politically. The Motherland of Socialism was now as revolutionary as a papal state. It tolerated nothing remotely radical except for its propaganda slogans, of which most people became so weary that they didn't hear the ceaseless noise pumped into their ears or see the ocean of ritualized huzzahs for the Communist Party waved before their eyes. Especially after 1956, when Nikita Khrushchev revealed some of Stalin's crimes, Natasha and Ivan wanted no more upheavals. What they did want was a piece of the action by such all-but-universal means as pilfering from their factories, cheating on their sick days, doing some (illegal) trading on the side. Yes, and to conceive any excuse at all for an extravagant celebration—"extravagant" in terms of their depressed income—that would dispel the daily dreariness. And, when the vodka had begun to do its work, to fantasize. If you were a member of the Moscow intelligentsia, your dream might be of somehow spending a day in Paris before you died.

OUR OWN MYTHS ABOUT THE SOVIET UNION, especially our sloganeering reaction to what we saw as the "global Communist threat," was also touched with fantasy, if not the dreamy kind. Now that the myths have lost their monopoly on our thoughts, it's time to look back with fresh eyes at the former "Motherland of Mess," as the nation was also quietly called. For it's now possible to reassess the Soviet Union in a less stereotyped, more personal/biographical way that recognizes the country's complexity. If not for most Americans' protracted failure to recognize that Russians were individuals even as Soviet citizens, I'd apologize for the commonplace that not to think of them as such—to lump them together as enemies—inevitably distorts.

Just after I'd written the above, George Kennan made a more cogent call for understanding how the actors in any historical drama perceived the facts. For that, argued the dean of American Russian specialists, the writer himself must enter the picture

> because he has to ask himself . . . how these historical personages were motivated. What was their own vision of what they were doing and why they were doing it?
>
> To explain people of other societies and ages, history's how as well as its what, historians must reveal something about themselves as well as their subjects. It is more than just an account of what happened in the past; it's an account of how, transposed into a different age with all the different environmental circumstances, we ourselves might have reacted.

The Cold War left little time or inclination for that. Looking back, distortion can be seen as among its richest achievements. Both Americans and Russians, deeply religious by nature despite all secularization, were powerfully inclined to regard the other side as evil. We were that to Russians because they saw the United States as the citadel of the cruel, exploiting capitalism that stood in the way of history's advance toward a better, fairer life for everyone. Russians were that to us because we, in our conviction of our God-given goodness, considered (and still consider) our adversaries evil almost by definition, all the more so after just having fought World War II's genuinely diabolical enemies of the Third Reich and Imperial Japan. Thus our thinking about the foe, or lack of thinking, turned our sound policy of containing Communism into a crusade for abolishing it. It didn't always make somber Russians *all* evil, but generally made them unworthy of much attention as people.

Of course, truly evil Soviet officials weren't hard to find, especially because power-loving nastiness gravitated toward the commanding positions in the Party and the state apparats, most of all the agencies that executed the repression. But how total was their totalitarianism during the final decades? Might it have been reformed? If so, might that have been better than wanting the whole creepy structure torn down? What of the vast majority of nonapparat people— those devoted first of all to their professions rather than state interests—who conceived (in both senses), nourished, strove, toiled, fiddled, loved, persevered, and sometimes succeeded? Trying to make sense of any given aspect of Cold War Russia, partly by contemplating the motives and abilities of the participant-protagonists, one remembers the old saw "There's no history, only biography." Other people in the same endeavors, even outward doubles in their education, ideology, and goals, would have reached distinctly different results. The four subjects to be examined on the following pages show strong evidence of that, most clearly in the remarkable Soviet space program, surveyed in Chapter IV, "The Secret Soviet Moon Mission."

It was true that the Communist Party played the "guiding role" in space and every other public activity. (So stipulated the Soviet Constitution, but the actual practice was closer to "control.") Not even a hiking club could be formed without its approval and supervision. But Party membership, even at top levels, did not end diversity of views, desires, and intentions. The Party that most of the West viewed as a monolithic abstraction could speak and act only through its members in every sphere of endeavor; and every member differed— some drastically, as we'll see. Powerful men, all supremely resolved to reap power and glory for the Soviet Union, clashed mightily about the means, and when and how to employ them. Even former labor camp prisoners quarreled, although their ordeal would have seemed to make them think alike. That, really, is the message here. If there's a key to re-creating Russia's "feel" during its final Soviet decades, it lies in illuminating the contrasts and conflicts of a much more complex society than was generally understood. The onerous state controls probably narrowed those contrasts and conflicts from what they'd have been in a nondictatorship. On the other hand, they also widened the variety of the tangle and disarray, since vast amounts of time and energy went to devising ingenious dodges from the restrictions. The wags liked to say that if there were no damn system—the kind you had to circumvent in order to accomplish virtually anything—Russians would have had to invent one.

In any case, the duped, duping, groaning, gopaking, fatalistic-but-believing Soviet people of the second Cold War period bore only outward resemblance to the way they were perceived in America. The popular image of supinely obedient, utterly dedicated captives of totalitarianism was 100 percent correct—but only, to make a seat-of-the-pants estimate, 6 or 7 percent of the time.

To RETURN TO CHURCHILL, HIS FAMOUS description of Russia as "a riddle wrapped in a mystery inside an enigma" also smacked of myth, despite its nice turn of phrase. Prolonged residence in Soviet Russia showed the country was mysterious chiefly because so little was known about it. When that was remedied slightly, the puzzles seemed to derive less from riddles and enigmas than simply from being *different* from the West.

The differences were large enough to invalidate some American reporting about the Soviet Union. (Correspondents who were getting around a bit more during the 1960s in search of stories that would click with their readers reasoned that Russian youths really wanted capitalism at heart because they loved jeans and jazz.) They were large enough so that no interpretations by a foreigner should be taken as received wisdom—my own included, especially since I was so restricted to the major cities and spent so much time among my counterparts in the intelligentsia.

This is the place for a cautionary reminder of that. In the 1960s, most Russians believed the Soviet economy would indeed "catch up to and surpass" America's, just as the Kremlin cockily promised. Many American economists were also grimly convinced of the same, citing central planning as the critical Soviet advantage. The prioritizing and control enabled state targets to be set and met, particularly the steadfast channeling of relatively huge investment to heavy industry and other powerful engines of economic growth rather than to "frivolously" nonproductive consumer goods. That would soon enable the crucial Soviet steel industry, for example, to exceed the output of our own, making the general overtaking appear even more inevitable.

But the Soviet economy began stagnating in the 1970s. Then the birth of the computer and of the global market demolished the predictions of its forthcoming triumph. When the new technologies wafted us to the postindustrial "knowledge" age, the very same central planning and control proved to be the Soviet economy's *undoing*, for the measure of strength shifted from tons of steel and cement poured to the usable, salable items fashioned from those primary materials—and, above all, to quick, innovative thinking. Now the greatest economic assets were flexibility, unfettered creativity, and rapid response to market turns—everything a command economy was designed to squelch. While most of the West and much of Asia raced toward the future on spaceships of individual ingenuity, the Soviet economy became a dinosaur mired in an earlier era's premises and meaningless production targets.

Our old, erroneous prediction of ultimate Soviet domination demonstrates the sometime feebleness of foreigners' interpretations. On the other hand, we now know much more than we did about the real "Soviet reality," as opposed to the fictions about it served up by Party propagandists and their free-world antagonists. It's worth repeating that the secrets are being exposed, partly by the PBS television series from which this book developed. (The series itself is the result of Abamedia's Archive Media Project, established for exploring the Russian Republic's vast collection of films and photographs, one of the world's richest treasuries.) Recent revelations from Soviet archives are providing better answers to many long-debated questions.

Another reason for looking back is the perspective provided by Russia's experience *after* Communism. Our far smaller emotional involvement with the new state makes it easier to contemplate the old one with less slant. So does the absence of fear (except fear that Russia's deteriorating nuclear weapons will fall into radical or criminal hands). Now is a better time to judge, for example, whether the Soviet victories examined in this book, which the anxious West saw as its own defeats, weren't really the opposite in the long run.

It's also a better time to ask whether the boundless suffering under Communism, symbolized by grisly interrogations of innocent prisoners, was all in vain—and not only the suffering but also the visions of a higher social good that drove the huge striving to build a finer society for the benefit of all humanity. Was it all really for nothing? The torture, shootings, hideous prison nights, gruesome decades in labor camps? The "free" majority's daily sacrifices—and, as we'll see, heroic labors—for reaching a better new world? To conclude that gigantic effort achieved nothing positive at all would go against the grain of American optimism; but despite many similarities to us in other respects, Russians differ in that one. Fundamentally pessimistic, they believe at bottom that life is essentially hard and tragic, thus the poetic references to fate being *downward*. That's why a Russian's "Oh God, why was I born?" doesn't necessarily suggest a personal tragedy, since that's often the perception of life in general, where lots of Slavic woe is inhaled with the oxygen. It helps explain the frantic toil to build the utopia. The poet Boris Pasternak, best known to Westerners for his persecution after his book *Doctor Zhivago* was published abroad in 1957, once asked the West why it so hated the Soviet Union. The Russians, said the victim of Politburo revenge, are only trying to put into practice the precepts of Western Christianity, such as justice and fairness for all.

Such notions may mystify outsiders, who were convinced they were fighting Soviet aggression, not Christian ideals. Still, to omit them would be to make reflections about Russia during the given period much too shallow. As for what to *cut* from our own heat-of-the-struggle view, the list is probably topped by attribution to Communism of almost all Russia's political, social, and economic failings under Soviet rule—a concept that the country's post-Communist troubles, some of which are even worse, should be laying to rest.

So although no interpretation will ever be final, new ones are needed based on amendments of our previous knowledge by the most recent revelations. Maybe they will provide durable insight on the following excursions into the four important aspects of Cold War Russia, even knowing how many exceptions there were to everything among its large population. The system's failings are fairly well known. Less so are the attitudes of exceptional and "ordinary" Russians, the latter represented by Ivan Ivanovich: John Doe.

Question by Ivan Ivanovich: Can Communism be built in America too?
Radio Armenia [an imaginary entity about which a little more is revealed in Chapter V, "Soviet Propaganda"]: Without doubt it can. But what did Americans ever do to you personally?"

Such gripes notwithstanding, however, the Ivans had a reservoir of faith in the idea that Communism put them on the right side of history and justice. Therefore, it would seem more useful at this calmer point to seek the sources of their conviction in the Russian national character, especially its view of the outside world, than in the ubiquitous Soviet propaganda that didn't always work. During each of my visits over the course of twenty-nine years—from 1959 to 1988, after which my son's perceptive reports of his visits kept me informed— native behavior struck me as ever more Russian and less Soviet, or to say that more precisely, the explanations for that behavior more and more seemed to lie in national attitudes and habits acquired *before* 1917. The disappearance of everything outwardly Soviet from the face of the earth is another reason for taking a fresh look at how accurate or mistaken earlier impressions were. The victors who write the history have a special obligation to think carefully.

II
Secret Victories of the KGB

In essence, from the perspective of my seventy-one years, I still think that brash youth had the right end of the stick.

—Atomic spy Theodore Hall, 1997

I justified it in my mind by believing that I was helping, in a small way, in building a new society.... It's never wrong to give your life to a noble idea and a noble experiment, even if it didn't succeed.

—Soviet agent George Blake, 1998

They believed in this country, this ideology. They found the ideals and goals of our society attractive, and that's why they decided to help us—and to help us without payment.

—Vladimir Semichastny, former head of the KGB

The enemy howls, and seeks a way inside.

—Old Russian saying

COLD WAR ESPIONAGE PROBABLY PRODUCED slimmer results for both sides than the furious struggle was worth in trouble and expense. If that view never becomes conventional wisdom, it will be largely because the public remains hooked on spy thrillers, the prism through which many still see the larger struggle. But respected experts support the doubt of Phillip Knightley, Britain's guru of intelligence and "Red Files" consultant. Knightley recently wondered whether the massive underground efforts had been "a vast international confidence trick to deceive us about the necessity and value of the world's second oldest profession...all a waste of time."

No less an expert than John Le Carré endorses that skepticism. Not long ago, that former spook turned maestro of the spy thriller remarked that only intelligence officers, their heads buried in their secret work and their eyes narrowed with resolve to defeat the enemy, could have missed major Cold War trends unmistakable to others. Citing instances of Western intelligence

KGB

The Soviet secret or "political" police changed its name as the bureaucracy sprawled and it was felt a new name might enhance its reputation. Its final incarnation of "KGB" was an abbreviation for Committee for State Security.

It had a long lineage. The tsarist secret police, organized as the Third Section of His Imperial Majesty's Privy Chancery under Nicholas I and reformed in 1880 as the Sections for Safeguarding Public Security and Order, melted away after the February 1917 revolution. The provisional governments (March–October 1917) then decentralized police authority, but after the Bolsheviks came to power, Lenin spoke of a need for a chain-mail fist: "The state is an instrument for coercion," *Pravda* quoted Lenin saying in a speech delivered on November 22, 1917. "Previously it was the instrument for the coercion of all the people by a handful of moneybags; but we want to transform the state into an institution for enforcing the will of the people. We want to organize violence in the name of workers' interests." Soon Lenin directed some of his toughest supporters to form a fighting unit—the VCHEKA.

Many refer to all Soviet permutations of the secret police as the "Cheka," the original Bolshevik operational agency under the leadership of Felix Edmunovich Dzerzhinskii ("Iron Felix"), created in December 1917. "Cheka" stands for the All-Russian Extraordinary Commission for Combating Counterrevolution and Sabotage, whose purpose Dzerzhinskii explained in 1918:

> We stand for organized terror—this must be frankly stated—terror being absolutely indispensable in the current revolutionary conditions. . . . We terrorize the enemies of the Soviet government so as to stifle them and their crimes at the outset. Terror serves as a ready deterrent.

The Cheka was criticized for the "Red Terror," for arbitrariness, and for operating without proper Communist Party supervision, which enabled it to act above the law. In 1922, after its victory in the civil war, the Soviet government replaced the Cheka with the GPU (State Political Administration), renamed the OGPU (Unified State Political Administration) the following year. Other names followed. During the worst of Stalin's regime, when millions were murdered, it was called the NKVD, initials some feared even to whisper, preferring "the organs." Folk wisdom held it was safer to use a former name in making any but the most official reference to the dreaded organization.

During the murderous Stalinist years, the Russian initials OGPU were some-times said to stand for "O Lord! Help Us Flee!" It was also cited as an abbrevi-ation, if read backwards, for "If you flee they'll catch you and cut off your head."

During World War II NKVD was briefly changed to NKGB. It was later called or became part of the MGB (1946–1953), the MVD (1953–1954), and the MB (1991–1993). A post-Stalin reorganization settled on the KGB designa-tion in 1954. Since the Soviet government moved to Moscow from Petrograd in 1918, its most influential bodies were quartered not far from the Kremlin in a complex of buildings on Bolshaia Liubianka Street. By far the most infa-mous, which formerly housed an insurance company, fronts on Liubiankaia Square. For decades, a giant statue of "Iron Felix" stood in its center, until jubilant crowds tore it down in the fury that followed a failed hard-line Com-munist coup against Mikhail Gorbachev in August 1991. The KGB's domestic and foreign operations were then separated as part of Russia's more or less democratic revolution under Boris Yeltsin. External intelligence is now under the SVR (Foreign Intelligence Service), and since 1993 domestic work is han-dled by the FSB (Federal Counterintelligence Service). How much the new or-ganization resembles the old remains a mystery: like the KGB, the FSB is shrouded in secrecy.

officers failing to see crucial Soviet developments because they never looked up from their underground operations, Le Carré regretted misleading the public about the significance of intelligence work. Richard Helms, a former director of the CIA, was only half joking when he said his analysts would have done better to conduct their research in the Library of Congress. Even Marcus Wolf, the virtuoso "man without a face" who was called the greatest modern spymaster for his artful command of East Germany's foreign intel-ligence service, agrees that the game was rarely worth the candle. Distin-guished writers about Cold War espionage now find it was not merely "a dirty, bogus business riddled with deceit, manipulation and betrayal," to quote Knightley again, but also an unprofitable one. Espionage agencies fell victim to their own ideologies and bureaucratic strategies. Their captains were beguiled into playing the furtive game more for itself than for the na-tional good. Reports that contradicted prevailing evaluations or attitudes about the sinister enemy were dismissed, often leaving their authors under suspicion, almost in proportion to the value of their information. Mistakes naturally abounded in the field officers' workplace of darkness and anonymity. The worst were made by their own jittery comrades, even their operational superiors, who unwittingly did more to get them captured and punished than the enemy's counterintelligence.

In a word, the huge expenditure on the morally corrupting, rarely fruitful enterprise was a kind of fleecing. Of course, the full record of success and failure won't be known until, if and when, all secret records are opened to public scrutiny. (That remains to be done for biological warfare weapons, although former scientists on both sides have made a start with their memoirs.) But a considerable share of material is already available, including more than three thousand messages between Moscow and its American spies in the 1940s that were intercepted by American counterintelligence and recently declassified. Judging by such examples, more could have indeed been learned by analyzing information that was easily accessible to the public without a password, and not only in the Library of Congress. Given the choice of a mole in the National Security Council or a subscription to *The New York Times*, one KGB officer said he'd take the latter any day.

Fairness requires some personal disclosure here. Of all Western journalism for the non-Communist press, it might have seemed that Moscow would have been least likely to be angered by my kind, which tried to portray the Soviet people, even the bureaucrats, as recognizable human beings. But the defenders of the official portrait of the forever patriotic and industrious Soviet citizen cared nothing about that. A friendly Soviet journalist once explained in the safety of London that mid-level bosses never considered the effect of any reporting on *Western* public opinion. "Those people are interested only in whether a given book or article meets the standards of *their* bosses, higher up—people who've never been abroad and have no way of knowing what the West is really thinking." Surely the man worked for the KGB in one way or another, but his disgust with the almost willful narrowness "upstairs" seemed genuine. "And," he added, "your writing annoys them because it reveals too much deviation from the prescribed image of virtuous Soviet behavior."

That was apparently why I was barred from returning to Moscow for almost the full decade of the 1970s. When I finally got a visa in 1979, I saw at once that a sea change had taken place in popular morale. *Why* was less obvious because living standards had decidedly improved, at least in Moscow. My in-laws had escaped from their detested communal apartments to blessedly private self-contained ones, and a cousin through marriage even had a car! Nevertheless, the formerly cautious family that had always avoided all talk with this American about politics—or, heaven forbid, discontent—could hardly stop complaining.

Sharper grievances sounded from my less inhibited friends and former classmates. In the trembling 1930s, Stalin's "Life's become better, happier" had rung with tension as well as hope. Now the old declaration was true in a way, Muscovites being less tense as well as better off than before. However, the change brought neither appreciation nor optimism. Increasing knowledge about the outside world had fertilized expectations to grow faster than the improvement. From old dormitory friends once staunch in their belief, to strangers standing alongside at public urinals, the Soviet people seemed unable to restrain themselves from muttering about economic stupidity and failure. Many spoke about the possible breakdown of a system that seemed to be losing its struggle to cope with modern developments.

It would have taken considerable pains to avoid the abundant evidence of demoralization. Much later, when glancing at some CIA reports about the Soviet Union at the very same time, I wondered whether their authors had taken just those pains. Some of the agency's evaluations seemed to pertain to a different country. Ignoring what a dozen conversations with Russians would have easily exposed, those stout documents, compiled and composed at vast expense by a brigade of tight-lipped professionals, represented the unraveling country in the usual way: as a frightening dictatorship whose threat to the United States was *growing*.

That experience nudged me toward the camp of the critics of intelligence work, for their attitudes more than their operational habits, about which I knew little (despite the KGB's stock conviction that I was an agent). It also reminded me that the few men I'd met whom I knew to be CIA agents inspired little confidence in their objectivity or the broadness of their views. That they were better specimens than the lowly KGB officers I personally knew was not high recommendation. Their primary concerns were secrecy and agency patriotism, not truth. They most valued information that supported their fighting spirit.

That insidious mindset fortifies my reluctance to buff the supposed glamour of intelligence work. Why give the old—even the newly discovered—operatives even more attention, especially knowing that both Cold War adversaries ended with little to show for their huge efforts? The reason for doing so lies in the significant exceptions, acknowledged even by the detractors of East-West espionage. The most important by far was help given the Soviet Union in the design and building of its atomic bomb by remarkably well placed, well informed spies.

IN 1952, LEE HARVEY OSWALD AND HIS FLIGHTY mother were living briefly in New York. Thrown off track there, the thirteen-year-old Texan often played truant to wander the streets, nursing a sense of injury to himself—until a protester handed him a pamphlet. Lee's elder brother would speak of that moment as a

Decoding Soviet Spies: Venona

The U.S. Signal Intelligence efforts to collect and decrypt Soviet NKVD and GRU messages in the 1940s was code-named "Venona Project," but sometimes also called "Arlington Hall" after the name of the building where the codebreakers worked. Venona's long-secret cryptographic marvels decoded intercepted Soviet espionage cables, the most important of which came after World War II, when reports to Moscow concerning the American A-bomb effort were cracked. To protect the Venona treasure house of Cold War information, American criminal prosecutors never used its documents directly. Instead, information derived from the intercepts was passed on to the FBI and CIA on a carefully vetted "need-to-know" basis.

Anatoly Sudoplatov, the son of the prominent KGB general Pavel Sudoplatov, explained why Soviet spies changed their coding procedures as the Cold War got under way:

> The Soviets didn't know exactly that the project was entitled "Venona" but they were aware of American efforts to penetrate into their spy syndicate. Noteworthy, they changed and you find no interceptions after July 1945. Some stuff was intercepted, I believe in traffic between San Francisco and Moscow, Canberra and Moscow, London and Moscow dating back to 1946. But the bottom line is that the cable decipherers for the New York residency [NKVD cover office] and the Washington residence were changed.

Sudaplatov reported that one of the Soviet Union sources who tipped off its spies that their cables were being decoded was in the "Signal Corp of the American Army."

After the Soviet Union's collapse, the scholarly senator Daniel Patrick Moynihan (D-NY), a leading proponent of glasnost in American government, prodded the U.S. National Security Archives to declassify and make public at least some of the Venona documents. Now many can be viewed online at http://www.nsa.gov:8080/docs/venona/. They include reports that indicate the information about Ethel Rosenberg's incapacity for espionage tasks was passed on to the FBI.

radical turning point because it enabled the adolescent to weave his personal resentments into a pattern of larger injustices. The pamphlet was about Julius and Ethel Rosenberg, New Yorkers who had been executed for treason the previous year. Outraged by the text's account of their "framing," unhappy young Oswald soon declared adherence to a movement whose protest appealed to him, although he barely understood its philosophy or operation. His Marxism would help take him to assassination ten years later.

Subsequent exhaustive research, the most recent of which draws on declassified files, has proved beyond reasonable doubt that the Rosenbergs *weren't* innocent, contrary to the absolute conviction of much of the American Left at the time. Ex-KGB officers proud of their exploits in atomic espionage deny that the couple ever aided such efforts, and that may be essentially true. But since Julius did pass secrets about advanced U.S. radar and sonar, we now know that punishment was deserved. We also know, however, that his *execution* violated American precedent and standards of justice. The government's prosecution was abhorrent in design and method. The sentence— especially against Ethel, whose involvement in her husband's secret work was extremely peripheral—wildly exceeded the crime.

Such, of course, were the times. In the early 1950s, almost anything could be believed about the Soviet viper. Moscow's acquisition of the atomic bomb many years earlier than predicted frightened and dismayed. The Rosenberg investigation and trial took place in the shadow of the Soviet mushroom cloud, further darkened by American wrath over the enemy's success in producing it so quickly. The emotional climate enabled prosecutors to use otherwise repugnant means to *stop Communist spying!* And the martyrs young Oswald saw in the couple helped him find a noble home for his sense of victimization.

There is no evidence that Oswald would ever ponder Stalin's legacy, let alone his skills in acting and dissembling. But those skills naturally concerned American statesmen and intelligence officers. In particular, an inexplicable response from the Soviet leader in July 1945 perplexed the handful who were in on the secret of the project to build an atomic bomb. The setting was the Potsdam Conference, held near Berlin, at which Stalin, President Harry Truman, and Prime Minister Winston Churchill were finalizing agreements about European dispositions that had been made after Germany's surrender some ten weeks earlier. Meanwhile, the gruesome war on Pacific islands continued, with Japanese forces promising to fight even more sacrificially on their sacred mainland. At Potsdam, Truman was advised from Washington that the Nevada tests of the world's first A-bomb had been successful. He took the occasion to notify Stalin that American scientists had developed

Agony and Acronyms

Even before the Soviet state was created from the ashes of revolution and civil war, its leaders believed they were engaged in a life-and-death struggle with capitalism. Convinced of Communism's inevitable triumph in the long term, they nevertheless feared the capitalist West might succeed in temporarily snuffing out Communism in its Soviet birthplace. In that fight for survival, espionage was assigned a critical role. Mere weeks after taking power, the Bolsheviks founded the first Soviet intelligence agency, the Cheka (see p. 32). Its emblems—later adopted by the KGB—were the shield and the sword: the former for defending the revolution, the latter for smiting its foes. From the beginning, Soviet intelligence directed its efforts inward as well as outward: the capitalist threat was thought to require eternal vigilance at home as well as abroad. In other words, it was entrusted to spy on its own people as well as foreign powers.

In all its acronyms—Cheka, GPU, OGPU, NKVD, KGB—it summoned visions of surveillance, of networks of informants, of the gulag, of purges and executions. To the rest of the world, however, the KGB was known primarily for the successes of its foreign agents.

The most impressive involved the recruitment of the British spies who became known in KGB lore as the "Magnificent Five." Students with Communist sympathies, they were recruited at Cambridge University in the 1930s. All later rose to high positions in British intelligence or in the Foreign Office. Donald Maclean, Guy Burgess, Anthony Blunt, John Cairncross, and Kim Philby worked for the KGB not because they were blackmailed or bribed but because they believed its cause was just. While Nazism spread across the European continent almost unopposed by the liberal democracies of the 1930s, Communism seemed to many the best hope to fight the fascist danger. Philby was far and away the most important of the quintet. His extraordinarily successful career made him a likely choice to one day head the British Secret Service. However, he came under suspicion in the 1950s, after which one of the most celebrated double agents in the history of espionage finally defected to Moscow.

Lesser known Richard Sorge, who was half-German and half-Russian, gathered information about Japanese military intentions by posing as a German journalist in Tokyo. The handsome, charming agent managed to gain the confidence of Japanese and Germans in Japan by pretending to be an ardent Nazi. One of his most important coups was obtaining certain information about the planned Nazi invasion of the Soviet Union, even the date of June 22, 1941. But Stalin ignored Sorge's reports. Having signed a nonaggression pact with Hitler in 1939, he obstinately refused to heed the signs that the Nazi dictator was planning an attack, even forbidding the Red Army to take proper defensive measures. That terrible mistake would cost the Soviet Union dearly in lives, territory, and resources.

Although the USSR and the USA were allies during the war, the Soviets continued to engage in active scientific and technical espionage in the United States, ferreting out the latest American developments in fields like radio engineering and aviation before stealing secrets from the Manhattan Project, America's covert program to develop an atomic weapon. American efforts to recruit Soviet spies were less successful—almost inevitably, in a closed society with high levels of surveillance and a profound suspicion of contacts with foreigners. Oleg Penkovsky, an officer in the Soviet military's intelligence agency (the GRU) who gave valuable information to the West during the Cuban missile crisis, came under suspicion for having an unauthorized meeting with a foreigner. He was placed under twenty-four-hour surveillance. The family living in the apartment above his was sent on vacation, and Soviet intelligence drilled a hole in their floor to place a pinhead camera in Penkovsky's ceiling. He was arrested, tortured, and shot.

Soviet agents who defected to the West risked retaliation on family members left at home. In addition, the KGB went to great lengths to track down and assassinate the defectors themselves, especially in the Stalin era. Even those who succeeded in defecting sometimes had a hard time convincing CIA agents, to whom distrust and deceit had become second nature, that they were genuine defectors and not "provocations," sent by the KGB to feed false information to the West. The CIA imprisoned a valuable officer named Yuri Golitsyn for over three years, while counterintelligence officers tried to force him to confess to being a Soviet mole. When he was eventually freed, it was too late to act on the most critical information he had tried to pass along.

Perhaps the most embarrassing failure for American intelligence was the CIA's refusal to heed many signs that Aldrich Ames was a double agent. Using lists provided by Ames, the KGB was able to identify and murder dozens of American agents. The Ames triumph was the last major one for the KGB, which—at least in name—died when the Soviet empire collapsed. As noted, its successor, the Russian FSB, lives on.

a new weapon of extraordinary power. The American bafflement lay in "Uncle Joe's" reaction. As deadpan as a virtuoso poker player, he asked for no elaboration, merely offering quiet thanks for Truman's courtesy.

The answer to the puzzle would be revealed only much later—in the case of some of the most important revelations, not until the late 1990s, after the passage of more than fifty years. It rested in brilliant intelligence work that had probably made Stalin more knowledgeable about the new weapon than Truman was at Potsdam.

How could that have happened? The secrecy of the Manhattan Project, the code name for the American venture to construct that first nuclear weapon, was thought to be as absolute as possible. Extremely elaborate means were taken to protect it, especially at a sprawling new complex at Los Alamos, New Mexico. Forty miles west of Santa Fe as the crow flies—much longer over the difficult roads into the obscure wilderness—Los Alamos ("the poplars") was hidden in the pine forests of the Jemez Mountains. From its founding in 1943, security there only began with the watchtowers guarding the fences and the highly restricted passes required to enter the gates. When scientists and technicians went out for dinner, military sleuths trailed them and listened to their conversations. John Rhoades, now director of the Bradbury Science Museum at Los Alamos, remembers the atmosphere of the secret settlement where the actual designing and building of the first A-bombs took place:

> Los Alamos as a name didn't exist, it was Box 1663. On people's birth certificates, it said "Baby born Box 1663." No word of Los Alamos could be used outside. Letters were censored, they'd arrive with big holes cut out of them. It was very, very tight security.

German agents never managed to penetrate the secret there or at the sites where preliminary work was conducted, such as Oak Ridge, Tennessee, one of the most important. If they had, the consequences might have been extremely grave, since Germany had the intellectual power to make its own A-bomb, although the German program was getting nowhere for lack of Hitler's support. But since Soviet physicists also had a theoretical understanding of nuclear physics and its potential applications for weaponry, the situation indeed became extremely grave for the West several years after Soviet agents—no less than twenty-nine of them, according to "Red Files" research—*did* penetrate the Manhattan Project. They accomplished that by recruiting Allied scientists: sympathizers whose pointers and diagrams of plans and installations saved the embryonic Soviet atomic program years of research and vast expense. It's no accident, as the old Marxists liked to say, that the first Soviet atom bomb, detonated in 1949, was virtually an exact copy of the prototype devised and engineered at Los Alamos.

But the information conveyed by the Rosenbergs—a drop in the bucket of Soviet espionage—played very little part in that; perhaps none at all. Their whole, strident case, a symbol of heinous Communist perfidy to some Americans and of sickening anti-Communist hysteria to others, was a sideshow. Outside a pair of tiny, extremely tight Soviet rings, no one knew that then. No one suspected that Moscow considered Ethel and Julius too unimportant to risk even trying to help them escape.

MUCH OF THE STORY OF THOSE OTHER supersecret rings, and how they managed to pour a stream rather than a drop into the bucket, is new. The Soviet code name of the American scientist at the center of the most important was *Mlad,* a variant of the Russian word for "young." That was appropriate, if imprudent. Theodore Alvin Hall had been invited to join the Manhattan Project directly after his brilliant undergraduate studies at Harvard, which he completed in 1944, at the age of eighteen. He was the youngest physicist working at Los Alamos that year and the next. A decent young man with honorable ideals and normal compassion, he shuddered at the news of the Rosenbergs' execution, going so far as to suggest to his Soviet handler that he give himself up. "Don't pin it all on the Rosenbergs," he rehearsed his never-delivered confession to the American authorities. "Because I was more responsible than they were."

Another ring whose yield was incomparably more valuable than anything the Rosenbergs passed to the KGB centered around a superb physicist named Klaus Fuchs. A refugee from Nazi Germany, Fuchs had settled in England before being invited to work on the Manhattan Project. Apprehended in 1950, he would be imprisoned for fourteen years for his dismayingly harmful spying, prompting renewed dismay among those who compared his sentence to the Rosenbergs' punishment for their far lesser damage. Released after eight years, Fuchs flew to high praise and position in East Germany.

Fuchs's Soviet control, a KGB colonel named Alexander Feklisov, told the makers of "Red Files" that Fuchs, practically speaking, had given full information about the first uranium and plutonium bombs. "He gave the whole theoretical basis." Even discounting any exaggeration by a proud veteran of the espionage war, Fuchs's contribution to the creation of the Soviet bomb, including instructions for converting uranium to plutonium and notations about its critical mass, was indeed priceless—almost a guide to the construction of the entire bomb. But the contribution of teenage Theodore Hall was no less valuable. (Neither had any notion whatever of each other's existence.)

While at Los Alamos, Hall was drafted into the army. In retrospect, that was a mistake because the prodigy was also a passionate political radical who now took some precious time from his urgent bomb-making duties to battle every possible form of military discipline. More to the point, however, his outlook and temperament inclined him to conclude that a monopoly of atomic bombs, even an American one, would menace the world.

Although Hall worked far from the giants of atomic theory, he became one of very few Los Alamos experts involved in the critical practicality of actually setting off a nuclear explosion. The distinctly unmilitary army recruit was in charge of the all-important field testing of simulated procedures and the process contributing to it. He knew, and told Moscow, that the American trigger for activating the bomb's big bang worked by implosion instead of ex-plosion. That innovation, among the century's great ones, was so counter-intuitive to Soviet scientists that it might have taken them years to conceive it on their own, without equation-filled summaries from their youthful coach inside "Enormoz," as the Soviet agents appropriately code-named the American uranium-bomb effort. Hall's information was priceless to the mostly young Soviet physicists who were burning with desire to end the ter-ror, as it was painted and perceived, of America's sole possession of the hideously destructive weapon. It prompted a sober recent account, entitled *Bombshell: The Secret Story of America's Unknown Atomic Spy Conspiracy*, to conclude that "the Soviets could not have hoped to find a junior scientist in a more sensitive position."

But how was the booty passed to elated KGB overseers and scientists in Moscow? Not by the Rosenbergs; nor by David Greenglass, a Los Alamos ma-chinist who gave Julius some shallow, garbled information about marginal matters; nor by any other of the fellow travelers who also worked in Los Alamos—now thought to number several dozen, according to books just pub-lished and still being written. No, the ferrying of the secrets was accomplished by a couple who would have attracted no attention whatever if they'd lived next door, except, perhaps, for their pleasant personalities. As "Lesli" and "Volunteer," their NKVD (an earlier designation of the KGB) code names, that team made itself into the prized Soviet asset in America.

IN 1961, TEN YEARS AFTER THE ROSENBERG executions, a British court sentenced a couple named Helen and Peter Kroger to twenty years in prison for helping run a KGB spy ring at the critical Portland naval base, on England's southern coast. The pair had used the most modern methods available to transmit to Moscow espionage information about submarines obtained by a self-

Trying Spies—A Cold War Passion Play

enerations of American leftists, progressives, and liberals saw the Rosenbergs as martyrs assassinated by a government infected with the virus of McCarthyism. Abroad, the Rosenbergs symbolized the hypocrisy of a country unable to tolerate political diversity at home while preaching it everywhere else. During the interval between the Rosenbergs' 1952 conviction and 1953 execution at Sing Sing prison, thousands protested their innocence throughout the world, many of the rallies orchestrated on Moscow's instructions.

We now know Soviet espionage officers asked the Kremlin to create an opening for commuting the Rosenberg death sentence. By admitting a link to them, Moscow could have signaled Ethel and Julius that they were authorized to satisfy the prosecutor's demand that they acknowledge their involvement with the Soviet Union. Stalin's government turned down the request, ordering all to remain silent.

Alexander Feklisov, the man who "ran" Julius when he had collected data on radar, sonar, and other electronic devices, called him "a great sympathizer of the Soviet Union, a true revolutionary who was willing to sacrifice himself for his beliefs." Feklisov now says he always felt guilty that the U.S.S.R. abandoned someone who had helped the country in its time of need. Other foreign nationals turned Soviet spies could never openly voice their ambivalent feelings about the Rosenbergs. Lona Cohen—about whom more on the following page—was more or less typical of those. Svetlana Chervonnaya, an English-speaking Soviet historian, was one of the few people close to Cohen near the end of her life.

> Whenever I tried to talk with them [the Cohens] about the Rosenberg story, I had a feeling that somewhere, very deep inside, they didn't want to show they had a sort of jealousy that they did something for which other people got credit. Credit is bad word, because they got death, death chair. Still the Rosenberg case is a landmark. They were much in the limelight. Maybe it's one of the landmark stories of the centuries. And theirs [the Cohens'] is still a rather obscure story, and rather obscure life.
>
> In their last days, they talked a lot about the need to write or maybe to film something about themselves. They were thinking about it, not in terms of Russia, but in terms of the United States because as I told you, that they

felt themselves very, deep inside, Americans. They want somehow to get back to their American compatriots and to explain themselves to them.

In 1992, Svetlana visited Lona in the hospital, where she was dying of cancer.

Several times I remember her just staring at me and saying, "Well, am I a traitor, Svetlana?" I think that that was her deepest thought at that moment— whether she betrayed her own country, or whether she and her husband did something worthwhile, not only for the Soviets, but for America. So at one point she said "but I didn't kill anybody, and I didn't destroy any American life. No American soldier died because of what I have done."

proclaimed Canadian businessman named "Gordon Lonsdale." Igor Prelin, a former high KGB officer, later described the good-natured Lonsdale as a man "who loved life . . . [and had] a huge sense of humor. . . . He certainly never behaved as an illegal should."

That limelight lover was actually an NKVD colonel named Conon Molody. In Moscow several years earlier, the same skilled Krogers had helped train him to talk like a native North American. Neither the British nor the American secret services knew that, however—or anything else about the Krogers' background. The pair's espionage tasks in Britain included playing roles as slightly eccentric rare-book dealers as well as mastering the fine points of photography, microdot procedures, and high-frequency radio operation. Their skill in those pursuits was quite enough to make both services feel relieved after their 1961 uncovering. Any idea about how much more valuable the devoted Lesli and Volunteer had been to the KGB and its predecessors might have upped the relief to rapture.

The Krogers had taken that name when they moved to England in 1951, posing as antique dealers from New Zealand. Actually, they were native Americans who'd left the country a year earlier, when they felt the breath of approaching FBI investigations. After a stop in Germany, they proceeded to Czechoslovakia, then to Moscow for further training—and NKVD missions that remain secret to this day. The peripatetic couple were actually Lona and Morris Cohen of New York. He was a peddler's son. She, née Lona Petka, was the daughter of Polish immigrants who worked in a cotton mill. Lona became a socialist at age fifteen, and it was she, with Morris's affectionate help and guidance, who served as the courier for Theodore Hall's information from supposedly impenetrable Los Alamos.

The first task for Soviet intelligence had been to find that deeply secluded, elaborately guarded sanctuary in the New Mexico wasteland. The NKVD had suspected since 1940 that Western countries might try to build an atomic bomb. Two years later, three years before Hiroshima, Soviet scientists guessed why and how it might work. But ferreting out the actual Anglo-American research station—which the first tips to Soviet intelligence located as "somewhere in Mexico"—was something of a feat in itself.

The Cohens' performance surpassed it. Lona-Lesli was a seasoned courier of information about American weapons and other secrets before she was chosen for her nuclear mission to New Mexico. Luck was generous in helping her cope with the things that usually went at least a little wrong even in the most carefully planned espionage operations, but her success was also due to tenacity and ability to improvise. Three consecutive failures of a contact to show up at a planned place of meeting—in this case, a drugstore in Santa Fe—might have thrown a less determined woman.

As for Morris-Volunteer, he'd found a soul mate in her—a true loving comrade, to whom he had introduced the Soviet experts who were skillfully exploiting them. Morris, who had demonstrated bravery as well as idealism when he volunteered to fight fascism during the grim Spanish Civil War of 1936–39, was a quiet pillar of faith in the profound morality of their underground activities. Together, their adventures make a classic story—a stirring one from the Soviet viewpoint, full of lone missions, close calls, the briefest of encounters with scientists bearing uniquely precious gifts, mistaken reports of the protagonists' death, and last-second decisions that turned out to be prescient, if unintentionally. As dramatized in "Red Files," Lona, faced by guards posted at a New Mexico railroad station to guarantee wartime security, hides a cache of invaluable information from Hall in a box of Kleenex. She asks one of the guards to hold the box while she opens her handbag and suitcase for inspection. Once in the train, she remembers the Kleenex box, which is handed back to her by the obliging security officer, who boards her car for that purpose. Whether that was dumb luck or superb intuition, present-day ex-KGB officers are not entirely hyping when they claim their old colleagues' haul deserves credit for the first Soviet splitting of the atom. "Obtaining the secrets of the atomic bomb from the United States," added Igor Prelin, the above-mentioned former KGB colonel to "Red Files" interviewers, was "the greatest intelligence coup of all time."

IT'S NO LESS TRUE FOR BEING COMMONPLACES that there will always be spies, and that many volunteer participants end as pawns. Although Ted Hall began by wanting to give the Soviet Union just a peek at Los Alamos doings, he was almost inevitably dragged in deeper. Although the Cohens were loath to leave their cherished America, they never saw it again after the NKVD ordered them to flee in 1951, following a tip by Kim Philby, the British master traitor who served as liaison with American counterintelligence. (Philby's most recent Russian biographer wasn't exaggerating when he described his subject, who was party to the inner sanctum of FBI and CIA secrets, as having "a unique knowledge of Western intelligence." Philby also figures in a second major spy story, discussed below; meanwhile, note that the alerted Soviets made certain to save the Cohens, as they hadn't the Rosenbergs.) Most of their remaining forty-plus years were spent in Moscow, which appealed to them less than they thought it would.

But does that trio's treachery say anything more than the truism that the amateurs never control the game or, ultimately, themselves? Perhaps it does by helping convey the spirit of their time. That spirit was also an essential element of a second great NKVD-KGB victory just over a decade later, one that again involved the Kroger-Cohens, although this time not as volunteers.

THE COLD WAR CONTINUED OBSESSING THE superpowers throughout the 1950s. The Soviets, as convinced as ever that the West's goal was to destroy Socialism, saw it as history's ultimate struggle. The American fear of the Communist peril was almost as intense, despite vastly greater geographical advantage, economic resources, and military power. The 1954 Doolittle Report commissioned by President Eisenhower warned that America confronted "an implacable enemy whose avowed objective is world domination by whatever means and at whatever cost." In such a struggle, it counseled, no rules mattered: "Hitherto acceptable norms of human conduct do not apply. If the United States is to survive, long-standing American concepts of 'fair-play' must be re-considered" in favor of ever more espionage to "subvert, sabotage, and destroy our enemies."

Whatever skirmishes were fought elsewhere, ground zero of the espionage struggle was Berlin, by that time divided into Soviet and Western zones. The British, French, and American ones formed an atoll surrounded by hostile Soviet-bloc territory. The CIA station there was a virtual neighbor of the world's largest concentration of Soviet troops.* The KGB station was critical enough for its chief to be deputy chairman of the sprawling agency. Both were

---

* The author acknowledges the important contribution of *Battleground Berlin: CIA vs. KGB in the Cold War*, Yale University Press, 1997, to this chapter's accounts of the Berlin Tunnel and other CIA Berlin operations.

convinced the other side was impatient to invade. Their feverish battle was a proxy for the entire East-West clash.

Although the Berlin Airlift had broken the famous blockade of 1948–49, the Kremlin remained determined to dislodge the bone in its throat called West Berlin. Washington saw that goal as a vital step in the Soviet intention to dominate the European continent by any means. North Korea's 1950 attack on South Korea swelled the American fear that NATO's embryonic defenses would be no match for the seemingly inevitable Communist onslaught in Europe. On raged the espionage combat to secure vital information about those and related matters.

The advantages seesawed. The Soviets scored one in the early 1950s by switching their radio traffic to more secure means. That put an end to American interceptions, since the CIA could think of no way to approach the intensely patrolled Soviet telephone lines. It urgently needed a new way to acquire intelligence about the vastly superior Soviet conventional forces and their orders from Moscow.

A promised answer to that need lay in a daring plan delightedly approved by Allen Dulles, the CIA's director. Its brilliant concept prompted selection of the relatively obscure officer who'd conceived it as the Berlin station chief, even though he spoke no German, had been with the agency only five years, and had none of the upper-crust qualities of his predecessors and current counterparts in other stations. Many were startled by the appointment of so junior an officer to head the world's largest and most prestigious agency station.

But some of William Harvey's other qualities made him a natural for the job. To call Harvey flamboyant would be like describing Babe Ruth as a good hitter. Despite his pear-shaped body and bulging eyes, he was labeled "America's James Bond"—although his personal comportment, for which J. Edgar Hoover had fired him from the FBI, was more like a caricature of the unorthodox private eye, with touches of John Wayne thrown in.

Outsized "Big Bill" was thirty-seven in 1952, when he arrived in West Berlin to take up his new post. Even discounting the legends he inspired there, the certifiable truth about the anti-Communist crusader was startling. He would share a claim with future president John Kennedy of never going a day without enjoying a woman. He often drank five martinis at lunch, and loved guns perhaps even more. Three or four loaded ones were always in his desk and two on his person, rotated daily from among his vast collection. "When you need 'em, you need 'em in a hurry," he informed a beer hall waitress who handed him a pistol that had slipped from his pocket. Actually, he had no such need in Berlin, thanks to a tacit understanding that

KGB and CIA officers didn't shoot one another. (A former head of KGB counterintelligence recently confirmed that although his organization was "one of the most vicious in the world," it decided not to kidnap or kill American intelligence officers.) Still, he required that all his Berlin personnel carry a weapon.

Harvey so differed from his Ivy League predecessors that the staff of the BOB, as Berlin Operations Base station was called, saw their new boss as "a creature from another planet." While their wonder quickly turned to apprehensive admiration, startled Europeans tended to see the lover of pearl handles and battle hyperbole as dangerously half-cocked himself: the archetypal anti-Communist cowboy. Actually, Harvey took pains to broadcast his passion for alcohol and guns, believing his macho image helped him get results although those results were more likely the product of astute hunches prompted by his street-smarts. Combining hunches with careful legwork, he had a rare ability to identify and mesh every relevant detail. That made him an excellent planner of operations as well as an outstanding case officer.

The massive operation he now conceived was a tunnel—an unthinkable one, he hoped. Beginning at a secret site near the border of Berlin's American and Soviet sectors, it would poke boldly into Communist territory to tap communication cables there. If the risk seemed huge, so were the stakes: nothing less, in the eyes of the espionage captains, than Europe's fate, and maybe the world's.

The new station chief had learned that British intelligence had tapped underground lines at the Soviet army's Vienna headquarters. Operation Silver, as that project was called, inspired him to try something similar in Berlin, but worthy of being called "Operation Gold" because it would be far more ambitious. Harvey had already taken the first steps—learning roughly where the enemy cables were, and what traffic each carried—while at his previous post in Washington.

Now, after arriving in Berlin, he directed a powerful effort to enlist East Germans who had knowledge of the cable network's routings. Since BOB officers never ventured into East Berlin, the actual recruiting had to be done by covert East German agents, mainly when they visited West Berlin for their case officers' instructions. Soon an East Berlin post office official procured bulky books with details of cable traffic. *Nummer Maedchen*—"the numbers girl"—provided comprehensive data from her classified post office switching room, which executed orders as to which cable should be used for what Soviet traffic. A prominent East German lawyer specializing in international postal matters took to arriving in impeccable dress for elaborate dinners at a West Berlin safe house. The starchy guest would begin the evening by lowering his trousers and ripping adhesive tape from his buttocks. *Et voilà*: invaluable cards appeared onto which the procedures of communications switching offices had been copied.

Slowly, with unavoidable stumbles and halts, new and old East German operatives helped BOB piece together a picture of the Soviet network. More time was consumed by vital checking to ensure the information from various sources tallied. Everything took even longer because Harvey was determined to hide the intricate undertaking from all but three top CIA officers in Germany. The handful of carefully selected BOB officers who tackled matters related to Operation Gold remained ignorant about the purpose of their assignments. Nor were they given any slack in their regular duties, heavy enough in themselves. An important BOB agent in an East German foreign exchange bank chose just that time to be recruited and switched by the recently founded *Hauptverwaltung Aufklarung,* the East German Main Intelligence Directorate that would become notorious under Marcus Wolf, that "man without a face." A BOB officer had to run the difficult new case while simultaneously supervising the recruitment of agents in East German telecommunications.

The urgency of the "normal" tasks made no dent in Harvey's iron resolve to preserve the project's secrecy. He didn't mention Operation Gold even to seasoned David Murphy when the latter was appointed his deputy base chief in 1954. (Murphy co-authored *Battleground Berlin: The CIA vs. the KGB in the Cold War,* which includes the best account of the tunnel undertaking.) The new deputy chief's briefing, which came only after he arrived in Berlin, was further delayed while Murphy worked—in vain—to recruit a key veteran of the KGB's Berlin compound.

That tightly fenced square mile was known as Karlshorst, for the district where it was located. Some three thousand people, including Soviet military guards and signals personnel, inhabited Karlshorst. A dozen miles away, exhausting work in BOB's cramped "Target Room" tellingly demonstrated the need for new sources of intelligence. The targets were KGB officers who occupied critical positions in the Soviet citadel nearby. However, the CIA's extremely thin, patchy information about them made it exceedingly difficult to determine which one might be worthy of a campaign to turn him. Meticulously collating wisps of information about possible candidates' duties and habits, BOB officers tried to connect their names and ranks with the faces on covertly taken photographs.

In the end, the Target Room's intent to identify, select, and finally recruit Karlshorst personnel by uncovering and exploiting their vulnerabilities remained a fond hope. Knowing the penalty for slips, KGB officers bolstered their steadfast professionalism with extreme wariness. Endlessly coached to avoid East as well as West Germans as potential "imperialist" agents, they were also carefully watched by the security specialists of several Soviet services in the Karlshorst compound—who, in turn, were reinforced by swarms of colleague-informers. More than 95 percent of the Soviet–East German social contacts reported to BOB were for quick, commercial sex. Counter-intelligence specialists of the GDR (German Democratic Republic, or East Germany) investigated the few meetings of longer duration. In the end, the grand total of CIA recruitments was zero. Soviet intelligence, with its longer pedigree and greater practice, was winning that war within the war.

That heightened Harvey's zeal for his tunnel gamble, especially after a BOB source in the GDR's Ministry of Post and Telecommunications provided copies of maps showing the locations of Berlin's cable traces. In the dead of a nervous spring night in 1953, an intrepid BOB agent in an East Berlin telephone office patched Soviet lines to a West Berlin circuit long enough to confirm that the Soviets were making ample use of the cables to transmit material of exceptional interest. Now Harvey and the literal handful of senior officials who were in on the plan were able to shape it more precisely.

Meanwhile, BOB's great majority of uninformed officers kept to their normal duties, which centered around their perpetual hunt for information from new targets or volunteers. Among the latter, a man none of them ever glimpsed was about to become one of the best. The anonymous benefactor would leave secret notes, some warning of KGB penetrations of Western intelligence services, in a West Berlin letter drop. He signed them "Sniper." For all Harvey's perspicacity, he could not have imagined Sniper's eventual involvement in Operation Gold.

BIG BILL'S BIG QUESTIONS IN THE SPRING OF 1953 were where to start and end the tunnel, and how to disguise the digging. More tests and precious additional information from East German telecommunications files indicated that the most promising cables lay along a highway that led to Karlshorst. They included a high-frequency line that linked Moscow with Soviet military headquarters in Wunsdorf, twenty miles south. After Harvey traveled to consult with technical experts elsewhere in Europe, designs were drawn to gouge an almost elegantly wide shaft to the cables. Harvey's necessarily frequent flights over surrounding East Germany were one reason he had diplomatic cover and carried a diplomatic passport: a plane might be accidentally or purposely brought down during one of his tense passages through East German airspace. All other BOB personnel were supposedly members of Berlin's American military garrison.

Technical consultations about another phase of the project had started even before Harvey took over in Berlin. In October 1952, he'd flown to London for meetings with specialists from the British Secret Intelligence Service (SIS). There, his resolve to protect Operation Gold's secrecy was hardened even further by his knowledge of British treachery. For the midwestern anti-elitist had just used his skills to sniff out Kim Philby, the British arch spy who had tipped off the KGB about the Cohen-Krogers and other more famous Soviet agents—even while Harvey's Washington superiors were still inviting the gentlemanly traitor to their classy clubs. Even so, Big Bill knew the Brits had the best expertise and greatest experience in making and operating suitable listening devices. Their technicians were the logical choice to plant the actual taps at the tunnel's far end.

Other research was pursued elsewhere, including testing soil conditions similar to Berlin's in England and in New Mexico. But wasn't it all still fantasy? Would ground ever actually be broken? Yes, the great day came in August 1953. The large hidden cavity was called "Harvey's Hole" by the still severely limited selection of people who knew about it.

No SUMMARY CAN DO JUSTICE TO THE IMAGINATIVE solutions and ardent exertions that went into the tunnel's construction. It began below another Harvey brainchild: a massive, semi-underground warehouse near the southern end of the border between Berlin's American and Soviet sectors. Specially built to hide the 3,100 tons of earth to be excavated, it would also provide cover, since the warehouse was disguised as a new radar intercept station, Americans' need for which would be unlikely to arouse Soviet suspicions. Earth-laden trucks rolled up and down ramps to the impostor radar facility's cavernous basement. From five meters below it, the tunnel would burrow 900 yards to the border, and then another 900 to reach the cables.

The incessant above-ground espionage war continued to serve as a spur. The Stasi, the KGB's near-paranoiac East German offspring, was now arresting many BOB informants. Together with tightened Soviet security, that made BOB's communications with its agents in the East even more difficult, inspiring the tunnel staff to *get the job done*—warily but swiftly.

Breaking though a wall beneath an old house, the diggers were drenched by the contents of a cesspool. To avoid the possible attention if foul-smelling clothing were sent to local laundries, an underground washer and dryer were installed. At the same time, the listening and recording devices—such as demodulation equipment for separating carrier channels in the Soviet cables and amplifiers for each line—were chosen or specially designed, and then co-ordinated. Warehouse admission was restricted to personnel already aware of the project. Harvey and his top subordinates avoided observation by visiting in closed trucks. Twenty-four-hour logs registering all movement of person-nel and vehicle traffic near the site were scrutinized for pattern changes. Mi-crophones for detecting intruders were placed along the border fence. Overlooking the tunnel's line to its target, a concealed observation post in the warehouse was manned around the clock. Following a Harvey trip to Wash-ington to obtain approval, plastic explosives were planted for collapsing the tunnel without causing a surface explosion in case of emergency.

Like its conception, the tunnel's construction was a dazzling display of CIA creativity and enterprise, technological expertise, and resourcefulness in overcoming daunting problems. It also seemed to demonstrate an exquisite ability to maintain the highest degree of secrecy in the world's most difficult environment for it, where armies of spies and double agents reported every rumor to debriefers at scores of secret service agencies. Normally, Berlin was an intelligence sieve where "everyone was a spy, and the spies were spying for everyone," as a colleague of Harvey's described the scene those seven years before the building of the Wall. Squads of "illegals," informers, double agents, and accomplices crossed back and forth between the hostile sectors. Preserving the security of so large and complex a project in those conditions seemed a demonstration of operational brilliance. Despite East Germany's police state, despite ardent surveillance by the KGB and Stasi, the digging proceeded undetected.

The caricature of hard-drinking, gun-toting "Pear," as his agents had nick-named Harvey, held true in its narrow way. Colleagues called luncheon at his suburban villa "trial by firewater": dry martinis were swallowed from noon to the serving of the meal four hours later. But his labors to give birth to the tunnel while heading Europe's largest, most active CIA station were remark-able. The project quivered with his huge energy. His work discipline and nose for potential trouble had never been more impressive. His inspiring single-mindedness fused with his talent for thinking of every detail.

CONSTRUCTION WAS COMPLETED IN FEBRUARY 1955. The massive excavation, high enough for a six-foot man to stand upright in it, ran beneath the high-way to Karlshorst and ended at its far shoulder. During the following month, the British experts dug a smaller vertical shaft up from the tunnel's end to near ground level, then built a small tap chamber for the equipment that had to be placed near the East German cables. The first of three taps was in place in May.

A new KGB technique of defending those cables with internal wires filled with pressurized air had convinced the Soviets their high-frequency lines were virtually immune to tapping. Those minuscule devices registered the most minute dip in the current, which was inevitable when even the most sophisticated apparatus was installed on a line. Now the contribution of British expertise became crucial, for it included an even more clever SIS installation that foiled the artful Soviet defense. Specially designed amplifiers on each of the several hundred telephone wires inside the three cables prevented any dipping in their current.

Recording began as soon as the first tap was planted. While taps on the remaining two cables were successfully installed during the following three months, BOB slaked its thirst on a continuous flow of information from one of the juiciest outposts of Soviet intelligence. *Eureka!*

Some 500 communications channels were active at a given time, enabling continuous recording of an average of 28 telegraphic and 121 voice circuits, the former producing some 4,000 feet of teletype messages daily. Hour after hour, hundreds of machines in the fake warehouse recorded every scrap of conversation and every telegram—about troop dispositions, personnel changes, tactical and strategic plans. Karlshorst and the Defense Ministry in Moscow discussed weapons acquisitions, operational planning, shortages and budget squeezes, technical deficiencies, code names for newly developed weapons technology, you name it. Sorted and analyzed, much of the traffic was considered to be of immense value. Four decades later, Marcus Wolf would marvel at the "intelligence man's dream."

Its value was unintentionally confirmed when a warehouse cook misread a road sign and drove toward an East German city instead of the West German one he wanted to reach. BOB had decided not to prohibit car travel by Operation Gold's nonsensitive military personnel, believing that to do so while other American servicemen were free to use their cars might prompt suspicion. Sure enough, however, East German border guards stopped the errant car and took its driver into custody, bolting the America station into alert. Although the cook knew nothing about the tunnel, clever interrogation might elicit revealing information. However, tunnel monitors were able to follow live East German reports about the incident. BOB sighed in relief when it became clear that its great secret wasn't suspected.

The mass of new intelligence simplified BOB's hitherto daunting task of cross-checking information provided by its Soviet and East German agents.

Analysis of the cables' river of Soviet orders and chatter made it easier to determine who were false defectors and double agents—maddeningly difficult puzzles in the pretunnel days. Back then, BOB had recruited a KGB plant posing as a Soviet code clerk, for whom the KGB had gone so far as to invent a special military unit where he supposedly worked. Now it was much harder to fool the Americans, and easier for them to spot clues about planned KGB and GDR operations.

With the Target Room's files much expanded by the new wealth of professional and personal details, it was also much easier to craft campaigns against KGB personnel. Tunnel material, rich in facts, hints, and gossip about them, was especially helpful for corroborating information from BOB's bona fide Soviet and East German agents. Meshed with reports from covert agents in the field, it could be invaluable.

As before, extreme security measures were observed. A sound-muffling wood had been chosen for the tunnel's floor. Insulating sandbags lined the underground tap-room at its end, and to prevent noises that might be heard from above it, cable transmissions were monitored and recorded only back in the warehouse. Otherwise, total silence was essential, as in submarines under depth-charge attack. Above ground, every possibly relevant field report, especially about Karlshorst communications personnel, was painstakingly checked for hints of a Soviet inkling of the operation.

There were none, but American whispers might also give the game away. So many recording reels were being used that BOB felt it necessary to stifle the curiosity of the officer responsible for flying some of them to Washington. "Let in" on a fabricated explanation—that the packages contained uranium ore from an East German plant BOB was trying to monitor—the flattered officer never again mentioned the vital "secret." Every other day, the Royal Air Force flew out a much heavier cargo for transcription and analysis in London. By any measure, the feat was greater than anyone other than the exultant Harvey would have dreamed. The remarkable yield—50,000 reels of magnetic tape with recordings of 368,000 Soviet and 75,000 East German conversations—continued during the early months of 1956. It aided almost every facet of BOB's work just when ever-stiffer Soviet security elsewhere was thwarting it, and it inspired new ploys suggested by the highly confidential Soviet traffic. Harvey's Hole had cost the United States more time, nerves, and money than any other intelligence operation in Germany, but no investment appeared to pay off more lavishly. Nothing better demonstrated the skill and value of American espionage, or undermined its detractors' arguments.

WHETHER OR NOT IT IS TRUE THAT A COLD, wet spring fills peasants' barns, as an old German saying comforts, it brought something even more weighty to Karlshorst in 1956, after almost a year of tapping. Uncommonly heavy April downpours plagued East German underground telephone and telegraph circuits with electrical shorts and other faults. And although both sides in the murky struggle of wits and dirty tricks tended to cheer at news of any difficulty for the other, BOB's reaction to the GDR's communications troubles was the opposite. The prospect of even temporary suspension of the precious secret harvest caused concern.

Apart from Soviet commanders' complaints of disturbances on their lines, nothing else seemed unusual in the flow of Russian and German chatter. When the threat of serious interruptions seemed to lift, BOB's personnel breathed easier—until shortly after midnight on the night of April 21–22. Armed with night scopes, the watch at the warehouse observation post detected some fifty men on the Soviet side of the sector border, just beyond the highway. They were near the tap chamber, digging at close intervals. Harvey rushed to the warehouse from a dinner party.

The diggers discovered the chamber's top at 2 A.M. By then, BOB cable monitors were picking up the work party's comments and conversations. Shoveling cautiously in case the site had been mined, they spied the tap cables after roughly an hour. Those cables led down to a trapdoor of tempered steel separating the tap chamber from the tunnel. As Harvey watched through night-vision binoculars, the monitors now recorded the diggers' excitement over their unexpected find. "Hey!" exclaimed one. "This cable's tapped!" The surprise evidently confirmed that the party was made up of communication engineers dispatched to deal with the vexing moisture problems on the lines.

IF ALL GOOD THINGS MUST COME TO AN END, Operation Gold's seemed spitefully premature, falling when it was in full, fruitful swing. Predictably, the Russians tried to turn their lucky discovery into a propaganda triumph. Their noisy campaign trumpeting the work party's socialist heroism maintained the diggers had found the tunnel's steel door open. When, it claimed, the astonished Americans manning the recording machines caught sight of the dauntless diggers, they dropped their coffee and fled into the body of the tunnel.

Ex-KGB officers continue spinning that tale today, but BOB's tapes make nonsense of it. Actually, it took the discoverers some fourteen hours to blow-torch their way through the steel door to "their" long-empty half of the tunnel. Accompanied by a film crew, the Soviets entered the tunnel's main body at 2:20 on the *afternoon* of April 22. Meanwhile, Harvey had requested authorization from the U.S. Army's Berlin commander to destroy the shaft with his planted charges. It was denied because there could be no guarantee that no one, particularly no Russians, would be hurt.

But Harvey did order immediate installation of sandbags and barbed wire in midtunnel, just below the border between the Soviet and American zones. "You Are Now Entering The American Zone," read a handwritten sign. At 3 P.M. the Americans heard the sound of cautious footsteps moving through the tunnel in their direction. Big Bill was fully in his element. He cocked the bolt on a machine gun that had been set up behind his barbed wire. The bolt made a loud, distinctive click. The footsteps stopped. The explorers scurried back.

But even if the Soviets had conceived more imaginative twists to the story, it's doubtful they'd have scored a propaganda coup. Western media acclaim for the operation's technical brilliance drowned out objections about the tunnel's unscrupulous eavesdropping. A prominent newspaper praised it as a "striking example of American derring-do." Even the aggrieved party inadvertently joined the chorus of praise. Protesting to the U.S. Army's chief of staff for Europe, the Soviet high command in Germany noted that the very expensive tunnel structure and equipment were "executed thoroughly, with a view to long use." Marcus Wolf would be less coy: "It was a perfectly designed underground listening post."

But no compliment could compensate for the rotten luck delivered by the April downpours. Or so it seemed for nearly five years.

NEVER-SEEN "SNIPER" SENT HIS HIGHLY USEFUL secret messages westward for three years, then decided to defect. On the tense winter day in 1961 when the mysterious source finally appeared at BOB's headquarters, he turned out to be a former deputy chief of Polish military counterintelligence. Although the good man was convinced he was heir to the imperial Russian throne, there was nothing delusional about his "business" reports. Safe in the West, he identified hundreds of informants working for Polish and Soviet agents.

One was a certain retired chief petty officer of the Royal Navy: the chief source of the secret submarine information Colonel Conon Molody, alias Gordon Lonsdale, had passed to the Kroger-Cohens for transmission to Moscow. Another was George Blake of Great Britain's Secret Intelligence Service. Seven years earlier, Blake had sat next to William Harvey during the first CIA/SIS meeting about the tunnel's conception. Responsible for taking the minutes, Blake compiled detailed notes. The KGB couldn't have planned it better.

Asset Protection Program

"**R**ed Files" research found new evidence of how far the NKVD/KGB would go to protect its valued assets, including taking risks to shield Lona and Morris Cohen from Stalin's increasing paranoia. Following instructions, the Cohens fled ahead of an FBI dragnet through nine countries, finally making their way through Germany to Moscow, citadel of world socialism, in 1950. Not speaking Russian then, they were at first unaware of the purges and the unholy repression, but were soon hustled off to Poland nevertheless. Why? Svetlana Chervonnaya later asked Lona. "So that Uncle Joe doesn't cut our heads off," she replied, using the nickname FDR and the American press coined to soften the image of the Soviet dictator during World War II.

> "Later I thought how could Lona and Morris, without any Russian, without any friends [or] acquaintances in the Soviet Union understand that Uncle Joe could have cut their heads off. I think that maybe it was some form of saving valuable agent... maybe someone just saved them for future mission and took them out of danger....
>
> "I think that [Lona understood the situation] retroactively, but it could be only retroactively. She meant the situation in the Soviet Union at that time, with purges, with massive arrests, with the anti-Semitic campaign, which was called anti-cosmopolitan campaign, with the doctors plot. Morris was also Jewish, and besides they were both Americans. And to be just a foreigner in the Soviet Union was dangerous enough then."
>
> *Q:* In other words, someone moved them to Poland so they didn't get caught up in the Stalin purges?
>
> "Yes, that's my feeling. That they were just saved as future valuable agents."

Was nothing sacred? Unequivocally trusted Blake seemed the very picture of superior intelligence in both senses. At sixteen, he'd been a courier for the anti-Nazi resistance in his native Holland. After a terrifying pickup by the Gestapo, the modest, highly principled teenager was smuggled to Spain—only to be imprisoned there, on general suspicion. Eventually released, he made his way to Britain, where he served in the Royal Navy before his SIS (MI6) recruitment. By the time he was posted to Korea, under diplomatic cover, his valiant background and sterling service made him one of SIS's most promising officers.

But he was even more valued as "Diomid," his KGB code name. Diomid became the then-best Soviet mole in the West by passing to his control in London the minutes of the CIA/SIS meeting, together with his sketch of the tunnel's position and layout. Thus the KGB knew all about it before the first shovel scratched the ground!

It turned out that the KGB's top strategists were much cleverer than suggested by the hype about the diggers' heroism. The tunnel's faked "find" was actually part of a plot to prevent the CIA and SIS from suspecting Blake. When Karlshorst's chief learned of the tunnel in 1955, he quickly initiated preparations to stage its supposedly unexpected discovery. Working with a KGB specialist in eavesdropping flown in from Moscow—the colonel who would lead the "work party"—he laid plans for the "accidental" find to be made by a fictitious Red Army signals unit supposedly on a routine detail.

Moscow orchestrated the tactics and timing. For maximum diplomatic and propaganda value, Nikita Khrushchev chose to stage the exposé on the eve of his first visit to London. He also ordered that the culprits be nabbed in the act, which may account for the Soviet struts about catching American personnel with their earphones on.

A 1959 Sniper warning of a Soviet mole in SIS, possibly code-named "Diamond," had prompted an investigation by MI5, the British counterpart to the FBI. It failed to find Blake, and BOB remained totally fooled by the Soviet theater until the Sniper fingered him those five years later. The consummate traitor's highly skilled protectors had manifestly outdone BOB in security. No member of Soviet counterintelligence in Berlin had the slightest knowledge of the tunnel. The KGB's top command instructed Blake to reveal his information to no one, not even KGB officers other than his control. As late as the summer of 1955, only three people in Moscow Central's First Chief Directorate (for foreign intelligence) knew his identity and were aware of Operation Gold's existence. All that security enabled Blake to keep spying for another five years. More humiliating for BOB, its extraordinary measures for protecting the tunnel's secrecy had all been for nothing!

Did that futility apply to the operation as a whole? Was the huge effort to record, transcribe, translate, categorize, cross-reference, and evaluate the sea of tapped material also for nothing? Or worse than nothing: Did the knowingly bugged Soviets feed the taps with massive disinformation, as some agents later claimed? While Operation Gold ended in *Soviet* success, that wasn't intended by the originators, to put it mildly. For them, the end result seems to fit the current fashion of dismissing most espionage as a scandalously exorbitant con. Writing after perusing archives on both sides, respected experts conclude that the tunnel's practical value was extremely limited. In that view, the massive adventure—a telling display of the futility of espionage in general and the CIA's efforts in particular—can be seen as supporting Phillip Knightley's dismissal of "the whole corrupt [intelligence] concern." With that kind of victory, who needed defeat?

Former BOB officers disagree, as would be expected. Recovering from the Sniper's stunning revelations, they sang the tunnel's praises despite everything, citing later Soviet documents as evidence in support of their denial that they'd been duped by disinformation. In general, they say, the tunnel's yield—1,750 intelligence reports by September 1958, based on 90,000 translated messages or conversations—was a huge asset even years after the taps were shut down. As they tell it, that treasury was essential for verifying and corroborating information provided by agents in the field, even for pointing them toward where to look and what to look for. That applied directly to the offerings of BOB's new star source, a lieutenant colonel of Soviet military intelligence who supplied invaluable information, especially after his fortuitous transfer to Karlshorst, also in 1957. His reports about the compound would have been far less valuable without the explanation, enhancement, and interpretation made from the tunnel transcripts. (Caught in the act, the lieutenant colonel would be executed for treason in 1960, despite a KGB plea to spare his life.)

Operation Gold also reinforced the defense against the persistent Soviet crusade to rid Berlin of its "spy-ridden" Western zones. Nikita Khrushchev warned in 1958 that unless the Allies accepted East German control over access to those zones, he'd sign a separate peace treaty with East Germany, ceding that power to the new, sovereign GDR. Rich tunnel documentation of Soviet undercover operations in West Berlin armed Washington's winning counterattack to that serious threat.

American enthusiasts are convinced the cables continued transmitting massive quantities of sensitive material even after the First Chief Directorate knew they were being tapped. Baffling as that might seem to laypeople, the reason makes impeccable sense to spies. Changing communication practices and procedures to negate the taps would have required an operation large enough to tip off BOB, whose search for the leak may have uncovered Blake. To protect its secret—that it knew the American secret—and thus shield source Blake, the First Directorate willingly compromised other KGB departments, together with fellow intelligence services and the Soviet army in Germany. Not even Karlshorst's commander was told about the tunnel until Blake's normal rotation from London to Berlin's SIS station.

Whether disinformation was leaked into the river of genuine stuff coursing the cables may never be known unless the most sensitive KGB files are one day made available to the public. Whether it's true, as Marcus Wolf believes, that his side would never have discovered the tunnel without Blake's tip-off is also a moot question. But Operation Gold does reveal some of espionage warfare's ironies. Too little hard evidence against the imprisoned George Blake could be found to prosecute him in court. A confession was needed, and an artful British interrogator went to work to obtain it. "Come on, George," the expert baiter kept taunting. "We know why you did it. It was for the money." In the end, that provoked the prisoner who had once wanted to be a priest. "No, not for money. I never got a penny! I did it for the ethics."

What ethics? When North Korea captured Seoul in 1950, the admired young Blake was imprisoned for three years. During that time, he took the initiative in serving Moscow by asking to speak to a Russian officer. What prompted him? Before his posting to Seoul under British diplomatic cover, he'd been assigned to take a Cambridge University course on the menace of Communism—which attracted the introverted young man instead of repelling him. Communist sermons—all for one and one for all; the need for means of production to be owned in common because people are more important than property—echoed the moral lessons he'd learned as a boy from his devoutly Lutheran mother. Thus a course on Communism's dangers triggered his conversion, which was reinforced by the sight of "the relentless bombing" of Korean villages by massive American planes. "I felt I was committed on the wrong side," he'd explain.

The tunnel's fate held more irony. "Blown" from the beginning, it couldn't be closed until serving its purpose for Soviet intelligence—Blake's protection, as well as American disinformation. Thus ended an elaborate illustration of the dividends and the waste of actual espionage operations and the sometimes strange rules of play in which some participants are more interested in demonstrating their skills than in contemplating the national interest. It was the classic modern spy story.

AFTER LEAVING BOB IN 1959, WILLIAM Harvey went to work directly for John Kennedy. The young president placed "America's James Bond" in command of Executive Action, a new CIA program for developing a capability to conduct assassinations anywhere in the world. Fidel Castro was among the first targets. Drinking more than ever, Big Bill negotiated with Mafia mobsters, who indeed attempted to kill the Cuban leader in the 1960s. During the potentially calamitous Cuban Missile Crisis of 1962, the Cold War cowboy took it upon himself to send sabotage teams onto the island. Much of the intelligence com-

Master Linguist and Mole

Dutch-born George Blake was Moscow's man of many missions. During the first extensive interview he granted after the fall of Communism, he traced his steps into the Soviet wilderness of mirrors.

Blake was born in 1922 and raised in a cosmopolitan setting. His father, from a Spanish-Jewish family living in Egypt, had served in the British army in World War I; his mother was middle-class Dutch. After the death of his father, the serious thirteen-year-old, intent on becoming a minister in the Dutch Reform Church, moved in with his extended family in Cairo, in whose schools he became acquainted with Arabic culture and the outriders of British Empire. Although young Blake resisted the influences of a beloved cousin who was a believing communist, the seed of a utopian dream was planted in that hot North African land populated by desperately poor millions. The outbreak of World War II in Europe found the youth at his grandmother's in Rotterdam. As a half-Jew in Nazi-occupied Holland, his life was in danger. But the sophisticated sixteen-year-old, still intent on becoming a Protestant clergyman, had the advantage of looking much younger. That helped his cover when he bicycled as a courier for the anti-Nazi underground.

Deciding to fight fascism head-on, he made his way to British-held Gibraltar, then to England. From the Royal Marines he was recruited into the British Secret Service, for which he worked chiefly in Holland. Four months after the Allies celebrated their victory over Hitler, London dispatched him to spy on Soviet forces in East Germany, which he did that enough for his MI6 supervisors to decide to add Russian to his languages. They sent him to tweedy, classbound Cambridge, where another seed of espionage was accidentally planted—in a Russian language class that supplemented his Communism studies.

In a way [that class] shaped another stage in my development towards . . . my desire to work for the Soviet Union. That was, the professor there was an English woman, but her mother was Russian, and she had lived in Petersburg, before the revolution. And . . . she had a great *love* for Russia, not for communism, but for Russia. And she inspired her students with that *love* for Russia, and things Russian. She took us to the services in the Orthodox Church, and I happened to be one of her favorite pupils. Her influence was of great importance, because it changed my attitude towards Russia, and things Rus-

sian. Inspired me with a great attraction. . . . Maybe a little bit naïve, or a little bit romantic, but still there it was.

Such love was not uncommon among students of Russian language and
literature. But MI6 was unaware of it—and of Blake's positive response to
the ideological aspects of Communism that the Cambridge lectures were
supposed to have innoculated him against—when it posted him to South
Korea under diplomatic cover. Blake's orders were to attempt espionage
penetration of the Soviet Union from what was assumed to be a soft under-
belly, its Pacific Far East frontiers. But his Cambridge language training had
changed his outlook, and he never forgot his formative years fighting
fascism in Holland. The regime of strongman Syngman Rhee—the Ameri-
can-selected president of the newly created Seoul government—prompted
flashbacks. "I got to know the political situation in South Korea," Blake told
"Red Files." "It was really in my view kind of fascist. So I had a certain sympathy for the North knowing very little [about it]." (Blake failed to penetrate
either North Korea or the Soviet Union.) His time in North Korea as an imprisoned enemy alien with diplomatic status turned that sympathy and an-
tifascist bent into devotion to the Soviet cause.

Insisting he never was brainwashed, Blake singles out American airpower
as a key factor in his turnaround:

> [What] acted on me as a catalyst [to change sides] was what I saw happening
> in North Korea: the relentless bombing of small Korean villages by enormous
> American Flying Fortresses. People: young women and children and old peo-
> ple—[old men only] because the young men were in the army—I saw them with
> my own eyes. I might have, we might have been the victims ourselves. It made
> me feel ashamed . . . of belonging to [those] with overpowering technical supe-
> riority against what seemed to me quite defenseless people. . . . I had seen the
> devastation in Germany after the war but it was nothing, absolutely nothing
> compared with the devastation in North Korea. . . .
>
> [The American bombing] and the other stages of my development made
> me . . . feel that I was fighting on the wrong side. . . .
>
> I didn't go too much into the wrongs, the rights and wrongs of the begin-
> ning of the Korean war. It was very difficult from the position you were in to
> decide exactly what started it. But now I realize that it was the North who
> started it. Still it was that experience of the war, which acted as a catalyst,
> and made me decide to join the other side.

Now, after revelations from Kremlin archives about Soviet flaws in general and Stalin's collusion with North Korea in particular, Blake may seem a naïve dupe. But his leap of faith came in the shadow of fascist destruction across Europe. After a personal evolution eased by ignorance of Stalin's huge blot on the Communist dream.

As for the Soviet experiment to which he had devoted so much of his adult life, Blake turned philosophical when discussing it with "Red Files."

Obviously it has failed. It has not been possible to build that society. I for myself have worked out why that is so. It is that a Communist society is in a way a perfect society, and we are not perfect people. And imperfect people cannot build a perfect society. And people have to change a great deal still. It would take many, many, many generations and perhaps thousands and thousands of years before we can build such a society. But I also think that it is a very noble experiment, which deserved to be successful. But which wasn't successful, because of human frailty.

munity shared his fury over the Kennedy brothers' refusal to provide air support for the ill-trained anti-Castro brigade facing disaster at the Bay of Pigs eighteen months earlier. But he went further by rebuking John and Robert Kennedy during a tense cabinet meeting at the height of the Missile Crisis. "If you hadn't fucked up in the first place," he was said to have informed the president, "we wouldn't be where we are now."

Exiled to Rome, he guzzled before and after episodes involving revolvers—one pointed at a policeman who'd stopped him for speeding—and on trips to relive his glory in Berlin. Among the handful of CIA colleagues who attended the legend's funeral in 1978, some remembered the gold medals awarded them for what the CIA believed, at the time, was the spy war's greatest coup.

Theodore Hall fared better. In 1950, Colonel Rudolf Abel, then the top KGB operative in the States, tried to re-recruit him. "No more," Hall is reported as saying. "I helped during the war, and now it's over." Nevertheless, prudence and anxiety convinced him to leave America for England, where he took extremely pleasant refuge at the same Cambridge University, where he would spend more than thirty years as a distinguished, sometimes brilliant physicist. In 1994, when almost all those with knowledge of his past were dead or dying, Morris Cohen predicted Hall's identity would remain secret for another century. Actually, American counterintelligence had known it in the 1950s, but Hall was never charged with anything, much less convicted. Retired to a pleasant English suburban house, he told the authors of *Bombshell* in 1997 that he was "quite convinced" he'd have "acted differently" if he'd known of Stalin's crimes. The "principled man of enormous integrity," as his daughter described him, never shared his secret with her or her sister until his activities became known. But despite the "great burden on him," his Cambridge life remained enviable until he died there in 1999.

The Krogers' luck held less well. In the wake of the Sniper's revelations about the former chief petty officer's betrayal in the Portland naval base, they were exposed and sentenced to twenty years' imprisonment in 1961. The authorities "let us know in no uncertain terms," Cohen-Kroger told Soviet interviewers in a film obtained by the series producers, "that if we did not allow them to take my fingerprints, they would force me." The documentary's larger revelation is that the ten-year American search for the Cohens ended when a match was found in two sets of fingerprints that had been taken as belonging to two different men. As David Major summed up for "Red Files," it was only then that the previously baffled FBI realized they had "this remarkable spy that had operated in both countries."

Despite that, and also despite KGB hints that the Cohen-Krogers were "worth a czar's ransom," as the authors of *Bombshell* put it, they were exchanged for three prisoners of the Soviet Union in 1969. That seemed a very bad bargain for the West, since the three were a university lecturer who'd merely been distributing "anti-Soviet" literature in Moscow and two men serving drug sentences. However, London was moved by Moscow's threat of a life sentence for the latter and the Cohens' poor health. Then interned in separate prisons, she was suffering from serious arthritis, he from painful skin problems and other disorders.

Back to the U.S.S.R. they went, via Poland—and back to their work for the KGB almost immediately upon their arrival in Moscow. After decades of training colleagues there, Lona Cohen was diagnosed with cancer. According to a memory offered to "Red Files" by Svetlana Chervonnaya, the historian of espionage, she wanted to return to America for her remaining time. However, she was still in Moscow when she died in 1990. Morris, now less certain he'd picked the right side, followed her three years later.

The couple had first heard of, and then met, George Blake as prisoners in London. After Blake's long-delayed unmasking by the Sniper—the full five years of KGB service after the tunnel's discovery—he was sentenced to forty-two years of incarceration, the maximum for three counts of violating British secrecy laws.

Some claim the forty-two years amounted to one year for each British agent killed as a result of the information he provided. He himself would express *gratitude* for the unusually long sentence, measured by British norms. "I must say," he told "Red Files" interviewers, "that in a way I'm grateful to the judge . . . because it made my position in prison very much easier." By that he meant that fellow inmates sympathized with him.

Blake's prison was Wormwood Scrubs, London's maximum-security facility, where he also met Molody-Lonsdale. Still the jolly optimist, Lonsdale predicted that before long they would both be celebrating in Red Square, and sure enough, he was swapped for a Western spy in 1964. Two years later, Blake, helped by devotedly admiring fellow prisoners, escaped from Wormwood Scrubs—in time to be smuggled to Moscow and join his honored comrade celebrating the fiftieth anniversary of the Bolshevik Revolution in 1967. Now Blake lives a quiet life in Moscow as a Middle East expert for the Russian Republic's successor to the KGB. Britain's most wanted criminal, who was named after King George V, Britain's monarch at the time of his birth, remains unrepentant—in fact, proud of his instincts, if not the outcome of the Soviet experiment

SOVIET ESPIONAGE ENJOYED A LONG HEAD START. Although far from perfect, its professionalism was distinctly higher than that of its American counterpart until the advent of high-flying U-2 spy plane, and then the satellite cameras that can photograph Band-Aids from space, provided unparalleled U.S. reconnaissance. Can the seeming contradictions and ironies of the Cold War's best tricks offer more enduring wisdom than that for the still-booming business? The new photographic marvels themselves may suggest something to consider: that thoughts of one's own country's spying rarely temper anger over the enemy's. When America got its superb technological act together, it became the uncontested espionage world champion. Sober observers say that the National Security Agency, still among our most secret institutions, eavesdrops not only on countries considered potential enemies but also on friends and allies, and that it can pick up foreign leaders telling their wives they're going to the bathroom. That might put Cold War espionage as well as current varieties in better perspective. In the outpouring of outrage about the recent alleged Chinese theft of nuclear secrets from Los Alamos, our far greater "coverage" of China—not only from the sky, surely—goes unmentioned. If their intrusion angers us, wouldn't it make foreign-policy sense to credit their resentment of ours?

As for the old Cold War, fading ideological commitment within the Soviet Union also dulled the radiant socialist promise to Western sympathizers. That brought a corresponding reduction of "classical" East-West espionage—the kind motivated by resolve to fight for human justice and welfare. When the once-enticing hocus-pocus about a "higher" civilization stopped playing more than a ritual role, recruitment of politically devoted Western spies fell to near nothing. The American providers of information changed from heeding a higher calling to peddling valuables. During the past several decades, all the major ones did it for precisely what miffed George Blake when that motive was attributed to him: for the money, with or without the thrill of courting danger.

The righteous Blake's doing it for *conscience* was once the rule, not the exception. If nothing can justify traitors, if allegiance to one's country is the highest good, the earlier band's motives nevertheless merit reflection because the danger is ongoing. They were moved by the same notions and yearnings that inspired millions of Russians to close their eyes to many realities during their furious "building of Socialism." Many pointedly refused payment for their contributions. Almost all acted out of what must be called authentic, if tragically misdirected, idealism. That and the Soviet ability to fool foreigners made their romanticized conception of the Motherland of Socialism understandable—at least until Nikita Khrushchev's quite different kind of bombshell at the Twentieth Party Congress in 1956. Khrushchev's famous "Secret Speech" there to the Party leaders began circulating in the Soviet Union and abroad almost immediately. It was a devastating, if partial, revelation of Stalin's crimes—or, for the critics of the Soviet Union who had long been talking about them, a confirmation. Either way, it made impossible any further denial that millions had died and otherwise suffered horribly, and it demolished every possible excuse for further serving the Soviet Union. Most of the diehards who continued to do so were daunted by the idea of admitting a dreadful mistake and renouncing the convictions and dreams that had propelled virtually their entire purpose. But their justifications in terms of their earlier ideals sounded pathetic.

Klaus Fuchs's allegiance to Communism came from a slightly different angle in the same general direction: he saw German Communists doing more than anyone else to resist the Nazis—a matter of additional importance to him when he was put on the Gestapo's wanted list. Resistance to fascism also moved the others, especially those like Morris Cohen-Kroger, who feared the Nazi-supported fascism they volunteered to fight during the Spanish Civil War would overwhelm Europe unless it was stopped, and who saw enough of its ugly face on the Iberian Peninsula to harden their convictions.

Highly principled in that respect, Morris confronted the beast in the best way he knew how. Never mind that in that civil war, the Soviets actually fought supposedly fraternal socialist parties as much as General Franco's armies; Morris didn't know that. What he did know was that Europe's burgeoning fascism imperiled the continent, and that the capitalist democracies, including his freedom-loving native land, didn't really care. There he was probably right, and might have preserved a fine sense of honor if he didn't let it take him further, to accepting recruitment by Soviet intelligence.

Another formative influence on the Cohens—and on almost everyone who then involved himself or herself with Soviet espionage—was the near breakdown of the American economy in the early 1930s. As an American counterintelligence officer named David Major reminded a "Red Files" interviewer, it was the era of the Great Depression:

> Everything about the West was put in question. Everything. From our values to our economy, people were looking for answers. Answers to problems they couldn't solve.

Beyond a cause of immense misery and injustice, the Depression seemed to some to be proof of capitalism's doom.

Theodore Hall's immediate problem came on top of the others: the danger he saw in an American monopoly of the bomb. (That's what it amounted to, although Great Britain also had its own.) It turns out that other Manhattan Project scientists shared his belief that a balance of terror might make the world safer by precluding the launch of unilateral atomic war. Fifty-odd years later, Hall remained convinced that a safer world was exactly what his espionage had achieved. It has even been alleged that "[I] changed the course of history," he told the authors of *Bombshell*, the 1999 book about him and his ring. He answered that allegation from his own perspective.

> Maybe the "course of history," if unchanged, would have led to atomic war in the past 50 years—for example, the bomb might have been dropped on China in 1949.... If I helped to prevent that, I accept the charge.

But Hall's fear for the world's future with atomic weapons available to a single power grew from a larger anxiety: that economic atomization and globalization after the war would return America to catastrophic unemployment, followed by fascism. That conviction, in turn, derived from an almost classic Communist worldview—which, as they say, he came by naturally. A family member recalled that young Hall "drank Communism with his mother's milk." His parents were indeed Communists for all the right reasons—resolve to fight injustice, help the poor, make America a better place for all—and all the ignorance, often self-imposed, of what the Soviet comrades were really up to, all the zeal to assert that ends of such overwhelming importance indeed justified the means. By the time the budding scientist entered Harvard, his ideological convictions were almost as strong as his aptitude for physics. If he hadn't roomed with two of the college's leading radicals, he'd have sought them out anyway.

Despite Morris Cohen's lower social station, he read some of the same far-Left literature as did Hall, and joined some of the same organizations that held the same rousing meetings about capitalism's evils and Communism's salvation. If those two, and Lona, had a problem with social concern, it was that theirs was not too little but too much, at least too ambitious. Everything they thought they were doing—even their resort to lying and deceiving—rang with devotion to "higher humanity."

Does it matter that they were more gullible than villainous? That they did their deplorable work for "good" reasons, making their tragic errors at a time when concerned Americans knew much less about the real Soviet methods than about the pain and suffering under the crueler capitalism of those years? None of that lessens their damage to national security by a smidgen—unless you share the increasingly popular opinion of natural and political scientists that MAD's (Mutually Assured Destruction) balance of terror between the superpowers *did* ensure an uncommonly long period of, of all surprising things, world safety. But that may be little guidance for a future in which the arsenal of many countries may include superweapons.

While ideology surges in the Middle East and elsewhere, it seems dead as a doornail in the West and in Russia. My children, puzzled by how on earth their parents and grandparents could have spent so much energy causing so much agony for an "obviously" unworkable utopia, feel certain that no such "naïve foolishness" will return. But cyclical history suggests that ideological fervor may be less dead than resting. Utopias have a way of returning to intellectual and emotional fashion. No doubt a crusading new fundamentalist Socialism will reemerge somewhere in the world, possibly as ever greater allegiance is transferred from the nation-state to something more embracing of civilization as a whole. If so, maybe the ultimate folly of the Soviet spies will restrain the enthusiasts of the new designs from convincing themselves they can put the whole world right, and from willingly risking everything for it. But I suppose that's wishful thinking.

MEASURING THE LONG-TERM VALUE OF espionage necessarily requires speculation, and here's a final item. Did the Soviet theft of atomic secrets eventually have an opposite effect to the one intended? The Japanese attack on Pearl Harbor, tactically and operationally brilliant as it was, produced the worst possible result for Japan: a fierce commitment in hitherto vacillating America to fight, *fight, FIGHT* the perfidious enemy that committed the dastardly attack. And dazzling as the Soviet success was in penetrating the Manhattan Project, the enterprise brought upon Moscow some of the same intensity to *defeat*.

Yes, it much speeded the urgent work back home to break the understandably feared Anglo-American monopoly. It also boosted the Soviet Union into the category of top world players. Precisely that, however, frightened Americans into retreat from some of our most cherished principles (while we shouted them all the louder). A revved-up national self-righteousness combined with the combat vision configured by (exaggerated) danger to nourish domestic witch-hunting in general and McCarthyism in particular. But if the widespread suspicion of "anti-Americanism" was bad for *us*, the final consequences for *them* were probably worse. Above all, the U.S.S.R. needed attention to its internal issues and problems, with some form of Western cooperation, as during tsarism's more progressive periods. Increased fear of the Soviet Union made that task—or pursuing world domination, if that was really the country's ambition—much harder. And greater fear was just what the Soviet atomic bomb provoked, together with hardening suspicion, distrust, and even hatred of everything and everyone Soviet. That happened most of all in America, which called many of the West's shots. So it can be argued that even the superb espionage coup against Enormoz, considered the greatest of the entire twentieth century by CIA as well as KGB veterans, produced lesser long-term results than it was worth in energy and effort.

But of course the Kremlin didn't know it would lose. History was supposed to be on its side.

ABOVE NKVD Badge, "The Sword and the Shield"

RIGHT "Iron" Felix Dzherzhinsky: a 1919 portrait by noted Russian-Jewish photographer Moisei Nappelbaum.

BELOW The profoundly feared Lavrenti Beria, Stalin's last Secret Police Chief, at Stalin's dacha, mid-1930s. While Stalin works in the background, Beria cradles the dictator's daughter, Svetlana, in his lap.

ABOVE A doctored photograph of CHEKA leaders clustered around Dzherzhinsky at his desk in Lubianka, 1922. Abram Bless, Lenin's chief bodyguard, is standing behind Iron Felix. Other Chekists, many shot during the purges, were cut out of the picture. Note the sharp edges on lower left and lower right.

BELOW The Stalinist leadership at a Bolshoi Theater ceremony, February 1943. In the front row, from left: Beria, Vyacheslav Molotov, Nikolai Bulgamin, and Boris Cheernussov. Behind Molotov stand Stalin and Semyon Budennyi.

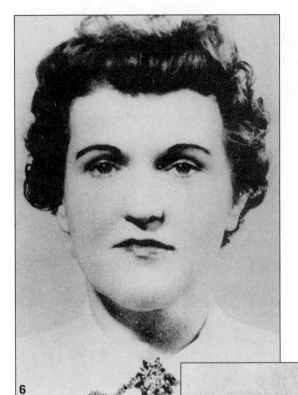

Lona Cohen c. 1941 photograph from the Russian Foreign Intelligence Agency. She pulled off the "ENORMOZ Kleenex Box caper" to ferry American atomic secrets from New Mexico.

6

Morris Cohen, a secret agent who kept his secrets secret, c. 1945. Only a portion of his long career as a Soviet spy is known even now.

7

LEFT Operating in England as "Helen and Peter Kroger" in 1955–61, the Cohens passed Navy secrets to Moscow.

BELOW Lona and Morris Cohen completed their careers in Moscow training new spies. Near the end of her life in 1992, Lona often asked a friend, "Well, am I a traitor?"

The Cohens' Moscow tombstone. President Boris Yeltsin posthumously named them "Heroes of Russia": probably the only Americans to have received that medal and honorific title.

LEFT Kim Philby: Soviet secret agent, top-ranked British Secret Intelligence Officer, CIA and FBI liaison in 1949. In 1963, he fled to Moscow just steps ahead of spy catchers.

11

12

КИМ
ФИЛБИ
I.I 1912 — 1988 II.V

RIGHT Philby's tombstone in Moscow's Kuntsevo cemetery. He lived in the Soviet capital as a kind of English gentleman on a lifetime pension award by the Communist Party's Central Committee.

Theodore Hall in 1944, when he was working at Los Alamos. Hall gave U.S. A-bomb construction secrets to Soviet agents, but was never prosecuted. The day after his death in 1999, his daughter stated flatly, "He did it. There is nothing they can do to him now."

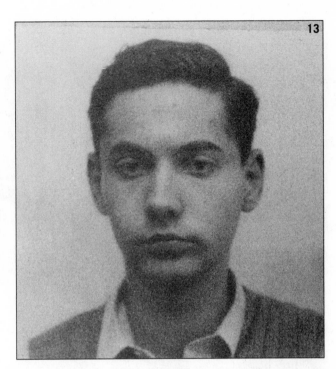

Karl Fuchs, who passed atomic bomb documents to the Soviets, in 1944–45. After Venona Project decryptions exposed him, Fuchs confessed and was sentenced to prison by a British court. He later lived in East Germany.

15

ABOVE Igor Kurcha-
tov, "the father of the
Soviet nuclear na-
tion," who supervised
the use of stolen
American secrets,
prepares to watch an
A-bomb explosion.
The soft-focused,
Stalin-era photo-
graph typically hides
details.

16

RIGHT Kurchatov
(right) in the lab of the
Ukrainian Physical and
Technical Institute in
Kharkov, 1932.

ABOVE Kurchatov, called "the beard" by colleagues, at the control board of the Ogra atomic plant. He died the next day: February 7, 1960.

BELOW Kurchatov (second from right) in a lab at the Ukrainian Physical and Technical Institute in Khrakov, 1932. "Kurchatovium," the 104th element of the periodic table, was named for him.

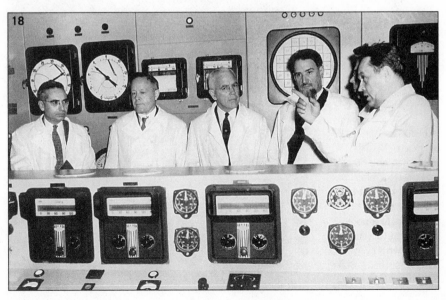

19

ABOVE   Kurchatov and British prime Minister Anthony Eden (right) at a 1956 reception at the Soviet Embassy in London.

RIGHT   George Blake, war hero, British diplomat, and Soviet spy, in December 1998. "I think it is never wrong to give your life, to a noble ideal, and to a noble experiment, even if it didn't succeed." Blake still lives in Moscow.

20

III
SOVIET SPORTS WARS

Sport in a socialist country is a state concern, and is structured according to the principles of amateurism.

—*Highlights of Soviet Sport,* Moscow, 1972

The Communist Party of the U.S.S,R. and the Soviet Government pay permanent attention to improving the welfare, health, and physical and mental development of the working class and students. Physical education and sports are increasingly a regular part of Soviet citizen's lives.

—*Moscow's Ready to Host the 1980 Olympics,* Moscow, 1979

I don't need any sports lovers but real sportsmen, champions.

—A sports official in a large Soviet factory, 1973

I turn to you with a very pressing problem. Our city has a large field house, sport schools and many sporting clubs. Everywhere, however, only talented children are wanted.

—A mother, to *Soviet Sport* newspaper, 1978

L ET'S BEGIN SOVIET SPORT'S SAGA OF brilliant wins and larger losses with an Olympian turnaround in 1952. Four decades had passed since Russia, well in its discredited prerevolutionary past, last participated in the Games. Stockholm, the host city in 1912, liked the amiable, well-spoken Russian contingent, but Marxist-Leninist historians were quick to point out that its blood was all blue; and doctrine had it that the exploiting privileged of tsarist Russia—or, as the propagandists often called it, the "rotten empire"—deserved no admiration. The supposedly all-new socialist republic that installed itself in 1917 claimed to be motivated by an utterly new approach to everything, down to the Games. Denouncing them as a capitalist institution, Moscow condemned the drive for victory in sports as bourgeois thinking.

As if to manifest the Dictatorship of the Proletariat's tendency to contradict its own revolutionary thinking, Soviet sports writers simultaneously criticized the performance of the prerevolutionary competitors. Still, logic was never the strong suit of Soviet exegesis. The point remained clear to everyone: upstanding Soviet athletes, *pures et dures*, were motivated only by love of their sport and of all humanity. Therefore, they would never take part in the profoundly antisocialist Olympics that duped its followers and distracted them from acquiring a class-conscious view of the world.

And so it went, for most of socialist Russia's thirty-five years—until Soviet teams entered the 1952 Summer Olympics in Helsinki. Depending on how seriously you took Kremlin statements—or on your view of how seriously *Russians* took them—the government's explications of its total reversal might

From Heroes to Bodyguards

Bursting onto the international stage at its first Olympics in 1952, the Soviet Union went from a sporting nonentity to the world's dominant sports nation almost overnight. The achievement was even more remarkable in light of the scantiness of the base, both Soviet and pre-Soviet. The Russian delegations to the Olympic Games of 1908 and 1912 won only humiliation: even tiny Norway captured more medals. Largely peasant, tsarist Russia sorely lacked the large number of city dwellers with free time to engage in organized recreation that was most needed for modern sports. Still, the embarrassment of the 1912 Games moved Tsar Nicholas II to create a government office for promoting sport. Fledgling sports societies of Moscow and St. Petersburg were encouraged. Soccer, already on its way to becoming the most popular variety, began drawing crowds of ten to twenty thousand to matches.

The Bolshevik Revolution of 1917 and the ensuing civil war quickly undid those modest beginnings. When the fighting ended and the Bolsheviks consolidated power, the country's new leaders were too preoccupied with rebuilding industry and agriculture to devote major resources to sport and physical education. Nevertheless, how to create a "Communist" sports system was vigorously debated. As in culture and much of economic life, the new Communist state aimed to erase all traces of bourgeois decadence. Thus, a new "proletarian sport" joined the new "proletarian art." Creative physical education teachers devised appropriate new games with names like "Rescue from the Capitalists" that emphasized cooperation and mass participation rather than competition and elitism.

While the Soviets argued among themselves, sports were becoming hugely popular in western Europe and North America. International sporting competitions that had been organized in the late nineteenth century leapt in significance after World War I, when competition among a handful of athletes acquired a much broader meaning: they and their teams were seen as representing their nations and their victories and defeats came to be considered a reflection of national strength. To be a great power now required great sports teams, especially since many varieties of "play" were now used for paramilitary training. As George Orwell put it, sports had become "war without the shooting."

With the Olympics and events like soccer's World Cup riveting global millions, the Soviets wanted to enter the new propaganda arena but rightly feared they were too weak to compete with the West's best. As an alternative, they created the Red Sport International. The Sportintern, as it was known, enabled Soviet athletes to compete in matches against teams from socialist clubs in foreign countries, of which there were eventually over a dozen. The official purpose was spreading goodwill and mutual understanding.

By the mid-1930s, however, increasingly well-funded and sophisticated Soviet sports programs wanted tougher competition. Soviet soccer players, boxers, and weight lifters were sent to Paris and Prague to compete against some of the West's best athletes—and they upheld the socialist Motherland's honor. Tentative plans to participate in full-scale international competition were postponed by World War II. Quickly dusted off and implemented at the war's end, they produced their stunning results.

For many Soviet athletes, sport provided an escape from poverty. Olga Korbut, for example, grew up sharing one tiny room with her parents and three siblings. Although her gymnastic skills propelled her into the Soviet elite, her career also illustrates the Soviet sports bureaucracy's conservatism and inflexibility. When Korbut and her coach introduced acrobatic elements into her routines, creating a faster, jazzier style, the Soviet press vilified them for desecrating long-held traditions and conventions . . . until her innovations won the gold and the adoration of the spectators at the 1972 Munich Olympics.

After the collapse of the Soviet Union and its vaunted sports bureaucracy, government funding dried up, and the commercial sports leagues that tried to fill its place have struggled to become profitable. Many of the best athletes from the former Soviet Union now play in Western professional leagues like the NHL. Others work as bodyguards for the Russian mafia, with only a memory of when they were adulated as socialist heroes. As for Russian sport itself, it's now a shadow of its former glory.

have provoked tears or laughter. George Orwell's *Animal Farm* best caught the spirit of the calculated Soviet flip-flops declaimed with a torrent of slogans for erasing memory of the old way and instilling devotion to the opposite new. When the pigs who took over the farm from humans wanted to shift gears, they altered the revolutionary bleat of "Four legs good, two legs bad" to "Four legs good, two legs better," and exploited the other animals even more callously than had the old human owners. By 1952, that had become a Politburo trademark, enabling the switching of all sorts of high canons to their antithesis, like some ice pirouette performed to hearty applause.

About Face! was ordered for a hundred policies and institutions. Soviet governments abolished and restored the death penalty as if zigzagging in waters patrolled by enemy submarines. "Revolutionary" divorce went from a wholly private concern—with a plaintive request for the parties to send a postcard to local registries so that they could update their files—to a matter of state importance, therefore very difficult to obtain. The superbly creative avant-garde painting, poetry, and theater that lent their hopes as well as their art to the revolution was squelched in favor of "socialist realism" (described in Chapter V, "Soviet Propaganda Machine"), a return to many of the stultifying conventions against which artists and intellectuals had originally rebelled. Officers' epaulets and other symbols of the old, despised imperialist militarism were brushed up and restored to service, sometimes on the shoulders of former tsarist aristocrats themselves.

So the U-turn in sports policy—its angles actually slightly softened by participation in a few international events during the five years preceding 1952—fit the Soviet pattern of restoring prerevolutionary goals and practices, even some of the most hated, when it was expedient. Good citizens didn't always know why they were ordered right when they'd been so righteously going left. However, the answer was clear about why teams were sent to Helsinki: After the decades of national trauma and the difficulties of devoting serious attention to sport, the Kremlin saw enticing possibilities for itself in the 1952 Games. Its athletes had trained their hearts out in postwar conditions that were meager at best and often severe. Now it was time for their hard-honed talent to sway the world—to demonstrate the Communist system's superiority, promote respect and trade with the outside world, capture Third World hearts and minds—by *winning*. Their achievements in the Finnish capital clearly justified the decision to send them there, for they amassed enough points to win the unofficial team championship. The feat was even more remarkable in light of the fact that many of the Soviets faced world-class competitors for the first time there in Helsinki!

Four years later, they captured more gold medals in skiing, speed skating, and ice hockey, the latter more stunning than the others because the sport had been introduced to Russia only after World War II. Whatever else those successes illustrated, they showed a country leaping from relative backwardness to proven supremacy in almost a single bound. Further evidence of the remarkable achievement came at that year's Summer Games in Melbourne, where Soviet competitors again won more points and medals than did any others. The almost unthinkable results astonished and dismayed the West, most of which—as in its underestimation of Soviet science before the launching of *Sputnik I* the following year—was confident of its athletic superiority over dark, disturbed Russia. The American reaction in particular bore a faint resemblance to the shock and outrage prompted by the attack on Pearl Harbor, which came while some of our highest military leaders were assuring the nation that the Japanese—not directly called "inferior," but so assumed—were incapable of mastering such a logistic and tactical feat.

Such was the premise of Avery Brundage, the long-serving chairman of the U.S. Olympic Committee (USOC), who later became president of the International Olympic Committee. The title of an ill-informed 1955 article by Brundage was a grudging "I Must Admit—Russian Athletes Are Great." Shortly thereafter, on the eve of the 1956 Olympics, a U.S. senator from Maryland called the Soviet athlete a "paid propaganda agent of the U.S.S.R., one more slave in the hideous chain of brainwashed individuals slavishly advancing the Communist cause." Although extreme, that senator, who further identified Soviet teams as "barbaric goon squads," was in good company during that boom time for bomb shelters and headlines like "The Reds Are After Your Child."

Less crusading Americans were also galled in large numbers by seeing the enemy's flag raised while Soviet winners stood on their platforms. Consciously or otherwise, the new challenge from a country previously considered to be a pushover in all but a few minor sports added to the anxiety about the menace from Moscow. Still more evidence of the Communist conspiracy was registered when the Supreme Soviet of the U.S.S.R. awarded high honors to a large number of its 1956 winners, coaches, and sports officials, including twenty-seven Orders of Lenin, the country's loftiest tribute. A perception that the Soviet goal in sports was the same world domination as in everything else tightened Western throats. Later Soviet moves, such as sending scores of coaches to Cuba to help *that* neighbor-enemy's Olympic program did nothing to temper that view.

Is the Russian System Better?

by Avery Brundage, Chair USOC

Russia is building the greatest mass army of athletes the world has ever known. Unless there is a sudden awakening in this country, Soviet sportsmen are almost certain to dominate the 1956 Olympic Games at Melbourne, Australia.

Is the Russian system better? As much as I was impressed, I can't say that I admire the Soviet sports program. By American standards, it is harsh and severe. It is both Spartan and puritanical. Most of the spirit of fun seems to have been bled from it, and it thrives on regimentation and fierce national pride.

What struck me most about the Soviet athletes was not their maturity, but their grimness. To them, sports seem not to be a pastime, but a dedication. It's a task to do for the country. You don't see the Russians cavorting and jesting the way Americans do, and there are no friendly, back-slapping demonstrations after winning performances. Everything is taken very seriously. . . .

The lives of almost all of Russia's 200,000,000 are touched by the government's emphasis on sports and physical training. First, young boys and girls are encouraged to participate in athletics on a general scale—light weight lifting, acrobatics and gymnastics. This is intended to build strength and condition. Later they are pushed into specialization, where they receive the finest instruction possible. Coaches and teachers are trained in institutes which deal scientifically with the mechanics and physiology of athletic competition, with biochemistry and psychology. There is a fierce drive to succeed, and, once successful, to go even higher.

From "I Must Admit—Russian Athletes Are Great!"
Saturday Evening Post, April 30, 1955

BY CONTRAST, THE RUSSIAN PEOPLE WERE PARTIALLY unwinding rather than further tensing in 1956, when the Melbourne triumph was prized more as a sign of joining the world than a promise of dominating it. Coming three years after Stalin's death, the Olympic successes seemed part of a blessed emergence from decades of intense pain and strain. The terror had largely dissipated. "Rehabilitated" gulag prisoners—survivors of the ghastly purges—were limping home, eager to forget their nightmare. The exhausted country was returning to a cramped but cherished "normal," still very needy but less hectic and high-strung. After too little relaxation and far too much isolation during most of the young Republic's besieged and besieging life, people craved a rest from struggle. A desire for peace, not war, underlay their very passionate rooting for their national sports teams in international competition.

The government even cracked its borders to a trickle of visitors from abroad: venturesome travelers who attracted (surprisingly cordial) crowds on on the streets because few Russians had yet to see one, even in Moscow. (If other indications somehow failed, natives invariably recognized foreigners by their shoes, which were like sports cars compared to their own dump trucks of inferior leather.) Foreign visitors remained exciting novelties even during the summer of 1959, when they included the guides to the first-of-its-kind American National Exhibition in Moscow who began their work by helping fit out the halls and grounds.

Wielding a hammer and paintbrush with the rest of the guides, I wondered what to do for exercise in the new powerhouse of sport. When our exhibits gave promise of being ready for opening day, a friend and I took a few hours off to hit some tennis balls, a seemingly bold undertaking, like all ventures then beyond tourist Moscow. On the other hand, an American passport magically opened many gates that Russians themselves would have stampeded if they could. Until I reread Orwell, it seemed puzzling that the more violently the Soviet media attacked Uncle Sam as a bloodsucking imperialist, the more graciously, sometimes even obsequiously, people in authority were likely to greet living visitors from the capitalist badlands. That pertained too to a pair of courts belonging to the Red Army Club.

The surface was red clay. Two young Russians were rallying on the neighboring court, under the eye of an attentive, if inexperienced, coach. Tennis still bore the odium of having been enjoyed by what Soviet writers had taken to calling "former people," meaning those whom Soviet rule had deprived of their wealth and power. It did the game no good that the relative handful of players in tsarist days were all from the wrong social class, topped by enthusiastic Tsar Nicholas II and his family. But when its U-turn would come several years later, the transformation of formerly "decadent and bourgeois" tennis would be as complete as in other flip-flops, and the old scorn for it would be repudiated as "Chinese thinking," meaning stupidly doctrinaire. Meanwhile, the congenial coach during that June afternoon in 1959 blinked at our manifestly non-Soviet sneakers and inquired about our nationality. Would we, he then asked, care to play some doubles with his boys?

We soon regretted having agreed: the young men were a lot less seasoned than their tattered rackets. But my partner and I didn't coast for long. Apologizing that the weaker of his players had a doctor's appointment, the coach replaced him with a decidedly better one. Five minutes later, we learned that the mother of the other Russian "needs him at home. Would you mind?" *His* substitute was better still.

Sweat flew. Moscow summers can be surprisingly hot, and the third and fourth substitutes moved fast and hit hard. At each insertion of a new one, always stronger than his predecessor, the coach explained, with fraying regret, why the old had to depart. So it went until play became tense—and I, as luck would have it, was to serve a crucial game. Feeling my own national pride was at stake by now, I peered across the net to picture my ace rocketing off the clay. The new ringer waiting there was a lissome Apollo who'd joined us without introduction. (At that point, why bother?) The rocket turned out to be his scorching *returns* of my serves. Game, set and match to the U.S.S.R.!

And a fitting synopsis of the essence of Soviet sport? Is it fair to say it was corrupted by resorting to *anything* in order to win, especially against foreign opponents? The answer to that question of questions about the subject depends on what purpose it was intended to serve in the first place, before the corruption did or didn't take place.

IT HAD STARTED VERY DIFFERENTLY. VERY EARLY after the establishment of Soviet rule, the Communist Party decreed that the task of sport was not to produce winners but to improve the physical and mental health, and the leisure time, of the people who were heroically working to build Socialism. Soon that was linked—as was almost everything, at least officially—to political purposes. "Physical culture must be considered not only from the standpoint of physical training and health," proclaimed a 1925 Party resolution, "but should also be used as a means to rally the broad working masses around various Party, Government and trade union organizations."

Things were different in practice, however. Despite the official dedication to sports for the masses, the desire to win, even among many state officials, was no weaker than under any other economic and social system. Nor was it true that the players on the court and in the field sought social good rather than victory. And shortly after the end of World War II, Moscow began joining international sporting federations and sounding the call to win the ultimate trophy of world recognition. In 1948, when the Party's Central Committee felt ready, it passed a resolution calling on Soviet athletes to heighten their efforts to beat bourgeois records.

Marching Sportsmen

"The Sportsmen's March," a hugely popular pre-World War II song, was written for *Goalkeeper*, a much-liked 1936 film. Reflecting the official face of Stalinist-era sports with its cheerful determination to march toward Communism's promise, it enjoyed increased popularity during the war, then became the high point of the sing-along segment of the sportsmen's parade through Red Square on Physical Culture Day.

The best-known first refrain and last verse reveal a clear line between sports and military readiness:

> Hey you, sunshine, shimmer brighter,
> Make us glow with your golden rays!
> Hey you, comrade! Liven up there!
> Keep up, step up, don't hold us back!
>
> *Refrain:*
> To make our hearts and bodies younger,
> Become younger, become younger,
> Do not fear the coldness or the heat.
> Harden yourself, like Steel*
> > Physicult-hurrah-hurrah-hurrah!
> > Be Ready!
> When the time comes to beat the enemy,
> Beat them back from every border!
> Left flank! Right flank! Look sharp!
>
> Hey you, goalie, prepare for battle!
> You're a watchman by the gate!
> Just imagine that behind you
> The borderline must be kept safe!

[Translation from James von Geldern and Richard Stites, *Mass Culture in Soviet Russia* (Bloomington: Indiana University Press, 1995), p.236.]

* Note that "steel" reflects the revolutionary moniker adopted by Soviet dictator Stalin (Stalin=man of steel).

By the mid-1950s, the desire to win had become ardor, and Westerners began thinking the Soviet government would pay any price for it. Episodes involving the nation's star athletes gave strong credence to that view. To cite just one of many similar episodes, a certain budding soccer champion wasn't included in a team that was playing a match in England—until his skills were suddenly determined to be needed there, and urgently. The young man happened to be enjoying the privileges of his status in a Black Sea resort. And securing permission for foreign travel—and to a capitalist country!—ordinarily took weeks, months, sometimes years! But never mind that now, when international prestige was at stake. Crisp orders sliced through the bureaucracies of the various institutions that had to give approval, all supervised by the KGB in one way or another. The necessary permissions having been almost instantly obtained from all involved offices, the young sportsman was rushed to a plane, flown to England, and driven straight from the airport to the stadium. Less than twenty-four hours had passed.

By that time, the Soviet media regularly, not to say incessantly, explained why Soviet sports victories testified to the superiority of the system that produced them—not just its supposedly mass physical-culture approach that reversed capitalism's exploitation of the athlete, but Socialism in general. They were proof that the country would indeed "overtake and surpass" the capitalist ones, as endlessly promised. According to that dogma, American sports prepared their participants to become "cannon fodder for a new aggressive war." Soviet ones, in supposed total contrast, helped the peace-loving side win the battle for the world's minds. A 1954 proclamation that each new triumph was "proof of the superiority of the Soviet socialist culture over the rottenness of the culture of capitalist countries" reflected the official perception of the stakes of international competition.

Time softened the widespread American view of the wearers of "CCCP" on their jerseys as soulless tools of a hellish state. Besides, America and the other major international competitors were hardly immune from their own passionate resolve to win and a willingness to close some eyes to irregularities in order to do so. By 1972, Soviet and American athletes were linking arms and jogging laps of honor together in stadiums—which became possible as the Kremlin dogma about the political significance of winning became less belligerent, starting in the 1960s. Still, the Soviet Union continued to see international competition not only in terms of political prestige, as did other countries, but also as part of the larger struggle for nothing less than the world's future. As in other spheres, Soviet sport had something ideological to demonstrate. As devotion to Socialism declined during the following decades, the urgency no longer gripped like fever. However, the habit of having to *prove* the Motherland's moral and political superiority lived on, underlying at least the official interpretation of why weight lifters set records and pairs danced dazzlingly to first place on the ice. "For Socialism!" "For Lenin!" "For the Motherland!" Or so it seemed.

THE POLICY OF TOTALLY SUBSIDIZING THE BEST and most promising competitors also lived on, together with the lies about it. According to some Russians, the KGB warned all recipients of the treasured gift of a visa to travel abroad—still a tiny group drawn from the most trusted, privileged cadres—never to reveal a certain secret about Soviet sport. Meanwhile, the official line was steadfastly propagated, as in a 1972 assertion that retired Soviet sportsmen faced none of the problems of Western ones. The reason, explained a sports journalist who wrote largely for foreign audiences, was that "there are no professional sports" in the Soviet Union; only unpaid physical development and recreation for people who earned their living in their regular careers and jobs. (More is offered below about the resemblance of that nonsense to American universities' fables about *their* athletes.) At the same time, however, the highly classified information about which the KGB worried was actually common knowledge in Russia, and it injected a trace of cynicism into the overwhelming pride in Soviet sports feats in contests against the world's best.

A further word about pride is needed here because it often goes unmentioned in Western analyses of Kremlin intentions, as does the universal motivation to be the best in any given sport anywhere. In the grandstands that roared when Soviet fans did see the best, the perception was that the West was stingy about giving full recognition to the extraordinary Soviet accomplishments in the Olympics and elsewhere. More than that, Soviet feats, no matter how exceptional, were thought to be intentionally downplayed. Of course, every country then wanted foreign recognition for its struggles and impressive deeds, and still does. But postwar Russia's thirst for it was intensified by resentment of the West for, as the Soviets saw it, refusing to appreciate their horrendous sacrifices in defeating Hitler. And now, when their athletes seemed to them to have raised the Red flag high for the first time since the end of World War II, their pride swelled further. They knew what few Westerners did, or at least credited them for: that the Olympic and other international victories came remarkably soon after the Great Patriotic War, as they called it, had decimated the ranks of their able-bodied men. (The casualty rate of Soviet men between the ages of seventeen and thirty was particularly horrific.)

Parades and Spartakiads

The gold medals and world records won by Soviet stars were the peak of a vast pyramid. Millions of ordinary athletes well below them, source of Soviet claims to have achieved miracles in "mass sport," were celebrated in spectacular parades and "Spartakiads"—from Spartacus, the gladiator who led a Roman slave rebellion in 73–71 B.C.E. During Stalin's reign, the annual "physical-culture" parades highlighted mass sport festivals. The largest was mounted in Moscow's Red Square, but thousands of smaller versions were held throughout the country. The spectacle awed General Dwight D. Eisenhower when he was invited to view the 1945 parade in Moscow. "We stood for five hours [on Lenin's mausoleum] while the show went on. None of us had ever witnessed anything remotely similar. . . . Every kind of folk dance, mass exercise, acrobatic feat, and athletic exhibition was executed with flawless precision and, apparently, with greatest enthusiasm." After Stalin's death, the parades were supplanted by even more grandiose pageants: the All-Union Spartakiads of the Peoples of the U.S.S.R. Held every four years as run-ups to the Olympics, those year-long competitions involved tens of millions of participants in dozens of sports all across the country.

Anyone with the remotest interest in international sports has surely guessed the nature of the above-mentioned secret that prompted the reported KGB warnings. It was that the supposed employment of the "amateur athletes"—chiefly as teachers and coaches in physical education institutes, but also in factories, collective farms, and other economy entities—was shamelessly fictitious. The same applied to the army and to schools at which the athletes were registered.

The Olympic Code limited competition to those who participated "solely for pleasure and for the physical, mental or social benefits [derived] therefrom." That definition of amateurism, which came straight from the English conception of true athletes as gentlemen who didn't have to work *anywhere,* was clearly outdated. Most American competitors, for example, could hardly be said to see their sole goal in terms of benefits not linked to the dollar. Still, the Soviet practice seemed more egregious, and its cover-up more thorough and more self-righteous. If the real measure of sport professionalism is being paid to spend one's entire working day in practice or competition, Russia's top athletes fully deserved that designation. Many visited the factories where they supposedly worked only to pick up their pay or to contribute an occasional afternoon to physical education programs.

Russians questioned that dodge as long ago as 1938, a year after the forming of all-star teams in, most notably, soccer, wrestling, and boxing—but before any participation in international competition. Reporting that large amounts had been spent on the upkeep of such teams, a sports magazine quoted a former soccer player who admitted he earned handsomely for playing in important meets. But the convention of giving stars sinecures kept growing and growing, prompting Yuri Vlasov, long-time world and Olympic champion in super-heavyweight lifting, to write in 1966 that "top sport is a profession, a sublime profession." His competitive career coming to an end, Vlasov predicted that the top level would sooner or later be separated from the lower ones, as professional art is distinguished from amateur varieties.

How much Soviet professionals were paid will never be known. No figures relating to the salaries at their nominal jobs—and their cash bonuses after important victories—can be nearly complete because the payment, in standard Soviet style, came partly in treats that were more valuable than money. One, as I've suggested, was possible selection for trips abroad. Another was access to good food in special cafeterias or at home, the latter thanks to permission to order from special suppliers that distributed the country's very limited goodies by priority. And with tens of millions of families living in communal apartments and dormitories, tolerable housing was probably an even greater lure. Even a shove toward the top of the list of people *in line* for housing or to buy luxury items was a perk because the wait for others could be insufferably long, as suggested by a popular *anekdot* of the time.

In 1977 a Moscow dentist who has managed to amass a fortune overcomes his fear that spending some of it would expose him to suspicion that it was made illegally. [All such suspicion was deserved, since wealth could not be acquired without them—in this case, by charging patients under the table.] Resolving to buy a Volga car, the would-be upwardly mobile dynamo finds the gloomy outlet, which looks more like a shed, and manages to convince its couldn't-care-less manager [who is rich on his own tricks, namely, taking bribes for his desperately prized cars] to accept his money. He plunks down a swollen wad in cash—the country has no checking accounts—and the manager consults a fat ledger.

"Okay now, you can have your car delivered on . . . um, let's see, how about August 24th, 1989?"

"Great! So it's agreed?"

"Just a minute, do you want that in the morning or the afternoon?"

"I . . . well . . . wait a second . . ." Suddenly, the dentist remembers and brightens. "Actually the morning, Comrade. The plumber's coming that afternoon."

Privileges in such fundamental matters as food, housing, and access to consumer goods added to the ample evidence that many of the American assumptions about Soviet international competition were true. Great pressure to win was indeed exerted, and great rewards—"great" in the Soviet context—were bestowed on winners because they were seen as carrying not just the hammer-and-sickle flag but also "History's" confirmation of which side would win the world's ideological and political war. ("H" was capitalized to emphasize history's religious-like place in Marxist-Leninist theory.) When sports stars fell into legal troubles, the favoritism could be flagrant, albeit hidden. Stories about the illegal protection from on high of prominent athletes fond of vodka and shenanigans—even some young ones who hadn't yet played for national teams—circulated widely in Moscow.

One of the most habitual concerned Eduard Streltsov, a superb young soccer celebrity whose nominal job in an automobile plant made him eligible to play for a popular team sponsored by the industry's sports society. In the virtual absence of critical reporting about such stellar performers—another perk, if a negative one—rumors served to distribute the news; and they often turned out to be surprisingly accurate. The talk about Edik, as his fans called him, was that he drank outrageously, beat his wife, and brawled in restaurants and on the streets—none of which, however, cost him his jersey. On the contrary, Streltsov's factory, worried that he might switch to another team, took pains to bail him out of trouble, including trouble with the courts. Not even a rare exposé in a major newspaper, evidently sanctioned when his behavior became *too* scandalous, brought him down. His fall from grace happened only after he'd raped a woman at a party—not just any woman, according to further rumors, but the wife of an important Party official. Sentenced to twelve years in a labor camp, he was released after only a few, in good time to spark the national team to more impressive victories.

In those ways too, Soviet sport was indeed an instrument of state design and purpose—which was also nothing new, since that's what it had been from its beginnings. As we've seen, the original subsidizing of sport had more to do with improving health and making the Soviet workforce fit, disciplined, and obedient than it did with love of a game. Officially, the goal was helping "improve the productivity of labor, the prevention of disease, and the conditions of active recreation."

It was only in 1931 that the spice of nationwide competition was introduced to the major, but still underdeveloped, sports of soccer, volleyball, cycling, and track and field. That concept went together with an advance into a kind of training program for a system called "Ready for Labor and Defense." The premise was that physical training would better enable the Soviet people to tackle their tasks of building Socialism and protecting the Motherland— provided, of course, that the ideological underpinning was understood. The newspaper *Red Sport* defined it in 1938:

> Only in our country, where there is no exploitation by man, where concern
> for the individual, labor protection, care for women, mothers, and children
> exists, where underage persons are not permitted to work, where, finally,
> people have sufficient leisure time and the right to rest—only in our coun-
> try can a healthy body be formed and develop.

Concern for that healthy body led to improving physical education programs in factories, residential complexes, and athletic facilities. It propelled a spread of Red Army physical-culture exercises to workers' groups that wanted to toughen their members. Parachute jumping, automobile racing, and the other paramilitary sports were promoted by what would later be called DOSAAF, the Voluntary [so-called] Society for Assisting the Army, Navy, and Air Force, which also supervised civil defense and helped organize paramilitary training. And although it's of course impossible to measure the actual help given to the armed forces, some contribution was indeed made to the mental and physical condition of Russian troops. Marshal Ivan Konev, a principal Soviet commander during World War II, had no doubt about that:

> Only physically fit people can stand the strain of heavy fighting, can march
> long distances under perpetual bombardment and quite often have to start
> fighting at the end of them. We owe the training of the Soviet people and
> their importing with such qualities as courage, persistence, will power, en-
> durance and patriotism primarily to the sports organizations.

Still, the goal remained conditioning the Soviet people, not winning international trophies—and, in any case, was of little concern to foreign sports fans because few knew about it. Nor did the Soviet leaders much consider the possibilities of sport winning world prestige, until the late 1940s. After something new was perceived in early triumphs over non-Soviet athletes, the Central Committee—in 1948, as mentioned—issued its summons to Soviet athletes to beat their Western competitors. As we've seen, that "something" was a propaganda weapon for demonstrating Communism's superiority. How ugly that seemed, even when—or *especially* when—Soviet individuals and teams performed magnificently.

But because that interpretation of the role of Soviet sport became the West's conventional one, it deserves a closer look. Concentration on the new state policy can mislead, again largely because every policy must be executed by individual people. In this case, their attitudes varied even when they generally approved the glory-to-the-Soviet-system message.

To put it more simply, state goals were one thing, personal ones often another. Beneath the crust of dedication to the former, the competitors and coaches, if not their political supervisors, were motivated by a variety of purposes that again ranged most of the human spectrum, from passionate commitment to state ideals to cynical, if hidden, self-promotion.

AUSTRALIAN MERVYN WOOD, WINNER OF THE 1948 Olympic gold medal for singles sculling, was favored to repeat his victory in 1952, until he competed against Yuri Tyukalov, the Soviet entry. Ten years earlier, while the young Tyukalov was struggling to survive the blockade of Leningrad, the corpses of his uncle, aunt, and cousin hogged space in the family's tiny room. The freezing cold that entered through the blown-out windows prevented them from rotting; and, in any case, the boy and his mother were too weak to remove them. They lived on four ounces of bread a day, while Wood was no doubt growing strong on Australian bacon, eggs, milk, and orange juice. Still, Tyukalov's victory seemed fated to him:

> I mean no offense to Wood. He's a fine athlete. I make the comparison with one aim only: to show that succulent steaks and a comfortable life aren't the only recipe for victory. Patriotism is also needed. For me, a Soviet athlete and citizen of Leningrad, it was incomparably higher than for Wood. That's why I won.

Maybe one had to live in Russia during the 1950s to accept that such gushing, which appealed so mightily to propagandists, could be entirely sincere.

During the following decades, however, *lack* of patriotism, at least to the

Scientific Sports Sense

Track and field medals were especially prized because they seemed to lend weight to "scientific Marxism." Robert Edelman, an American authority on Soviet spectator sports, explains:

> The Russians and the Soviets refer to it as the queen of sports and it really is this wonderful; it's the most basic of all and fundamental of all sports. To that extent it . . . allow[ed] the Soviets to see the link between track and field as this most pure expression of physicality in sport, to see the link between that and the ancient Olympic games. By doing that they established themselves as being part of this sort of long humanistic tradition that the founders of the modern Olympic movement intended. . . . On the other hand what was really attractive about track and field to the Soviets is that it was the most statistic of sports and it was the sport that you could most clearly use statistics to measure the improvement of human performance.

Soviet state, was one reason why more traveled, sophisticated competitors began to contemplate defecting at matches or tournaments abroad. That happened more and more often as the willingness to sacrifice subsided together with ideological commitment. When Anatoly Firsov, one of the national hockey team's great stars, was invited to play in America's National Hockey League in 1968, he accepted and requested permission to leave. (After it was denied, Firsov "finally" saw the light. "I understood you can't tell these people [the authorities] "anything. . . . I took off all my medals," he told "Red Files." "I'd had enough of our system.")

A great long jumper named Igor Ter-Ovanesyan also became indifferent to the Party line, with its heavy emphasis on rousing patriotism. With top Russian athletes handled almost as tightly as Maya Plisetskaya, the premier ballerina who disabused me of the notion that fame protected celebrities from state abuse, friendship between them and their Western competitors was rare. Two leading long jumpers were among the most prominent exceptions. One was the American Ralph Boston, the first man to jump farther than the great Jesse Owens. The other was Igor Ter-Ovanesyan, a young Soviet who, at the 1960 Olympics in Rome, introduced himself to Boston while they were weighing in. That year, when Boston beat the Olympic record and

Ter-Ovanesyan placed a distant third, the Soviet felt that American domination of track and field was so strong that it was "absolutely impossible to imagine how we can come close to them."

Over time, however, he succeeded in becoming more than close—while he and Boston managed to carve out a friendship, sometimes in moments hidden from the KGB watchers. Ter-Ovanesyan's first trip to America in 1962 opened his eyes very wide. He especially loved the steaks, the apartments, and the cars. He adored wide-open California, where the meet was being held, specifically at Stanford University. "I remember the climate," he told a "Red Files" interviewer. "I remember the orange juice. I remember the nice, nice girls around, and the friends and the humor and laughter—the sun!"

Above all, he was captivated by his sense of what friendship could be when people weren't watched by cordons of security agents, when teammates and others weren't pressured to "pay something back to the Soviet state that made you" by reporting suspicious activities and conversations. Meanwhile, Ter-Ovanesyan was catching up to Boston in the field and was on his way to giving the American what Boston himself would describe to "Red Files" as "the worst whipping I think I ever had"—in New York's Madison Square Garden the year after the Stanford meet. Meanwhile, too, he was probing Boston about American life and weighing suggestions that he defect on one of his foreign trips. In the end, he didn't, chiefly because he worried about retribution to his family if he committed that act of "betrayal."

Soviet gymnastics became an even broader study in contrasting attitudes. Larrissa Latynina, who launched an era of Soviet domination of the sport by winning three gold medals in 1956, proudly stood near the end of the spectrum where patriotism surged. "I believed in our system," the model Communist athlete said recently. "I believed and believed and believed....My gymnastics was not only mine. It belonged to my Soviet Motherland and all the people." And if the training was very hard, "sacrifices [were] necessary" in order to win, which was "all that mattered."

But it wasn't all that mattered to teenage Natasha Kuchinskaya, the coaches' favorite among the succeeding generation. Although Kuchinskaya also won big, in 1968, her personal position approached the opposite end of the spectrum. Brooding about the price of victory, she became convinced that winning *wasn't* the be-all and end-all. She saw the monastic, sometimes grueling training—constant practice sessions in an isolated camp, relieved only by the dining hall and surrounding forest—as making sense solely from the government's point of view. From her own, she wanted a life, not to remain a servant assigned to feed a government hungry for the prestige of Olympic medals. Returning from Mexico City the "Bride of Mexico," Kuchinskaya, felt too exhausted even to go to the gym. The flag-waving Latynina interpreted that—and, later, Olga Korbut's "prima donna" demands for attention—as a failure to recognize patriotic duty in heads turned by fame. "That's not how *we* were raised!" But another interpretation is that the game eventually wasn't worth the candle to Kuchinskaya and Korbut, whose political inclinations sharply differed from that of the elder Latynina, now their coach. "I realized I competed for government, not for myself [and] not for the public," Korbut would say later. "I was in a big prison. You can't live without freedom."

So although it's largely correct to say that the Soviet Union saw sport as a Cold War battlefield and considered athletes as soldiers—and that it programmed its sports machine to mass-produce world champions—that wasn't the view of many champions themselves, those who *didn't* equate team loyalty to state loyalty, except in a way Americans would consider normal. Even when they saw their goal as all-for-one effort and achievement, denying any wish for individual glory, that was as likely to derive from deep roots in Russian history as from the mouthing of Communist slogans. As Anatoly Kolessov, a former Olympic wrestling champion turned high sports official, put it, collectivism "is part of our very nature...[and] ingrained in the Russian mind. It's our power."

Few Russians were extreme about that. Many even mocked societies that seemed to them slavishly conformist. Nevertheless, their own collectivism was noticeably stronger than the West's, especially powerfully individualistic America's. It underlay their thoughts about the good society and fair economy in general. It made them less resistant than the average American would be to calls for sacrifice for the common good, less resentful of even callous dictates that appeared to have been issued for the nation's sake.

In the end, the state ordered and cajoled; each Soviet athlete complied or resisted as well as he or she could, in keeping with individual attitudes to his or her calling—which increasingly differed from what the state declared right and necessary for athletes. Of course all competitors wanted to win, but sometimes more for the game itself than for reflecting glory on their nation and its system. Anatoly Firsov, the dazzling hockey player, spoke for many when he told the makers of "Red Files" that the propaganda about contributing to Communism and the "unbreakable" Soviet Union "just passed through our ears.... For us, nothing mattered except playing hockey.... We just had our game. We didn't care about anything else."

Or if they did, it could just as well be self-interest as anything else. In ways well known among the American poor, outstanding athletic achievement promised a far better life, in this case by way of the system of bonuses and awards that was common to most Soviet undertakings. On the other hand, some didn't want to win *enough*—like Kuchinskaya, who in the end dropped out of the gymnastics program, climbed down from the machine, and suffered rebuke and ostracism but nothing more serious. During World War II, Stalin had ordered the shooting of military commanders who failed to accomplish their missions. The quite different post-Stalinist times, however oppressive in their own ways, punished much less drastically.

Soviet sport suffered setbacks even greater than the loss of Kuchinskaya because its political bosses jammed a surprising number of sticks in the spokes. The extraordinary Anatoly Tarasov, who essentially founded and launched Soviet hockey in 1946, was rightly known as its father. And in a country where fledgling teams often had to build their own homemade rinks and fashion their own primitive equipment, such fathers had many more concerns than those in nations where the sport was long established. "As kids, we had no money," recalled star player Firsov to "Red Files." "So we'd chop down cherry trees for wood. Then, at night, we'd sneak into barns and steal horse bridles" to make hockey sticks by gluing them to the wood.

Starting at that level, Tarasov—procurer of men and materials and all-around fixer as well as coach, strategist, and inspirer—somehow managed to make his national team world champions in an amazing eight years. The culmination took place in 1954, when, to universal surprise and Canada's dismay, the Russian team defeated the seemingly invincible Canadians, who were playing their national sport. But since the defeated Canadian team included no professionals, Tarasov began dreaming of playing their pros, and then preparing to, together with the hockey establishment.

At last given their chance in 1972, almost twenty years later, the Russian team came within a whisker of winning. But Tarasov had made bureaucratic enemies along the way, largely by trying to protect his team from governmental interference. And when the superb team flew to Canada to play that World Series of Hockey between the game's two superpowers, he was left home! More than that, the great coach was fired! Firsov, his top star, stayed home too, out of solidarity; and when the team returned to Moscow for the final four games of the eight-game series, he was even barred from the dressing room!

Such happenings further complicate the picture of Soviet sport. It was true that teams above the pickup level couldn't play a match without one or another form of the state's administrative guidance and control. But it was also true that the authority of the full government ministry at the top was regularly

End of the Cold War Melts Soviet Sports

When Anatoly Firsov tried to join the NHL in 1968, his request to leave the Soviet Union was quickly turned down on the standard grounds that his talents were not his own but were owed to the state that had trained and nurtured him. That attitude changed only in 1989, under Gorbachev's *perestroika* (restructuring of the economy). Even then, however, only older stars were permitted to become professionals in the West, and the Soviet sports bureaucracy took a substantial cut—usually about half—of their earnings. Still, that was a vast improvement over the past, when stars like Olga Korbut received not a penny of the substantial profits earned during money-making exhibition tours abroad. Ironically, Soviet stars, now that they can sign foreign contracts, face a different problem when they send money to their families back home. Their precious dollars or deutsche marks attract the attention of the Russian mafia, who sometimes use their foreign-based thugs to threaten them with dire consequences unless they pay "protection" fees.

diluted by the maneuvering of its subordinate sports organizations, clubs, and leaders. As in all bureaucracies, they had their own rivalries and priorities, usually local. The supposedly well-oiled national machine often sputtered with parts that didn't mesh and egos that wouldn't be suppressed, even if their owners were careful not to express them publicly. Other examples were less significant only by comparison. Barred from foreign travel, Olga Korbut emigrated. Even Larrissa Latynina was eventually driven to resign.

Who made those decisions? Weren't some of them more in settlement of personal scores than in the state's interests? Come to think of it, what *was* the state's interest when push came to shove? If it was primarily to win the international competitions, the best athletes should always have been sent abroad—which wasn't the case, as we've seen. Very occasionally, a last-minute change of mind caused a star who'd been sanctioned for foreign travel to be removed from a plane waiting to take off. That happened after the fear of the security personnel that he or she might defect was convincing enough to move a higher authority to deprive the suspect of all opportunity while there was still time.

A good number of highly valued players and performers were also grounded on suspicion that they might say or do something politically incorrect while abroad. From the professional point of view, the damage of that practice was wide-ranging because the gifted—as in ballet, concert performing, and other activities that could win national prestige—were likely to depart, in their various ways, from the habits decreed by the standard sermons and strictures. Most great talent wants to set its own agenda rather than submit to that of political overseers—which was precisely what the watchdogs feared. Those who actually administered the exclusions considered them beneficial, since nothing *wounded* Soviet prestige more than insufficiently patriotic talk and defections.

Those considerations kept the state's sports and security units in constant disagreement, even when they shared an ultimate goal—which was far from always. To the one, winning was being victorious on the fields and in the stadiums, something for which the competitors had to be given every chance to develop and shine. To the other, winning was keeping the Soviet image clean by guarding against all possible blemishes.

There was also disagreement about the conduct of sports programs, some of which even spilled onto the pages of the national press. While the West nurtured an image of a Kremlin totally, dictatorially dedicated to victory abroad, sports writers and others increasingly, if still cautiously, criticized the practice of giving top, essentially professional athletes their bogus jobs in factories and collective farms. More than that, some enthusiasts disparaged the whole tendency to promote the breeding of winners instead of succoring amateurs.

TO WHAT DEGREE SOVIET SPORT AS A WHOLE was unbalanced in that way will also never be known. As with crime statistics and figures pertaining to almost everything else considered of possible use by the capitalist enemy—even accurate maps and reliable demographic information—Soviet data about allocations to sport was highly unreliable, especially because the real financing came from a variety of sources (even if the state was the ultimate one). But letters to editors, as well as major articles, griped that sports clubs spent some 90 percent of their money, and roughly the same amount of their coaches' time, on seeking out and developing top players rather than encouraging mass participation. For example, an enthusiast stated in 1979 that the club of his sprawling Moscow factory had that year given not a single kopek for mass sports.

Four years later, no less an authority than *Soviet Sport*—whose every word was reviewed by censors, as was the case with every other newspaper and magazine—complained editorially that

> as before, sports clubs keep paying most attention to preparing various teams and fixing their selections and contests. Much less value is placed on

developing mass sports and sports for fitness. Considerable amounts of money are spent on top sport, to which the activities of sporting officials are often limited.

"The eternal conflict between sport schools and parents; the eternal problem of talent," commented one of the newspaper's journalists. "How many words have been written about this problem in the press—including our own paper—over the years?" Even the hard-line, flag-waving *Soviet Russia* chipped in with a 1984 letter from a mother whose son, lacking the prospect of developing substantial skills, was left without an opportunity to practice. By that time, resentment of the abuses of the star system was becoming a recurrent theme, even in Party newspapers (which were often even more rah-rah than others, although the differences were usually very small).

Certain forms of public criticism pervaded Soviet life. Although the dictatorship stifled any challenge to the system, the media abounded in reproaches and condemnations of people in almost every occupation who broke the rules, hid a life of personal enrichment, or otherwise wandered from the socialist path to commit all sorts of infractions and abuses. Stealing, lying, bamboozling, failing to meet quotas and fulfill official duties, building private little fiefdoms, and otherwise cheating and making bad or illegal use of economic and political authority—exposés of such shortcomings (which often saw print only after the responsible Party overseer had incurred the displeasure of a higher-up) were a staple of the Soviet press. All such criticism was directed not to policy itself but its execution. The canon remained that although Soviet society's socialist base ensured its essential health and humanity, isolated despots, thieves, and scallywags caused damage and pain to particular people and thus to the nation in general. As early as the 1960s, however, criticism of sports practices began going beyond that.

Dissatisfaction with the star system itself was growing, as in a distinguished professor's letter to *Soviet Sport*. Reminding that Lenin had called upon libraries to measure themselves by the number of users they attracted rather than the number of rare books they owned, the professor drew a comparison. Surely, he concluded, "Lenin's words apply equally to sport?"

SUCH OPPOSITION, LIMITED AND MILD AS IT WAS, made Soviet society less monolithic than it seemed from afar—and less frightening too, except to those whom it considered its internal enemies. In 1969, a referee in a crucial match, on which hung the championship of the highest league, disallowed a goal from the adored team of Anatoly Tarasov. As shown in "Red Files," the father of Soviet hockey responded by removing his players from the ice, disappearing with them into the locker room, and leaving the huge, supercharged crowd bursting with impatience—including no less than Leonid Brezhnev, the chairman of the reigning dictatorship, who was among the most avid of the fans. For some forty minutes, the general-secretary of the Communist Party, premier of the Soviet government, and recipient of everyone's endless accolades was forced to cool his heels in a special box for Politburo VIPs while match officials, then the head of the Hockey Federation, and then the U.S.S.R. minister of defense pleaded with Tarasov to come out and resume play. He finally agreed after aging, tired Brezhnev made his own unsteady way to the locker room; but that was hardly a demonstration of the totalitarian powers and fear of them that are usually attributed to the Soviet Union.

TWO FINAL COMMENTS SHOULD BE MADE about the essentially accurate conventional wisdom that Moscow saw sports as a Cold War battlefield. The first is that—contrary to the usual accompanying assumptions about the "weaponry" of Soviet sports' elite forces—the favored living conditions as well as the sports facilities and equipment were nowhere as luxurious as usually imagined. Soviet allocations for military hardware were indeed huge in terms of the gross national product—up to 40 percent, by some estimates. However, sports victories had a far lower priority. When Soviet tennis players began

Freedom of the Stands

"Spontaneity is the greatest danger," said Nikita Khrushchev, who himself was nothing if not spontaneous, Kremlin leaders feared emotional outbreaks, not to mention drunken hooliganism, that sometimes erupted at soccer and hockey matches. Yet those popular spectator sports provided one of the few channels of more or less legitimate freedom of expression, when fans could get away with behaving badly. For a few hours in a stadium, Homo Sovieticus could enjoy the release of feeling slightly beyond the controls. Nikolai Starostin, a famous soccer player in the late 1930s and 1940s, remembered that during those often terrible years, "soccer was separated from everything else. It was in some way not under the authorities, a healthy thought for a generation of sinners.... For the majority, soccer was the only, sometimes the last, possible hope for maintaining in one's soul some small piece of humane feeling and humanity."

competing at Wimbledon in the 1970s, one approached me to trade some Dunlop rackets for caviar because her own sponsors "just don't give us what we need on court."

The second is more important. Despite the "militarization" of sport, as some Western commentators have called it, many of its "peaceful" achievements were also striking. "From nearly a standing start," as a Scandinavian journalist described it, "the Soviet Union increased sports participation from 50,000 people to 50,000,000." Whatever the accuracy of those figures and whether or not the socialist scorn for prerevolutionary sport was justified, the regime hugely developed from their very limited footings before the Soviet era, in a time when the international competitors were indeed drawn chiefly from the rich and leisured and women of every class were all but excluded. For all its squeezing of other thoughts and activities, Soviet rule greatly encouraged women to participate in more "muscular" activities, including sport.

It can be argued that other countries did the same or better, and without the twisting wrought by compulsion in both senses. Still, no one who saw Soviet sports facilities actually being used can easily dismiss them all as cogs in a war machine, if only because much of the action was in *domestic* combat between the teams of the various leagues and associations. The fans, as devoted and rabid as anywhere, worked up their passions to beat not the capitalists but the goddamn team from the rival city. And they were loud of voice as well as great in number, no doubt partly because other forms of nonartistic recreation were restricted. Before Leonid Brezhnev loved ice hockey, Nikita Khrushchev had loved soccer. Whenever a player kicked a ball, the latter once declared, it was he who did it, "and whenever a player gets kicked in the shins, it's Khrushchev who gets kicked."

As with the statistics about how much sports money went to whom, those supposedly registering the size of the nation's physical plant—the number of gymnasiums, ski lifts, basketball courts, and so on—could never be trusted because only the most favorable figures were published, cleverly selected and doctored. Although the country claimed to have 1,081 rinks for long-distance skating in 1972, a deputy chairman of the National Skating Federation was convinced that was a serious exaggeration because many of the listed "rinks" were actually patches of ice, barely fit for training.

Despite the questionable statistics, however, despite even the self-glorifying propaganda, one was often deeply impressed by the essentially consumer-poor country's attainments, from the building of Moscow's 104,000-seat showpiece Lenin Stadium to the installation of Olympic swimming pools to the assignment of a multitude of excellent (if badly paid) coaches to train youths in gymnastics and ice skating. If sports were a huge success in the eyes of the Party and the world, many Soviet citizens whose interest in participating was entirely personal also saw it as such. Those who somehow managed to emigrate in the 1960s cited their and their children's free access to facilities as one of the most liked features of the country that otherwise made them unhappy enough to leave it. Please don't believe Russians said that only because they were duped—which was my father's conviction. Being of the generation that considered it its duty to enlighten its children about everything, he'd explain to me, even after my returns from long Russian stays, that the entire Soviet sports program was a front for the ruthless crash effort to win international trophies. That was the simpleminded message of his American newspapers and magazines.

Despite the critics' complaints about the star system, you could see for yourself that the overwhelming majority of the very large number of users of the sports facilities (poorly built, as most of them were) were far from being potential medal winners. They were just boys, girls, men, and women letting off steam, having fun while they learned, giving their all to a safe expression of their individuality. Even the practice of dispatching scouts throughout the country to recruit very young talent for very serious training—just as in ballet—wasn't necessarily nefarious, at least not more so than college recruiting in America.

On the other hand, big shots of one kind or another, or people with connections to them, hogged many of the supposedly public facilities. Without bribes or a push from on high, it was extremely difficult to secure training time in the best of them. (Toward the end of the regime, when corruption and the black market had taken over much of the consumer economy, the coaches and administrators of some of the less visible institutions, such as small collections of tennis courts, ran them almost like little private clubs, generating relatively handsome private profits from under-the-table charges for admission.)

That was true throughout the Soviet Union, or at least the parts foreigners were permitted to see. On any given day, you were never sure whether to cheer the undeniable accomplishments—in medicine, public health, education, and cultural activities as well as sport—or boo the glaring failures. In fact, you went from one to the other, depending on your mood as much as what you saw. If it was good, you viewed the sports summer camps and even the specialized schools as part of a worldwide trend. If bad, you suspected the widespread Western assumption that in scientific and technological institutes, medical personnel who worked with sports trainers to devise complex machines for measuring such things as energy patterns and hormonal development were also supervising the administration of drugs. (So far, post-Communist investigations have not shown that doping was unusually widespread, at least in comparison with other nations. East Germany was by far the greatest offender.) All in all, however, the big picture—or what one made of it from one's spotty glimpses—was distinctly more positive than one had expected. More positive meant less ideological as well as more inclusive and better served by knowledgeable, often devoted coaches—whom other countries were delighted to welcome as visiting trainers. In short, Soviet sport was more like sports everywhere, even recognizing that hidden parts of it were indeed girding for war.

In that sense, the huge, cumbersome, but often constructive Soviet program can't be called an unqualified failure. And judged in terms of the metaphor of international war, it was, as we know, a dazzling success—thanks chiefly to the competitors' ingenuity and stamina. Unless it's found that Soviet world champions relied on drugs, nothing can take away from their achievements, so quickly realized against so many odds.

STILL, SOVIET SPORT, THAT WINNER OF startling victories, was ultimately a disappointment. For all its spectacular victories abroad, it lost at home—for reasons linked to the "war mobilization," but broader.

One might have thought, perhaps hoped, that in sport as in no other aspect of life Marxism-Leninism would do its uplifting thing. One might have reasoned that encouraging and facilitating healthful activity for the greatest number would have offered a Marxist society a splendid chance to show its noble stuff. One might have imagined that fairness and fair play to all would be honored; honesty and humanity would be practiced; that openness and decency would reign; that the ultimate criterion would be benefit to The People. Where else, if not in games and physical development, should it have been possible to attain Marxism's ideals for the cherished masses to whom the whole movement was supposedly devoted?

But that wasn't to be, as in many other spheres. Under Soviet rule, the gap between city and country perhaps widened instead of closed. Industrial pollution became far worse than under despised, voracious capitalism. Millions of workers—*workers!*—toiled in conditions that enlightened capitalism would not tolerate. And the state that was supposed to wither away only grew.

For Moscow's Marxism was very Russian, and the bureaucracy wasn't significantly less self-serving or bent than when Gogol satirized its cronyism and chicanery. What mattered in daily life was access, connections, something to trade. The real system of scratching backs was in some ways more entrepreneurial—at least more convoluted—than in the West. You fancied a pair of imported boots? You had to locate someone who had one, and offer cash or an exchange; virtually everyone traded and bartered. You needed to use a restricted library? You had to find someone to know for that. You wanted to learn tennis? You plotted a way to interest a coach. Thus the worthy ideals seemed farther and farther distant, at least when I got my impressions of Soviet sport. Supposedly creative, inspiring, educational, and "pure" as nowhere else in the world, it was increasingly contaminated by the political and social defects of the country as a whole.

Russia may have had slightly more than a normal European share of petty tyrants and fiddlers, and although Soviet athletes demonstrated consistent sportsmanship in competition abroad, that was less true in domestic meets and matches. As a whole, the country was less than fully familiar with Western behavioral norms and, curiously, more naïve in its ways—in many cases, less inhibited in cutting corners and banging heads in order to win. However, the real curse wasn't that but bureaucratic practices. The unpleasant types gravitated to the positions of power about which Marxism had little to say, and exercised their authority there with too little exposure. Exaggeration of the Soviet economy's production statistics was endemic because it helped everyone "fool" everyone else, warding off criticism for failing to meet targets while all who could kept their hands in the till. With that instinct deeply implanted, it was natural to do the same with claims for sports facilities and participation.

The Soviet media sometimes complained about that too, but marginally; and they delayed, minimized, or entirely ignored stories of more damaging cheating. For example, *Soviet Sport* waited almost a year to publish, very inconspicuously, a story about key soccer clubs of several major cities fixing the results of 1976's competition. Other deceptions, such as changing athletes' names and falsifying their ages, went unreported for years. While that was related to the primacy of international *winning* at any cost, its larger cause was the hierarchical Soviet system of bestowing rewards for excellence, real or claimed. In the economy as a whole, the production figures were bloated also because they, not sales, determined payment. Similarly, domestic sports clubs were judged by the numbers of such things as the medals and trophies their members won, often meaning numbers on paper. In the end, it was less sport's militarization that spoiled much of it than that kind of fraud: the trickery, lying, bribing, arranging intentional losses, cover-ups, corruption, favoritism, fabrication, deceit. Above all, the cause was the pretense and the secrecy in which such fraud took place, qualities that had become inherent in Soviet society, with the predictable results.

This is not to argue that sport driven essentially by money is necessarily better than sport controlled by state interests; that would depend on what those state interests were. Nor that Western ways were free of the Soviet defects. It's now clearer than ever that American sports life, far from being a model, suffers from its own forms of lying, corruption, and cynicism, caused mostly by the pull of profit and prestige. If Soviet athletes were awarded cozy "jobs" that demanded no real work, how many American athletes enjoyed the equivalent in win-hungry colleges, where their education was a joke? Applying the same criterion of devoting full time to their sports, how many of those supposedly amateur college students were actually professionals? Surely the American sports scene suggests that billionaire owners of major teams don't *ipso facto* better serve the general welfare than state officials do. (And if Soviet athletes' bonuses for winning—often a month's salary, or the rough equivalent of $100—prompted American fingers to wag, are our own players' contracts that now exceed $100 million of no social concern?)

But Soviet officials were doubly burdened with their mission to build an Eden *and* to teach the world how to live, starting with the need for liberation from capitalism. The country's lifeblood ran with ingrained combativeness. The people who wrote the sports copy, like all other copy, were trained to attack capitalism's flaws and failings—and also to present almost everything in terms of fundamental conflict.

In that sense, all official Soviet life was militarized: permanently girded for the war that lay at the heart of governmental thinking. On top of that, or beneath it, came the Russian habit of making secrecy a major state interest even though many improvements depended on its sharp reduction. (But since part of the improvements might have been the leaders' removal, the idea had little appeal to them.) Although the unreliability of Soviet statistics makes it impossible to say for certain, it may be true that capitalist America, for all its slim state interest in the general welfare, did more for amateur sport during the 1917 to 1990 period—merely by letting individual interests and expanding incomes do the developing—than the beleaguered land of the workers and peasants. In any case, the Soviet aspirations for the general public never came close to fulfillment. Mirroring society as a whole, Soviet sport scored great wins in some areas but fell far short in ultimately more important ones. The marvelous achievements were diminished by the bluster, braggadocio, and crooked vision of incompetent leaders from a long line of conniving Russian bureaucrats, whose true motives greatly departed from those they preached. As a whole, their proclaimed *goals* for Soviet sport were more admirable than Western ones, in the sense of proclaiming a state policy to spread the benefits to everyone. Failing to achieve them, however, they took well-practiced efforts to mask the real state of affairs. Although The People weren't entirely left out, the leathery commanders gave primacy to their own ambitions, whose connection to the public welfare was as tenuous as that of the Mississippi sheriffs they resembled in their attitudes about authority and loyalty to "the boys" who drank together in back rooms.

The final irony was that the very marshaling of so much energy and so many resources to *win* speeded the corruption and the eventual total loss. The grabby self-interest in which Soviet sport operated contributed heavily to Communism's collapse, leaving many of its peerless stars in utter despair. "We athletes used to call out to our people: 'Go forward!'" the great Larrissa Latynina remembered after deciding, much later, that all that had been "cheap propaganda." "Now all my work and all my beliefs have left me with nothing," she told "Red Files" interviewers. "Absolutely nothing."

That too was exaggerated, but entirely understandable in the star's gloom over the death of her ideal. As with many other facets of Soviet life, it went from rags to riches to rags in just a few generations.

LEFT 1938 Physical-Culture Parade in Moscow. The Zenith Sports Club salutes Stalin by "sailing" the Battleship Aurora, which was supposed to have fired the shot that launched the 1917 revolution, through Red Square.

21

RIGHT Physical-Culture Day, 1939. The rifles clearly display the linking of sports training and military preparedness. (Photo: Kinelovskii).

22

BELOW Led by Stalin, Soviet high command moves to meet the visiting General Eisenhower and to review the 1945 Sports parade.

23

ABOVE   A 1947 sports parade reflects the Cold War cult of personality. Party organizers staged this postwar spectacle at Moscow's Dynamo Stadium.

RIGHT   Athletes from the Armenian Republic take a cue from the popular musical film extravaganzas of Grigorii Aleksandrov, a student of Busby Berkeley, in the 1947 parade. (Photo: L.Dorenskii).

LEFT   Stalin's cult emphasized his role as the wise "father of the Soviet peoples." The smiling man seated behind him, Enver Hoxha, ruled Albania from 1944 to 1985.

ABOVE Two medal winners in the javelin throw. At its first Olympics, the 1952 Helsinki games, the Soviet team—especially the women—emerged as international stars. (Photo: Savostianov.)

LEFT Igor Ter-Ovanessian realized his dream of beating his rival and friend, the American star Ralph Boston, in the long jump at a 1962 meet in Madison Square Garden.

BELOW Soviet track and field stars (left to right) Ter-Ovanessian, Valery Bulyshev, Valery Brumel in Moscow, 1962. (Photo: Dansin).

Olympic Champion Olga Korbut's luxuries, such as the stylish fur coat shown below, came more from her pop-star husband's status than her own. Non-comformist Olga made the staid Soviet gymnastic establishment very uncomfortable. Frightened by her individualism and popularity abroad, the establishment tried to cage her. "They didn't let me do anything. Believe me. I was in [a] big prison." (Photo: Ivanov).

BELOW Olga grew up in an ordinary Soviet family of humble circumstances in the Belorussian Republic. Gomel, 1973. (Photo: Iu.Morgulis).

ABOVE   Coach Larisa Latynina, a pillar of the Soviet sports establishment, with Tatiana Palamarchuk, one of her first disciples, in 1964. Latynina's faith in the Soviet system that developed her remained powerful for two more decades. (Photo: D. Donskoi).

LEFT   Natasha Kuchinskaya, beloved Soviet gymnastic star. Her 1968 Olympics triumph as "the bride of Mexico" so burned her out that she stopped competing. (Photo: Shadrin).

RIGHT   Latynina established Soviet dominance in gymnastics by leading Olympic teams in 1956, 1960, 1964. (Photograph by Dorensky).

ABOVE The VIth World Youth Festival in 1957 accelerated the Soviet Union's post-Stalin "thaw." Thousands came from abroad for the opening ceremonies in Moscow's huge new Lenin Stadium. (Photo: Savostianov)

BELOW The Pioneers' regimen inculcated physical fitness along with "correct political thinking." Morning exercises at a Moscow factory's camp, 1958. (Photo: Preobrazhenskii).

RIGHT   Anatoly Firsov on the receiving end of a "passing" Canadian blow during the USSR-Canada Hockey World Championships in 1966. (Photo: Naumenkov).

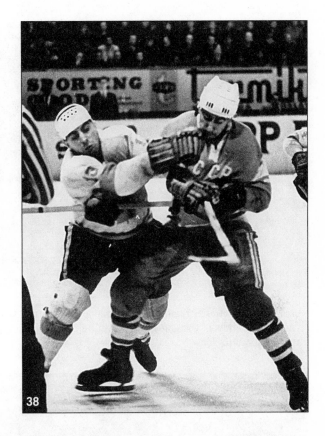

BELOW   Anatoly Tarasov, the coach of the USSR National Team and the "father of Soviet hockey," watching a game in 1967. (Photo: Shadrin).

40

ABOVE   USSR National Team vs. the Canadian NHL Stars. Canadian Paul Henderson: "The first minutes of the game and—and their conditioning was just absolutely unnerving."

41

LEFT   Smooth skating, fast passing, and graceful stickwork were hallmarks of Soviet hockey. They swept past the Canadians in the opening matches of the USSR-Canadian series in September 1972, Montreal.

RIGHT Unlike North American ice matches, said to be "fights at which hockey games sometimes break out," Soviet ones were essentially noncombative. But when attacked, the Soviet champions quickly learned to pull off the gloves and to punch their way out of trouble.

BELOW The USSR-Canadian series in Moscow 1972. The Party packed the stands with grey, staid Soviet officials.

RIGHT Soviet track and field star Igor Ter-Ovanessian about the 1972 series: "It was a shock. It was [an] event for the whole country. I remember those days. When it was on TV, just looking at this battle. This, this... oh, this war."

BELOW The Champion USSR Hockey team takes a victory lap in 1966.

IV
SECRET SOVIET
MOON MISSION

No, Mama, it's my life and my decision. My place is in aviation. I've decided.
—Eighteen-year-old Sergei Korolev, answering his mother's
pleas to consider other professions, 1924

Even now, ordinary propeller aircraft can't give us the needed superiority.
—Prisoner Korolev to Joseph Stalin, 1938

Don't lecture....Too many academicians give lectures that aren't worth a
shit.
—Chief Designer Korolev interrupting the academician
who headed the Institute of Biophysics, 1961

EVERYTHING CONSIDERED, THE SOVIET SPACE effort demonstrated more brilliance and ingenuity—certainly greater courage and tenacity—than did the victorious American one. More important for what was achieved and what more would have been in an open society, it displayed the fusion of intuition and laboratory slog that propels the best science. Here, technological mastery coupled with the Russian propensity to dream big—in this case, about something relatively old. The pursuit of the moon did not originate in Cold War military needs, nor was it a flash in the Kremlin's pan of sometimes overboard schemes. It had a substantial tradition when the planning began in earnest in the 1950s.

Eighty-odd years earlier, a twenty-seven-year-old nihilist named Nikolai Kibalchich was condemned to death for his part in assassinating Alexander II in 1881. (Russia's revolutionaries were as muddled as its reactionaries. The murder of that tsar, probably the country's most liberal, caused a huge setback to every good cause.) Days before his own death, Kibalchich wrote from prison that he'd meet it calmly, "knowing that my idea will not perish with me." He meant neither his political goals nor his bomb-making expertise. Kibalchich was also revolutionary in scientific thinking.

A Russian writer later praised him for making "the first step in the history of space flight." That accolade was based on Kibalchich's prophecy, the world's first as far as is known, that a flying machine might be propelled by an engine fueled by "slow-burning explosives." In other words, a jet engine—which other Russians soon imagined might be suitable for travel in space. Robert Goddard, often called the father of American space flight, was born the year after Kibalchich's execution.

Russia's scientific and artistic achievements benefited from certain advantages of backwardness. Backwardness spares the mind from filling with nuts-and-bolts considerations. It frees thinkers from the saddle of current styles and technologies and from reluctance to scrap existing machinery because it doesn't exist. It enables potential creators to seize on the very latest from the most advanced countries. Most importantly, it promotes dreaming. To call late-nineteenth-century Russia backward in the sciences would be misleading; exceptional achievements in physics, mathematics, and chemistry were then made, including chemist Dmitri Mendeleev's 1870 plotting of the all-important periodic table of elements. Still, it's good to remember the country's political, economic, and educational underdevelopment during the decades when a few remarkable Russians envisioned interplanetary travel.

Of those inspired by Kibalchich, none would become as important as Konstantin Tsiolkovsky, a high school teacher of mathematics and physics who'd been deafened by scarlet fever as a young boy and then orphaned. Poor Tsiolkovsky worked from dawn to whenever his eyes would no longer stay open at night. His teaching occupied the middle of that very long day. The remaining hours were given fervently to the theory and practical needs of space travel, of whose possibility the eccentric was utterly convinced. Months before the Wright brothers took flight in 1903, he was demonstrating mathematically that a device would achieve earth orbit after attaining a certain velocity, and he was predicting a moon landing. Tsiolkovsky's contribution—including promoting the liquid hydrogen and liquid oxygen that would fuel American rockets more than half a century later—is honored by a museum in his birthplace in Kaluga, two hours south of Moscow. Here, it may be enough to cite his turn-of-the-century insistence that mankind would not remain earthbound. Pursuit of light and space would take it beyond the atmosphere until "all of circumsolar space" was conquered.

Kibalchich and Tsiolkovsky were the forebears of this chapter's protagonist, Sergei Pavlovich Korolev. Korolev may have met the latter in 1929 or 1932, when the master Tsiolkovsky was in his sixties and his admirer a twenty-something newcomer to aviation. Russian sources disagree about whether such a meeting actually took place, but not about the influence of the elder upon the bold young man who would pilot the Soviet space effort during its glory years. Simply put, the mature Korolev would begin building what Tsiolkovsky had conceived. Meanwhile, the vigorous neophyte, still bearing no signs of his destiny, devoured the high school teacher's oeuvre, including *The Reaction Engine, Jet-Propelled Aeroplane, The Theory of the Jet Engine,* and *The Maximum Speed of a Rocket.* He also learned of Tsiolkovsky's amazingly foresighted concept of assembling several rockets to build an interplanetary space station—precisely the kind of device the Soviets would launch in 1971, and keep in operation almost continuously thereafter, presently as the ailing veteran Mir. In the 1920s and early 1930s, those notions were no longer considered science fiction by everyone—but by almost everyone.

I'VE ARGUED THAT RUSSIANS, AT LEAST FROM the 1960s, little resembled many Westerners' impression of them as an ant colony. Only from abroad could they have been seen as heroically devoted—and/or ruthlessly constrained— to producing ever more blast furnaces and weapons for use against the West. While there was *some* truth in that view, it more reflected our reaction to their bluster. Of course they wanted Socialism to win, if for no more reason than why almost everyone roots for the home team. But since victory was historically inevitable anyway, it prompted only mild fervor unless a need for the Motherland's *defense* was felt. In that case, even the Russian leaders tended to cool their socialist ideology, as during early World War II, when the fighting started as extremely grim and Stalin appealed to his people's devotion to Holy Mother Russia.

It's true that all had to meet, or to fudge, their production targets; but that was usually accomplished during several days of "storming" at the end of an otherwise fairly stagnant and muddled month. It's also true that they produced great quantities of (generally inferior) goods, but usually under discipline applied from above, as if to confirm the old proverb that Russians "can do anything, even make a watch" when beaten. In their own hearts and minds, however, the average man and woman, inasmuch as the large population *can* be averaged, were resistant to regimentation. They tended to be lackadaisical about their jobs, nearly all of which paid painfully little. A popular saying threw light on their real attitude: "The State pretends to pay us and we pretend to work."

But no pretense was necessary when they were inspired. During the early Soviet years, commitment to building the noble socialist society drove millions to tackle the punishing work of crash electrification and industrialization. The great canals, dams, railroads, mills, and plants—the monumental achievements and monstrous ecological mistakes—were built by voluntary as well as slave labor. However, state goals tended to fade after World War II, when the promised radiance seemed as distant as ever, even after the terrible hardships and privations already endured on the supposed path there. Now the inspiration was more likely to come from a personal dream, for which amazing feats could be achieved in seemingly impossible conditions when powerful leadership and a great deal of luck chipped in.

Russians were inclined to work like they ate, which was usually not at regular hours unless they were dictated by factory or office jobs. Otherwise, observing a set timetable for meals, making life nice and orderly—*ugh!* Since the native instinct was more for gratifying impulses and desires, people often skipped food until their hunger called, and then attacked a meal that prompted sympathy for the boa constrictor. As for drink, many didn't touch a drop for weeks until a display of heroic consumption, often in celebration of a holiday or anniversary. I never saw an opened bottle returned to a Russian shelf. The thought of saving something for a later day seemed laughably stingy and sissyish. In fact, there was no way to reseal most bottles, it never having occurred to the makers that anyone would want to do such a silly thing.

In short, fondness for indulging the appetites tended to weaken admiration for moderation. And when the appetite was for achieving a dream—for doing something more satisfying to the soul than getting a job done for its own diligent sake—Russians could work their Western counterparts under the table, as with their legendary and real capacity for drink.

Sergei Korolev's dream probably began in 1913, when the bright six-year-old with a facility for arithmetic saw his first certified hero. Although the barnstorming little air show to which his grandfather took him hit their Ukrainian town only ten years after the world's first flight at Kitty Hawk, the Russian pilot was already famous. Despite the dislocations of World War I and young Sergei's troublemaking streaks, the boy read voraciously. After his family moved to Odessa in 1917, he was among the first to enter a new kind of Soviet vocational school that largely replaced the old European-style gymnasia. Sergei's was for students of construction, but it gave advanced courses in physics, mathematics, and drafting.

He had a normal quotient of patriotism, normal being generally very high during the early years of Soviet rule, when the promise of Socialism shined and everything seemed possible. His growing fascination for planes was fed by the formation of new national associations to support the country's baby air force. Posters exhorted the population to "answer the imperialists' crazed armaments development with new squadrons built by Soviet workers and peasants, friends of our Air Force." Sergei helped patch up some old biplanes. A pilot who'd taken part in the storming of St. Petersburg's Winter Palace—the Revolution's most rousing symbol (at least as re-created on film by the great Sergei Eisenstein)—took him on his thrilling first flight.

A glider he took upon himself to design after graduation won praise from professionals. A second glider followed in 1925–26, when he was a student at the Kiev Polytechnical Institute. Soon he set records for distance and duration on yet another glider built with a colleague. Later, he switched to light planes. His senior-year project at the Moscow Higher Technical School to devise such a craft was supervised by Andrei Tupolev, one of the most promising of several highly creative Soviet aeronautical designers.

Despite desperately strained resources and the lingering effects of the catastrophic civil war, Soviet science and technology made impressive advances during the early and mid-thirties. Korolev's ascent to design excellence and management responsibility took him to an upward succession of jobs where highly charged young colleagues pursued many goals. He helped found the organization in which he chiefly learned and rose: the Group for Studying Jet Propulsion (GIRD), which was also an experimental laboratory. Meanwhile, he dreamed of designing a jet plane, wrote books, headed engine development shops and various structural, armament, and equipment departments, worked in factories, helped create the Scientific Jet Research Institute in Moscow, and experimented with rockets—for whose maiden flight in 1933 he lit the fuse. Five intense years later, he was, among other things, working on the development of a rocket-powered modified glider and testing the prototypes in hundreds of flights.

Then disaster struck, as so often happened among the scientific and artistic elites under Stalin. Korolev was a thrusting, trusting thirty-one years old.

In May 1937, a year of such devastating purges that many recall it simply as "evil 37," Stalin liquidated the Soviet army's top brass, including Field Marshal Mikhail Tukhachevsky. The widely admired Tukhachevsky was the driving force behind army modernization and *the* patron of the rocket scientists. In a typical Stalinist pattern, the ripples of a patron's purge soon reached his bureaucratic dependents. Among the elite (the educated, party members, celebrities) those guilty of nothing more than contact with the plague-bearer, the individual unmasked as an "enemy of the people," were often swept off to the gulag.

After visiting the Group for Studying Jet Propulsion seven years earlier, the Soviet army's farsighted commander in chief became, as an involved scientist would put it, the "spiritual leader of [Soviet] military rocketry," supporting it as actively as he could until his arrest. That boded ill for anyone associated with him, although no such link to an "enemy of the people" was needed to charge any or all of them with spying for Germany or participating in other "counterrevolutionary" activity. Sure enough, Korolev was arrested some five months after Tukhachevsky's execution. The new prisoner was snatched from his wife and three-year-old daughter in the middle of the night, in keeping with the standard operating procedure. Soon he was being beaten, and his relatives, although they knew nothing about where he was or what was happening to him, were sending imploring appeals to Stalin, like letters in bottles. (A jaw broken then or in later imprisonment would contribute to Korolev's death twenty-seven years later.) He was neither shown any evidence against him, nor given a trial. But after being shifted from one prison to another, he confessed to the usual participation in "counterrevolutionary activity," specifically "subversion in a new field of technology."

Maybe it says enough about the contrast between the settings of the Soviet and the American space programs to mention that almost on the day of Korolev's arrest, the generous Guggenheim Foundation told Robert Goddard, American rocketry's much older father, that it would be sending more money to finance the latter's experiments. Korolev and his fellow Russians were far ahead until a tyrant's madness interrupted them in 1937. Personal conditions for Soviet and American rocket scientists can be said to have been night and day, but only if you have a particularly dark night in mind.

KOROLEV PASSED SOME MONTHS OF HIS GRISLY solitary confinement wondering who profited from the spy mania and inordinate vigilance. "Could no one really tell the truth?" a Russian biographer named Aleksandr Romanov quotes him as thinking. That was typical for the majority of prisoners who began by believing that Stalin or a subordinate would soon correct the terrible mistake of their arrest. What made them so pathetically naïve isn't fully clear even now. Why the highly advanced, admirably cultured German people allowed Hitler to lead them to ruin remains largely a mystery these 70-

odd years later. The same applies to the Soviet people's collusion in permitting Stalin to hypnotize and brutalize them, although Korolev's prison musings throw some light on the puzzle.

He granted that if the great Tukhachevsky hadn't been able to prove his innocence, the likes of his inconsequential self stood little chance. However, his rationality stopped where it approached sacrificing his belief in Socialism's promise by accepting that much of it was being demolished before his eyes. He and most of his like were unwilling to think that, especially because they had only the dimmest notion of the scale of the national dementia and pain. It was far easier to attribute them to error than to grapple with the terrible thought that Stalin might be a monster. "No," biographer Romanov quotes him again. "I don't want to believe what's happening is intentional."

> It must be the work of the Motherland's hidden enemies, disturbed by my experiments that strengthen our national defense. I'm convinced that in the near future, rocket flight will develop widely and occupy its fitting place in the achievements of socialist technology.

As if to confirm the gulag saying that people convicted "for nothing" got ten years, that was Korolev's sentence during the prime of his energy and endurance. He hated his "enemy-of-the-people" label. According to Romanov, he was prepared to endure anything and everything, but "I'll never accept the slander, *never*." Soon he was indeed enduring some of the worst purge punishment this side of shooting. In the autumn of 1939, he was in a region of far-eastern Siberia called Kolyma, one of the gulag hell's lowest circles. Even before the publication of Aleksandr Solzhenitsyn's accounts, Kolyma's labor camps were known to be among the most brutal in the entire system. Up to 20 percent of their inmates died every year, chiefly of malnutrition, tuberculosis, and exposure to temperatures of minus forty to minus sixty degrees. Korolev felled trees, pushed wheelbarrows, and dug in the vicinity of his camp's gold mine. He lost all his teeth and may have suffered heart damage.

Then the purges swallowed the supervisor of the horror, the diabolic minister of the interior himself. After five months of murderous Kolyma, Korolev was summoned back to Moscow for reinvestigation of his case. The brutal conditions of his return trip from perilous Siberia—which he made on his own, without guards or, practically speaking, money—were second only to those of the camp he'd left. Death breathed on him several times—

and again back in Moscow, where it was decided to return him to Kolyma, his sentence reduced by an insignificant two years.

Now the condemned resolved to write directly to Stalin. His letter to the man who had his cavalier way with every Soviet life mentioned his perilous situation only in connection with the aviation that had become his life's blood and guts. It resounded with his conviction about matters involving national defense and prestige. "Soviet planes must have decisive technological advantages over all possible enemies," the prisoner began.

> There is only one solution: rocket planes, as proposed by Tsiolkovsky.... My
> life's dream and goal has been to create such powerful weapons for the
> U.S.S.R. I repeat: designing them is of exceptional and vast importance.

Since appeals on grounds of innocence, loyalty, utter devotion to the Party, and supreme fealty to Stalin himself left The Boss unmoved, it may have been Korolev's no-nonsense practicality that saved him. Intervention by prominent pleaders, including two of the country's celebrity pilots, didn't hurt, even though similar petitions were futile in other cases. Whatever the explanation, he wasn't sent back to Siberia but to a Moscow *sharashka*.

That uniquely Soviet institution was a kind of labor camp for scientists and engineers, with relentless pressure to quickly *create* for the state and with matching controls but tolerable living conditions. A better comparison might be a military installation (although here run by the secret police) whose personnel were kept under guard but given time for rest and decent food—in some cases, better than the general public's. The head prisoner at the *sharashka* to which Korolev was sent was the same Andrei Tupolev who had taught him at the Moscow Higher Technical School, and who probably requested him for his design staff. Tupolev's military craft would soon win distinction in World War II, and his civil ones would continue doing the same well after the war. They were designated "TU," as in the TU-104, a relatively modest modification of a twin-engine bomber that became the world's first passenger jet in widespread service.

IT WAS LATE 1940 WHEN KOROLEV RETURNED to his work and ardor. Although he wouldn't be fully, formally rehabilitated until after Stalin's death, and would receive notification of it only in 1957, nearly twenty years after his arrest, his incarceration now and the "enemy-of-the-people" shadow that would linger little retarded his professional life. (A good number of the best and brightest were in the same situation.) Nor even his military one:

Pyrrhic Victory?

Sergei Korolev and his team of aerospace experts launched the space race when they sent *Sputnik I* into orbit on October 4, 1957. The cosmos became a battleground not only because "victory" there promised military or scientific rewards but also because in the Cold War propaganda war, no achievement by one side could go unmatched by the other without a loss of face.

Ironically, Khrushchev had approved the Sputnik program with qualified enthusiasm. Although he was always glad for an opportunity to best America, lofting a 184-pound object into orbit did not seem the most exciting way to do it. But he was surprised by the great wave of fear, envy, and acclaim triggered by *Sputnik*, and President Eisenhower, having dismissed the warnings of American experts that the first artificial satellite in space would be a propaganda coup on a par with the development of the A-bomb, was shocked. The president considered the near hysteria misplaced, all the more because he knew the United States could easily have been the first to launch a satellite, if it had chosen to do so. Satellite programs of both the army and the navy had been puttering along for years, but without high priority—until *Sputnik*. As it was, America launched its own satellite just four months later, but the damage to national prestige had been done.

America's shock lay in fear that Soviet science and technology were progressing more rapidly than the West's. The achievement also seemed to support the Communist Party's claims that it had produced a superior society. *Sputnik*, *Pravda* gloated, proved "the most daring dreams of mankind" could be achieved under Communism.

The sight of *Sputnik* in the night sky diminished Americans' sense of invulnerability, previously provided by inhabiting a continent protected by oceans on both sides. Just a decade earlier, the United States alone had atomic weapons. The Soviets' explosion of an A-bomb and an H-bomb had ended that monopoly, and now the ability to launch a satellite, that vivid demonstration of rocket power, substantiated Soviet claims to have developed intercontinental ballistic missiles (ICBMs)—which could send atomic bombs to American soil in thirty minutes.

Despite the resounding public relations triumph, however, *Sputnik* can be considered a Pyrrhic victory in the long run. What the United States did not know—thanks to the great secrecy of the Soviet space program—was that it, like other remarkable achievements, was attained by extraordinary bursts of effort. Success came only after a project had been given a top priority and allocated scarce resources that might have been more usefully used in agriculture or industry. Meanwhile, the American fear of slipping behind awakened by *Sputnik* sparked a broad-based, long-term commitment to scientific education and research.

The federal government assumed an unprecedented role in education, spending heavily on science and math, and establishing the National Aeronautics and Space Administration (NASA) with the mission of making the U.S. the world's leader in space. Those efforts helped lay the ground for America's technological superiority in the long term.

In the short term, however, victory in the space race seemed uncertain. The Soviets favored heavy payloads and "firsts" (first dog in space, first woman there); the United States preferred smaller satellites with microelectronics and advanced espionage and scientific capabilities. A new Soviet triumph in 1961—sending into space the first human, Yuri Gagarin—could hardly have come at a worse time for the new Kennedy administration, which three days later would be humiliated by the Bay of Pigs fiasco, in which poorly equipped Cuban exiles made an even more poorly executed attempt to invade Cuba and overthrow Castro. With American prestige at stake, Kennedy quickly moved to launch the Apollo program, which would lead to Neil Armstrong's "giant leap for mankind" in 1969.

Cold War rivalry left the Soviets with virtually no choice but to try to beat the Americans to the moon. Their effort was spearheaded by charismatic, cunning Korolev, by far the most dominant figure in Soviet rocketry and space exploration. He was skilled at everything from winning funding for his projects to getting edible food for his bleak space compounds.

While American space exploration was kept largely separate from military activity, the two were closely intertwined in the Soviet Union. Thus Korolev often worked on military applications as a necessary compromise, even while much of the brass saw his projects as needless and wasteful. Their view—that scarce resources were best spent on technology with direct military value—explains their opposition to the moon mission just as they'd opposed *Sputnik*. That probably doomed it to failure, defense funds going instead to ballistic missiles and submarine delivery systems.

Despite losing the moon race some three years after losing Korolev himself, the Soviet Union continued to make achievements in space—and even cooperated with the United States when international tension was relatively low. In 1963, President Kennedy had proposed a joint endeavor to reach the moon, which the Soviets, publicly claiming to be uninterested, quickly rejected. Twelve years later, however, during the era of détente, American and Soviet spacecraft linked together in orbit to achieve the Apollo-Soyuz "handshake in space." But the emphasis returned to competition by the 1980s, the main contestants now being the Soviet space station Mir and America's shuttle program.

The fall of the USSR and the end of the Cold War led to rapid deterioration of the Soviet space program. The present Russian government would have little interest in spending the billions required to keep competing, even if not for the country's falling living standards, drastic declines in industrial output, and crumbling infrastructure. While Western funding is helping prop up Korolev's former Baikonur station, Russian space efforts reflect hardly a hint of their former glory.

---

in 1945, as the Red Army was about to assault Berlin, he was appointed a colonel. (The Communist Party took him as a member in 1953.) Meanwhile, he was one of a scientific corps that worked their heads off, ignoring the mad, ongoing injustice they'd suffered. Korolev kept it up on days off too.

International tension was growing, despite the 1939 Nazi-Soviet friendship pact. With Europe frightened by the seeming inevitability of major war, the most urgent task was to design new warplanes *quickly*. While helping with that, however, Korolev also pursued his passion for rockets—in Moscow and at the sharashka in Kazan to which he was transferred. Freed to leave the latter in 1944, he stayed on for roughly a year to continue his rocket work.

As coincidence would have it, the Soviet Union and the United States launch satellites on the same day in the early 1960s. They circle in opposite ways.

"Hi there!" cries the shiny American one on their first encounter.

"Zdrastvui" sounds the deep Russian reply: "Hello."

The same greetings are exchanged on their higher second encounter, then on their third and fourth. On the fifth, the tough Russian capsule booms a big *"Allo, Kollege!"*

"What's that mean?" asks the American.

"Come on, *mein Freund*, we're far enough away to speak German now."

Such Soviet stories were told to poke fun at the bombast from Moscow and Washington about their respective space triumphs. Few Russians knew their program had been boosted by espionage that began even before World War II. Soviet intelligence reported to Moscow about German rocket efforts as early as 1937, in particular those of a brilliant young scientist named Wernher von Braun, whose test flights Soviet spies observed. But far more, and more important, information came immediately after the Third Reich's surrender in 1945, when a battalion of Soviet scientists, including the new colonel named Korolev, was dispatched to Germany to scoop up all possible rocket technology and equipment. (Korolev arrived in Bleicherode, Germany, just three months after the German surrender.) And scoop they did—more accurately, they *shoveled* every drawing, model, calculation, and page of notes on which they could lay their hands into crates for shipping back to Russia.

The booty included superb blueprints and many of the ingenious scientists who had drawn them. To keep things in perspective, however, the cream of the crop had already departed for the United States under "Operation Paperclip," the gathering by American intelligence of a team of Nazi rocket experts, V-2 documents, and hardware. They included the same Wernher von Braun, then chief designer of the V-2, and some 130 of his team's best, who had fled the Soviet zone to give themselves up to the Americans. That both sides' postwar efforts began with copying the V-2 supports the charge that early Russian and American achievements were actually largely German. Again for perspective, however, it should be remembered that before the arrest of Korolev and other prominent scientists and designers, before the senseless shooting of so many talented men and women, Soviet rocketry was at least on a par with Germany's. It was also well ahead of the American effort, which most profited from Germany's wartime advances. And despite the Soviet lag that had developed during the severely disruptive 1937–45 period, it was Stalin who ordered the exact copy of the V-2, dismissing Korolev's promise that he could design a better rocket with newer technology even then.

In fact, Korolev's unfailing instinct was to improve on German technology, even when borrowing very heavily from it, as was the case for the first ballistic missiles. By the time Stalin died in 1953, Korolev had acquired vastly greater experience as head of the construction and firing of a substantial series of rockets, each more powerful and refined than its predecessor. Step by inventive, extremely laborious step, he advanced to designing the R-7, the world's first ICBM, following Khrushchev's order for a nuclear missile that could reach the United States. That mandate imposed a monumental task on the Korolev group: to design a vehicle that would carry a five-ton warhead no less than five thousand miles. Although still much indebted to the latest V-2 model (whose range was some two hundred miles), the new vehicle was twenty times more powerful, its technology eclipsing that which von Braun was using for the U.S. Army, although great weight diminished its efficiency. If one breakthrough can be cited as paramount, it was upping the thrust to a far greater scale than previously attained. "What the Soviets lacked in advanced Western technology," a space historian would write, "they made up for in brute force." But harnessing that force required massive innovation every unending day.

Khrushchev would soon be a regular visitor to various rocket design offices, delighting in their prototypes like a child with a dazzling new toy. He gave final approval for the R-7's testing in 1956. Although only four were ever made op-

But Stalin Didn't Know!

Korolev's daughter Natasha would recall her father's respect for Stalin, which was typical of the time.

Paradoxically as it may seem my father had a very good attitude to Stalin. He did not believe that Stalin had anything to do with his arrest. As many others, he believed that that was a misunderstanding and Stalin was simply not informed. He had two meetings with Stalin, already after the war.... Interestingly, he was struck by Stalin's erudition....At the Kremlin Stalin asked him questions, which he answered. Father told me that he was impressed how competent Stalin was in such issues, which were very far from his competence in politics, it was technology. When Stalin died in 1953, my father cried....In those years nobody knew of Stalin's guilt.

erational as rockets, the R-7's relatively huge power would make it a valuable space booster, for which over a thousand would be used during the following years, the first time with stunning effect. "Good old 7," as it came to be called once the Korolev team worked out the bugs in its five big engines, was fueled by a lethal mix of kerosene and oxygen. They designed it to be the most powerful missile in the world, and its simplicity helped make it the longest-lived.

The world knew nothing about the Korolev group's many failures perfecting the R-7. (It would also know nothing about later failures with even bigger rockets, all of which were kept secret.) Outside of a tight circle of scientists and just a few Kremlin politicians, no one knew about their first successes, either. In August 1957, after five failures, an R-7 flew more than four thousand miles, becoming the world's first intercontinental ballistic missile. The initials ICBM would join the American lexicon only after the country was shocked into learning a little Russian space vocabulary. The jolt came in October 1957, when the same rocket was used to launch *Sputnik* ("fellow traveler") *I,* the earth's first artificial satellite.

"This achievement," wrote *Pravda,* "embodies the genius of the Soviet people and power of Communism." That crowing, on top of the remarkable event itself, shook the West, America above all. Our military chiefs hadn't expected the Soviets to master the technology and build the system necessary to propel a rocket beyond the atmosphere. As if asking "What is wrong with this picture," Americans began a frightened self-examination of the national commitment to education, especially scientific. Within a week of *Sputnik I*'s bleeping orbits of the earth, a *New York Times* headline admonished, "Nation Is Warned to Stress Science—Faces Doom Unless Youth Learns Its Importance, Chief Physicist Says." More dismay followed quickly, for the Kremlin, realizing it had won a propaganda bonanza, ordered another space spectacular. "Our leadership suddenly understood that space was good propaganda," recalled Vassily Mishin, Korolev's lieutenant for rocket fueling. "We'd all gone on holiday, but we were ordered to launch another satellite within a month." In three-plus weeks of brainstorming, the scientists cobbled together *Sputnik II,* capable of carrying a dog into space. Unfortunately for the little terrier named "Laika," the rush to meet Khrushchev's order to demonstrate Socialism's prowess by November 7, 1957—the fortieth anniversary of the Bolshevik Revolution—left the Korolev team with no time to design reentry equipment. But Laika's flight riveted the attention of American specialists, including Robert Seamans, soon to be appointed deputy administrator at NASA, a new organization created to meet the Sputnik challenge. "It was obvious," Seamans would explain, "that where they had actually already put a dog in space, they were leading up to a manned program and that they were gonna carry it out as soon as they could."

More American dismay was on the way. During the following years the Soviets put the first man, then the first three men, then the first woman into space. The first spacecraft to land on the moon, long the object of Korolev's ambition, was also Soviet, as were the first photographs of the moon's far side. The first flyby of Mars was also Soviet, as well as the first impact on Venus, where Korolev had long dreamed of sending a manned flight. During the course of forty-three months in the late 1950s and early 1960s the "backward" country produced an astonishing succession of feats.

That first manned space flight came in April 1961, Korolev having personally selected Yuri Gagarin, the pioneer cosmonaut, as the brightest and most balanced of twenty candidates. Those qualities probably weren't needed to boost Gagarin high among the relatively few propaganda heroes whom the public genuinely prized. Instead of making their ritual nods in the direction of political chiefs and Heroes of Socialist Labor, the Soviet people cheered the handsome man—and no less when he developed a reputation for fondness for the national pleasure that came in the bottles that couldn't be resealed.

The space program as a whole intensely excited most Russians, even those bored by the hosannas to other socialist accomplishments and the smaller number who repeated stories about Valentina Tereshkova, the first female cosmonaut, trembling with terror as she boarded her craft. Although the sources of their enthusiasm, seemingly a good cut higher than Americans', can't be fixed without scientific analysis, we know that Russians were old fans of grandiose projects. "Under the tsars," a former director of the Soviet Space Research Institute recently mused, "the [church] bells always had to be big. The same thing with the Politburo"—and with many among the masses too. They cherished their elaborate metro system, even though (or partly because?) its construction and operation were better than almost anything above ground. They loved the Bolshoi Theater's opulence amid the pervading urban drabness. State accomplishments with which they associated themselves gave them a large dose of pride. That pertained especially to those that seemed to confirm—despite the mess in which the majority lived and worked—the essential truth of their daily hectoring about Soviet superiority and the better new world toward which they were supposedly striding. The space achievements were broadcast and received as further testimony that "the future is ours, Comrade." In private, people frequently griped about their consumer-poor country lavishing so much foreign aid on the Third World, but rarely about the cost of the space ventures. And when Americans were

What Space Race?

As much as the technical accomplishment, the propaganda triumph Korolev delivered put President Dwight D. Eisenhower on the defensive. "The speed of progress in the satellite project cannot be taken as an index of our progress in ballistic missile work," the president tried to assure. "Our satellite program has never been conducted as a race with other nations."

first to land on the moon, the Russians' congratulations were also genuine, despite their great disappointment.

Meanwhile, the cheers for Korolev came only from an inner circle of trusted colleagues and subordinates who worked anonymously and in isolation from everyone who didn't "need to know." So hidden was the work that Korolev himself became a state secret, which gives "Red Files" a quality of memory-capsule discovery. The year after *Sputnik I*'s maiden flight, Party Chairman Nikita Khrushchev, the prime mover of de-Stalinization, conveyed the sense of pride and importance attached to the space triumphs, and also explained his reason for the secrecy:

> We'll erect an obelisk to the people who created the rockets and the artificial satellites. We'll inscribe their glorious names in gold to make them known to posterity for centuries....But now we protect their safety from hostile agents who might be sent in to destroy those outstanding people, our valuable cadres.

Maybe it wasn't entirely pathological to believe, as Khrushchev claimed he did, that Soviet scientists, engineers, and technicians might be targeted. Some Washington hawks of the time were pitching assassination as the solution to international problems. In any case, special anti-CIA telephones were used and the key Soviet personnel weren't identified, Korolev most strikingly of all. Fat encyclopedias of the Soviet space effort published before the mid-1990s identified thousands of Soviet participants, from prominent to obscure, but not the boss. Even a memoir of Andrei Tupolev mentions a test pilot named Korolev, but not Sergei Pavlovich.

How was it possible for aviation scientists not to know the previously very visible designer? Some obviously did; but they followed their instructions well enough that his name fell from use. Korolev himself was less than fastidious about his anonymity. He was a full-fledged hero when he visited Kaluga in 1957, roughly a month before the launch of *Sputnik I*. The occasion was a celebration of the hundredth anniversary of Tsiolkovsky's birth there. The little museum's guides failed to recognize him, but he introduced himself by name before silently watching the ceremonies in the main square. So the secrecy

Journey through the Memory Hole

The "blank spots in our history," as Mikhail Gorbachev called the pre-glasnost Soviet accounts of the country's achievements and failures, included the "LK" (*Lunniy korabl'*, or lunar landing craft). A marvel of design simplicity, it was hidden from public view, and when Korolev's heirs accepted that they'd lost the moon race, they deposited it in a corner of a forlorn space warehouse. The relic went unseen by Western eyes until Gorbachev was presiding over the end of Communism and the Cold War.

In 1990, a handful of MIT experts who were touring the Soviet space complex happened to look through a door and ask their guide what was inside. The guide mentioned the lunar lander. Later Robert Seamans, a retired NASA executive, would declare that that was the first hard evidence the Soviets had one. "And that they undoubtedly could have achieved a landing about the same time we did, perhaps even before, if they'd been successful with their big booster."

The big booster was Korolev's huge, ill-fated N-1 rocket. Seventeen days before Buzz Aldrin planted the American flag on the moon's surface in 1969, an unmanned N-1 exploded on takeoff during a test launching. Before the month was over, the Soviet leadership, watching Aldrin and mission commander Neil Armstrong land on the moon, knew they had lost the race. On Kremlin orders, Soviet engineers fired the remaining inoperable rockets straight down the memory hole. One was recycled into a pigpen. Although the Soviet moon program never existed officially, some of its heroes still reflect on the "what ifs." "When *Apollo 8* went around the moon I was very proud for mankind, and I wished the astronauts every success," said cosmonaut Alexei Leonov. "But it was very, very sad for us. We'd held everything in our hands—after spending huge amounts of money and years of our lives, we let it slip away from us. It was a pity."

wasn't complete, especially after Korolev began using his public relations talent to stimulate interest in more appropriations for space.

But it was apparently secure enough. Some of the laboratories he created didn't know they worked for him. Even the cosmonauts spoke of him as the "Chief Designer" (of Missiles and Spacecraft), unaware of his identity, or pretending to be. Alexei Leonov, the first human to float "free" in space—after venturing from an orbiting Korolev craft—would report that "his name was never spoken. We wondered, 'Who is this man, whose name is only a whisper?'"

Despite the general reliance on rumor for information, the public's ignorance was virtually complete. It was a little like knowing nothing about a blend of Thomas Edison, the Wright brothers, and Admiral Hyman Rickover, the father of the American nuclear submarine.

The context makes that somewhat more believable. Relatively large numbers of Soviet VIPs in other fields were also unknown, or known only as names, without a hint of their personas or residences. Much economic activity was similarly camouflaged. If you asked someone where he or she worked—a young woman, say, with whom it was hard to associate anything menacing—the answer was often "Post Office Box" this or that. A post office box number meant she couldn't mention, let alone describe, her place of work because it was involved, as so many were, with military or police projects, like a thousand cousins of Los Alamos. But even in that context, with secrecy blanketing the country like a heavy snowfall, Sergei Pavlovich Korolev's anonymity was extraordinary. When Swedish officials asked for his name in order to consider him for a Nobel Prize, the Soviet government declined to give it.

CONSIDERING RUSSIA'S STATE DURING AND after World War II, the appropriations for the projects of Korolev and his colleagues were generous. In the immediate postwar period, rocketry and space were among the strictly rationed economy's highest priorities. That, however, didn't end, and in some ways only intensified, fierce squabbling about which government agency and research institution would get what—standard institutional in-fighting, but richly nourished by secrecy and the kind of fragmentation that flourished in the Soviet system. From the space program's birth in 1946, parts of it were assigned to a wide range of organizations in many separate industries. In addition to the government's powerful Military-Industrial Commission, no less than seven ministries—of Defense, Armaments, Aviation Industries, Means of Communications, and Machine Building, as well as two others—supervised aspects of the work. For example, the development of missile gyroscopes was under the Ministry of Shipbuilding.

So much for the assumption that dictatorships are better than democracies at establishing clear chains of command. On the contrary, personal fears and jealousies, including the fear of the dictator himself of giving too much power to any one subordinate, tend to make an ever-shifting collage of the organizational chart. But thanks partly to Stalin's direct interest in Korolev's work and the Chief Designer's personal relationship with Nikita Khrushchev, Korolev was often able to secure funding by outflanking the layers of bureaucratic organizations with their prerogatives and self-interests. That was a function of his charisma and charm, some of which came down to plying Politburo politicians with alcohol and misrepresenting his intentions as more military than they actually were. The combination sometimes worked even on ministers of defense, even when they suspected it shouldn't have.

(Khrushchev's decisions about missile appropriations were especially vital to the dazzling successes. In some, the effervescent Party chairman and premier acted as he would when authorizing the 1962 publication of *One Day in the Life of Ivan Denisovich*, Aleksandr Solzhenitsyn's powerfully liberating account of labor-camp existence, which Khrushchev put to use in his campaign against Stalinism and Stalinists. The intelligentsia dropped everything to read the sensational revelation in one quick sitting before hurriedly passing it to friends. Tears came even to men and women who had shed none when they themselves served their terrible time in the gulag. Khrushchev's sanction of the politically risky book resembled the old story about Abraham Lincoln announcing "the ayes have it" after hearing "nay" from his entire cabinet to an idea he favored. In the *One Day* case, the other Politburo members, cautious as usual, remained silent rather than oppose the proposal to publish—whereupon the irrepressible premier declared that "silence is a sign of consent." The incident provided a peek at Politburo politics. Just as in the relationship of supposedly fraternal industries, organizations, and bosses, Politburo members and the factions they represented were rent by quarreling competitions that could be even sharper, because hidden, than those among their counterpart Western entities. In the case of space, an American correspondent who worked in Moscow found that "the Soviets were as much at war with themselves as with us." Korolev had a number of rivals in both technological and bureaucratic matters. One of the strongest was the chief maker of large military rockets: a former superior, Petrovich Valentin Glushko, who was beaten until he testified against Korolev in 1937, and then himself sent to the gulag.)

Therefore, the Soviet leadership was entitled to feel it was handsomely, even luxuriously, underwriting the various competing space programs. However huge the CIA's exaggeration of the numbers, the agency *knew* how very

Spies in the Sky versus Yuri Gagarin

As Korolev advanced his plans to send Yuri Gagarin into space, he ran into the powerful industrial complex, with its own, very different priorities for using the equipment. "Korolev wanted to use the capsule to send a man into space before building a spy satellite," Lieutenant General Kerim Kerimov would recall. "He allowed no debate. Frankly, we in the military began to fight him."

much weaker than America the U.S.S.R. was in military missiles. Once again, old Russian insecurity fueled the Soviet swagger—insecurity great enough for Khrushchev to reject the 1963 proposal by President Kennedy to collaborate on space. The Soviet premier feared American domination of any joint project—and discovery of just how skimpy the Russian missile arsenal was.

The view from the ground, by contrast, showed great need and constant hardship. (The general public had effectively no opinion about the financing because it wasn't given a clue about it—not that Americans knew a great deal more about the real costs of their own program. Russia's anti-authoritarian haute intelligentsia suspected the expense was monstrous, but only from intuition; no facts were available.) And although very few organizations, Soviet or other, ever feel their appropriations are sufficient for their work, the Soviet space program truly labored in conditions difficult enough to require knowledge of World War II's achievement-despite-deprivation. Indeed, many of the space workers were veterans of that war, now uplifted by the promise of more victories.

If the American space program rode in a shiny new Grand Cherokee, the Soviet vehicle was a Model T stripped of everything except its chassis and moving parts. It was only because the scientists, many with ragged boots or none at all, got out into the mud to push that jalopy's flimsy wheels that they kept turning through the tangle of the bureaucracy, intellectual isolation, and general suspiciousness—and the severe difficulty of coaxing inputs from the overtaxed Soviet economy. A top Korolev aide wasn't exaggerating when he later described the building of Soviet-designed missiles as "unbelievably difficult for our country. We had to develop many technologies from scratch. And where to get the materials?" Many technologies were totally new to Soviet industry, whose technicians had to first devise ways to produce them, and then make their own searches for materials.

In Korolev's first Moscow factory after the war, the young team "had to start from nothing," as another key team leader put it. Nothing meant missing bones as well as bare bones. It meant no solid roof over their heads, let alone a snack bar; the staff had to grow their own vegetables on nearby plots. No amenities, from schools to hospitals, were available. (Soviet institutions of every kind were vertically integrated, self-sufficient little communities, each with its own day care, medical services, vacation facilities, etc.) The abandoned plant, which was actually just outside Moscow, previously manufactured artillery. Its condition was shocking, especially to the scientists who had seen some of the unbombed German installations while scouring them for every particle of knowledge. Western teams might have taken an order to build modern missiles within those walls of crumbling bricks and mortar as a joke. Korolev's team swept, patched, shoveled, and searched for boxes to serve as design tables for the engineers.

That plant's conditions were positively palatial compared to those at the first test launch site in southern Russia's Astrakhan area, where "the hot wind chased swirling dust and tumbleweed balls [and] there was essentially no water," according to a major rocket constructor's description. Another described the State Central Range at Kapustin Yar ("Cabbage Ravine") as a "bare lifeless steppe with dry sagebrush gray from dust." Compared to conditions at the American launch center—inaugurated in the same 1947 at Florida's resort-country Cape Canaveral—or even to the Los Alamos "campus" during its earliest war years, Kapustin Yar's were startlingly primitive. Most military officers assigned to the tests were somehow accommodated in a small town's already overcrowded housing, but soldiers lived in tents and dugouts. The scientists and technologists expected, and got, no better.

Ten years later, in the late 1950s, the principal range was shifted to the arid steppes of distant Kazakhstan, whose scratchy soil and relentless temperature extremes kept the area scarcely inhabited. (Khrushchev's monumental effort to catch up to American agriculture by planting corn in nearby steppes, where grass had a hard time growing, would end in a very costly failure that helped his enemies remove him in 1964.) The new center would become known to the world as Baikonur. Actually, that settlement was hundreds of miles distant, but the raw "cosmodrome" was named for it in order to fool the CIA. The safety and comfort of all who worked in the virtual desert remained near subsistence levels—"and moreover, there's nothing for people to live in," another Korolev aide complained. Even officers began by resorting to underground pits covered by makeshift roofs. Barracks, when they were finally completed, were unheated, despite winters of below-zero days and nights. A young engineer would describe the living conditions before then as "awful" and "terrible," in summer too.

> We lived in railway cars. The temperature at night was maybe 85 degrees.
> Very hot. Our food was very bad. Sanitary conditions were also awful.

Note that eighty-five degrees was the *nighttime* temperature, and remember that air-conditioning was then not even a dream. When the forsaken area wasn't unbearably hot, it was unbearably cold. Korolev's cabin had the envied luxury of hot water. Inspecting it decades later, an American biographer named James Harford found "a bed, a bureau, a desk, a table, a fridge, a toilet, and a sink." Korolev's colleagues, however, saw those virtually monastic quarters as a palace. To save themselves from having to stay in Tyuratam—the real name of the railway stop nearest the Baikonur cosmodrome—they tried to arrive just before test launches and leave just after. Only Korolev and a team of engineers habitually stayed over. His staying had more to do with his deep involvement in the details of the launching preparation and their evaluations than with his more tolerable sleeping quarters. For the others, however, the "terrible" conditions—almost all their descriptions use that adjective—included sleepless nights with bedbugs in addition to the sense of desolation deepened by "long roads to nowhere." Even years later, it took Korolev's pushing—in quest of a reward for some particular achievement or to please visiting bureaucrats—for key staff to be assigned an apartment. (Although Korolev saw to it that hefty cash bonuses were paid for major breakthroughs, the base salaries of scientists, engineers, and technicians were not significantly higher than in other industries.)

Still, it was a thrilling venture, lovingly embraced. One of the critical young scientists would remember that "none of us cared" about the living conditions—"actually enjoyed it," as engineer Sergei Krykov remembered—because they were so passionate about their work. The growing corps of specialists laughed, sang songs about the bedbugs and "awful food," relished the challenge, and felt immensely proud as well as perpetually anxious about making mistakes, which would surely not escape Korolev. Knowing they led the world in an endeavor that so clearly represented the future in their eyes, almost all of them interpreted that as vindication and proof of their political teachings, especially about how Communism united science and morality. Intense professional satisfaction went hand in glove with the gratification of fusing the promises of science and Marxist history.

Yet ideology isn't enough to fully explain why they were there, since the first reason was that young people would have been unwise to refuse a top-priority job for which they'd been selected. That more or less obviates the question of what kind of person took on the trials of working in gloomy plants and living in conditions more fit for infantry maneuvers than for a collection of scientists distinguished by theoretical and practical achievements. But although they *had* to do what they were doing, almost all wanted to. As for their other common qualities, intelligence, creativity, and industry were pivotal, together with a willingness to sacrifice that was furthered by the still-fresh memory of World War II, which dwarfed their present hardships.

I LEARNED DURING MY SEMESTERS AT MOSCOW State University that great numbers of the very brightest Soviet students chose to be scientists. I explained the considerably higher percentage than in America in terms of the unappealing alternatives. Although the arts and humanities were slithering toward less galling constraints, the often numbing Marxist-Leninist line still couldn't be contradicted. In science, however, the opportunity to call it as you saw it was much greater. Although under Stalin, ideology had wrought terrible damage to some scientific disciplines, especially genetics, by this time it played very little direct role, even among the considerable number of dutiful Party members. (Korolev was among those who rarely attended Party meetings, and he offered only a few platitudes when he did.)

Because the scientists, especially physicists, were so bright and so relatively free of dogma, they tended to be impressively informed and reflective about the arts and humanities too. And they craved—and got—much more information from the outside world than did people in other fields. Continued expansion of their role, which seemed inevitable, brightened the prospects for Soviet society.

Meanwhile, science offered an escape from mouthing political clichés as well as a crack at a fulfilling career (although the monetary awards were puny compared to those in the West). Even the privations afforded Korolev's little battalion an occasional "perverse" self-satisfaction. Many weren't much older than the student "volunteers" who were drafted to help with the national harvest every autumn—and who returned feeling proud about their two weeks of privation. For example, the young engineer who remembered his railway wagon's stifling heat had a critical assignment despite having been a mere three years on the job. The heavy responsibility served to intensify commitment and to charge the vodka-flowing celebrations of success. This was the happiest, as well as the most difficult, period in the lives of most who toiled the feverish days for the cause of Soviet leadership in space. "It was an amazing time," recalled Sergei Krykov, a young engineer who would go on to great responsibilities in the program. "We worked together with enthusiasm in the face of this incredible challenge, with a creativity we did not know we possessed."

Even skipping the prison experiences of some of those supremely dedicated people, a movie about them might be entitled "The Right Stuff Doubled." The Russian space effort was even more glorious than the American one—and also more thrilling, appalling, astonishing in a dozen ways. The best accessible computer in 1956, operated by the Academy of Sciences in Moscow, ran on vacuum tubes. Crude, slow, and unreliable, it was also often unavailable, as were lesser electromagnetic devices and even older mechanical computers. Korolev's team, including the many young members, had only pencil, paper, and slide rules to make their extremely complex calculations about fuel, velocity, payloads, trajectories, orbit apogees, and the like—and to factor in weather conditions much more difficult than Cape Canaveral's winds and occasional cloud cover. "In good weather and bad, sun and snow," marvels James Harford, author of *Korolev*, "they rolled their rockets to the pad...and sent them off"—some 150 a year—"with a remarkable success rate." During the course of forty years, more than 98 percent of some seventeen hundred launchings of the R-7 would go as planned.

As for Korolev's qualities in particular, any summary of them must begin with his rock-solid resolve to continue his work, even when he faced disaster in prison and the gulag. Alexei Leonov, the first man to walk in space, described him as "fanatical. Space was his entire life." If his passion for his goal and his single-minded focus on it were exceptional, so were his decisiveness and what an admiring subordinate called his "cold rationalism." By the time he worked in Tupolev's sharashka, the quintessentially driven Korolev was known for his furious ability to work and for his quick strokes that cut straight to the core of problems—or "sucked them out," as a colleague would put it. Those attributes helped him develop into a sterling organizer and rouser of others. His ability to turn the most complex theoretical ideas and technological dreams into the nuts and bolts of space machinery further helped. Like most successful warship captains, he opened up his men to the best in themselves, which often exceeded their own estimates. He himself remained inspiringly cool in crises, which abounded in a hundred forms. His energy was legendary. His physical bravery was evident from at least 1923, when a plane on which he was flying crashed into the sea.

But Sergei Korolev's many virtues were not the whole of the complicated man, any more than they were for Mikhail Tukhachevsky, his old champion.

Nikita Sergeyevich Khrushchev on Korolev

In his memoirs, written in virtual exile at his dacha outside Moscow, the former Communist Party leader recalled a Korolev report about his work to a Politburo meeting, not long after Stalin's death:

> I don't want to exaggerate, but I'd say we gawked at what he showed us as if we were a bunch of sheep seeing a new gate for the first time. When he showed us one of his rockets, we thought it looked like nothing but a huge cigar-shaped tube and we didn't believe it could fly. Korolev took us on a tour of a launching pad and tried to explain to us how the rocket worked. We were like peasants in a marketplace. We walked around and around the rocket, touching it, tapping it to see if it was sturdy enough—we did everything but lick it to see how it tasted. Some people might say we were technological ignoramuses. Well, yes, we were that, but we weren't the only ones. There were some other people who didn't know the first thing about missile technology. We had absolute confidence in Comrade Korolev. . . . When he expounded or defended his ideas, you could see passion burning in his eyes, and his reports were always models of clarity. He had unlimited energy and determination, and he was a brilliant organizer.*

As for Khrushchev's willingness to take a chance on the R-7 lofting of *Sputnik I,* his son, Sergei Nikitich Khrushchev, had an explanation.

> My father [had] a broad goal: he wanted to beat Americans in all spheres of life and to prove that our Socialist system is working better. A small portion of this was [in] space. So when Korolev presented his rocket, my father's first goal was defense: the military usage of the inter continental rocket. But when Korolev told we can launch this ball in space, and will be ahead of Americans, my father only asked, "Will you hurt our defense program?" Korolev answered "No." So my father said, "Go ahead."

* *Khrushchev Remembers: The Last Testament,* translated and edited by Strobe Talbot (New York: Little, Brown and Company, 1974), p. 46.

Although images of Stalin's victims as shining heroes help satisfy an apparently innate human need for stories about good struggling with evil, they make better drama than history. The executed field marshal was indeed heroic in some ways—and, like Korolev, blessed with rare foresight and energy. But that didn't make him a decent person, let alone a nice one. When the Soviet regime chose to suppress some early revolts by peasants and workers—the very people for whom it had supposedly created the whole huge turmoil of revolution—it sent Tukhachevsky to do the job. The distinguished military thinker was ruthless. Blood ran in the villages.

Korolev too had his darker sides, although none of the known ones involved violence of any kind, let alone killing. Some were probably deepened by his nightmare in the gulag, memories of which never left him, according to associates. A colleague once received no reply to a question he'd asked him—apparently a fairly common reaction from the sometimes "uncommunicative" leader. He later reasoned "that the black period of [Stalin's] repressions, prison, Kolyma, Magadan [another horrific gulag location] had made him [Korolev] cautious, and he avoided opinions on disputed [political] matters as if he feared that everything might be repeated again."

Another colleague saw him after the war as neurotic, basically pessimistic and still worried about being shot: "I think he was badly damaged, physiologically and mentally." Even well after the worry about more punishment had been replaced by honors and full knowledge of his importance to the country, he never forgot his time in the labor camps. Other rocket makers who had also been there managed to dismiss Stalin's villainy with what's called Russian stoicism, remembering the awful purges as "natural events." But Korolev seems to provide evidence that even those who look back on them in that fatalistic way may have more scars than they like to admit. The positive aspect was that he also never forgot the many fellow former prisoners in his programs, and sought to advance their careers. The negative was that draconian, utterly unjust imprisonment tends more to squash than to elevate spirits—and so it was with Korolev too, at least with respect to some of his moods.

Other evidence suggests he was not only extremely driven but also cynical, scheming, manipulative, threatening, very severe, and almost always feared. He shouted and swore at people who made the smallest mistake, especially if they tried to cover them up. He could fire such scoundrels in the blink of an eye.

As for the "Chief Designer" honorific, it somewhat embarrassed him, perhaps because he, like von Braun, had shifted from designing to managing, or in his case commanding—like Napoleon, one high subordinate remembered. Or like Lee Iacocca in the sense that his wizardry lay much more in corporate-like inspiration and management than in anything purely technical. Besides, not all veterans of the Soviet space effort are happy with his being awarded, very soon after his name was finally made known to the public, the lion's share of praise for its successes. The critics are convinced that lone-hero romanticism deprives others of credit that should be equal to his, especially in the case of a handful of younger scientists and designers who solved many of the most difficult problems, built many of the best engines, and wrote some of the analyses that were attributed to the boss.

More than that, some Russians now feel he was a losing horse for the moon race to begin with because his designs were inferior to those of other rocket makers, even though his salesman's charm sold them to the Politburo. An elite committee of scientists and engineers almost unanimously favored one such rival design, of a single large rocket instead of Korolev's thirty much smaller ones harnessed together. But the Chief Designer's maneuvering pushed his rival out of the internal moon race, and the fact that Korolev's admirers are writing most of the history now serves to obscure the superb work of the captains of other Soviet space empires.

Those arguments may never be settled, just as his personal qualities must remain a matter of interpretation. Yes, he was cunning and manipulative, but a Soviet shoe factory couldn't be run without those attributes. And despite his intimidating eyes and voice, those who got to know him more or less well—to the extent he permitted that—saw warmth when he relaxed, which could include solicitous interest in his workers. Alexei Leonov would recall that just before he embarked on the flight that would include the world's first space walk, Korolev wished him "a fair solar wind," and then embraced and kissed him—traditional Russian gestures to be sure, but heightened by Korolev's calling him by his diminutive, "Alyosha." As for fear of Korolev, it was tempered because he was almost always embarrassed on the mornings after his blowups, when he customarily ignored or countermanded his firing of personnel. In any case, the anxiety rarely extended to reluctance to suggest something new, even when it contradicted the wisdom of the moment. The rules-be-damned boss was not only open with young specialists but also protected them against revenge by any supervisor who took new ideas as a personal challenge.

All in all, however, the Soviet space effort was more complicated, especially in design creativity, than the subtitle of James Harford's well-researched biography suggests: *How One Man Masterminded the Soviet Drive to Beat America to the Moon.* Still, it's hard to deny that Korolev was never less than a first among equals. This is more than a case of selecting one contributor for the convenience of name recognition. Korolev of the "bulldog tenacity," in Harford's phrase, truly *was* the driving force, if not always the mastermind. He surrounded himself with superb scientists who had great technical understanding and creativity. A few even had fine management skills. But only Sergei Pavlovich combined those diverse qualities with his iron will, skill in making political connections at the top, and extraordinary ability to fulfill many functions simultaneously. The West had no counterpart, not even in von Braun.

THE ANSWER TO WHETHER KOROLEV'S HEART lay with rocketry's military or exploring-the-cosmos possibilities is also not fully clear, especially since all striving for personal goals took place in the context of the relentless bureaucratic infighting and squabbling for funds—and in a military obligation imposed on everyone. His admirers point to evidence that he always saw his ventures into space in general, and his conception of space in particular, much more as stepping stones to the planets than as an effort to contribute to military prowess. "Always more interested in spaceflight than ICBMs," one expert has stated, Korolev tailored his rockets for the one as well as the other: they could be used to launch space probes as well as warheads. That may be true, even though the sponsors of his various agencies were often the military entities that had the money. On the other hand, there is no reason to believe he had anything against the military use of space, and even some evidence that he took on some not-directly-military projects because he failed to get financially juicier ones for weaponry.

Space Squeeze

Korolev knew he could count on his cosmonauts' necessarily sterling ability to improvise. Alexei Leonov, the first man to walk in space, remembers being reminded before the blast-off that emergencies were entirely possible during the experiment. "But I know you are ready for them," Korolev told him. "I can't give you any instructions. Nobody has done what you are about to do." Korolev was again prescient: although the space walk went well, an exhausted Leonov couldn't get back into his capsule because he didn't fit. Alone in space, his oxygen running low, the seeming victim of bad Soviet planning saved himself by deflating his spacesuit and squeezing back through a narrow hatch.

Whatever his mixture of motives, however, he'd dreamed of a moon land-ing for decades, except that he'd have spoken of a work in progress rather than a dream. One day in 1946, he saw his daughter was reading Jules Verne's *Voyage to the Moon,* and emphatically told her that she would see human be-ings there during her lifetime. When the little girl (now a prominent lung surgeon) objected that that was impossible, he responded with a firm No. "Please remember this day. I tell you man will walk on the moon."

The Soviet race to the moon can be said to have started with that, or even with Tsiolkovsky's visions of space travel. And the push necessary for takeoff can be said to have come in 1955, when Korolev raised the possibility with gov-ernment officials; or the following year, when he addressed the Academy of Sci-ences about the voyage; or in 1959, when, after at least five previous failures, *Luna I* flew past the moon at a distance of some thirty-seven hundred miles.

Whatever date makes most sense—even Khrushchev's 1962 authorization after a day of feasting with designers in his Black Sea villa—the Soviet pro-gram had a head start and a good lead at the turn of the 1960s decade. The N-1, the launch vehicle's colossal new thirty-rocket power plant—the world's most powerful—would dwarf the R-7 and surpass the thrust of the larger *Sat-urn V* that would take the first American to the moon. The first orbits of the moon were scheduled for 1964.

Russian claims to have invented the lightbulb, radio, telegraph, airplane, baseball, you name it, had long been the butt of merry jokes by Russians themselves as well as foreigners. Actually, most of the self-congratulation was based on early Russian foresight and inventiveness, even if few of the experimental projects bore fruit as usable products. (Baseball was said to have derived from *lapta,* an old game played by hitting a ball with a stick.) More importantly, the ventures exhibited an enthusiasm for believing in "miracles" and intuition. And the present claims for rocketry were largely justified. There was every reason to believe the Russians' next prize would be the moon.

AFTER VISITING THE YOUNG UNITED STATES IN 1831, a twenty-eight-year-old French statesman-to-be named Alexis de Tocqueville made the first serious assess-ment of New World society. His *Democracy in America* predicted that a sec-ond country too was bound to attain great prominence among nations, although it started from a very different place. De Tocqueville's prescience was all the more remarkable because emergent America and awakening Russia were both rough-and-tumble. The free-wheeling young republic was tackling its "wild" frontier, the slovenly old monarchy was bogged down in autocracy—and both were still hobbled by forced labor (although Russian serfdom was less onerous than American slavery and lacked a racial component).

Although which of the two went on to fulfill the young Frenchman's promise is a no-brainer, the extraordinary accomplishments of Korolev and his Soviet counterparts in other fields make one wonder. If not for the political disasters that shook the "loser" country, would the twentieth century have been more Russian than American?

At its turn, the empire with the youthful excitement and drive in selected areas was still retarded in many others, especially social development—which a benighted tsar was sworn to stop. In that, it lagged perhaps a century behind western Europe. Still, literacy was soaring, along with education in general and commercial development, particularly industrial. With no help from the throne, the judicial system operated independently and well. In literature, the visual arts, music, theater, film, ballet, and several scientific disciplines, Russia had surged to the forefront or was making its way in that direction. The country's resources were vast; its scientific, technological, and industrial life, although patchy, raced ahead, promising huge potential. Full of energy despite the proverbial Russian passiveness—or because of it, since zest sometimes follows awakenings—the country had taken off toward almost certain realization of de Tocqueville's vision.

What would have happened in space, for example, if a corps of visionary scientists, among them a few probable equals of Korolev, hadn't been repressed in the late 1930s? And if the survivors hadn't been severely hampered by ideology, rigidity, and dictatorial absurdities? What would have been achieved in other fields whose shining lights, inspirations, and teachers—up to five million of the country's most talented innovators—hadn't been executed or otherwise silenced?

This is not the place to fix the blame for that measureless tragedy, but it should be said that the main share can't go to Soviet rule. Tsarist Russia's painful transformation from essentially feudal to modern industrial begot immense problems. All social and political institutions, from local hospitals to the fledgling parliament, needed remaking; and even Nicholas II's most slavishly devoted, archconservative counselors beseeched him to accept reform. Shutting his eyes and saying *Never,* the rigid, insecure emperor doomed his country to the breakdown and chaos predicted by his despairing supporters. Severe demoralization advanced to popular hatred of the regime, then to revolution.

That's obviously another story, but it can be summarized by remembering that Lenin took power from the streets, which the obscurantist Nicholas had done more than anyone else to put there. This point is relevant here for showing that the stunting of political and social development practiced by Politburo warriors and minions during the Soviet period had a non-Communist heritage. Without that stunting—or, to put it the other way, *with* the minimum of royal compromise that would have enabled the country to avoid revolution—it would have been a good bet that the first earthlings to land on the Orb of Night would have been Russian.

The country was wonderfully rich in the necessary human qualities. Its people had the science and the technological mastery—and, more important, the inventiveness. They had the fire in their bellies, the tradition of single-minded sacrifice, the "can do" and the "Yankee" ingenuity, all in spades. They even had more concern for safety than suggested by many signs and rumors to the contrary: in the end, their space program lost fewer men than the American one. What they didn't have was the means to compete with the National Aeronautics and Space Administration, which, as mentioned, had been created in direct response to *Sputnik I*. Reversing the Soviet promise that its economy would catch up to and surpass America's, NASA did just that to the front-running Russians. In the end, the money allocated to the two programs determined the results. As an American expert would write in 1999, "The competition revolve[d] on the ability of the two nations to come up with the enormous sums of money needed for a serious effort. Facing this challenge, Moscow proved bankrupt, as it so often would in the twilight years of the Soviet Union."

Since the economy couldn't supply enough for the "spendathon," as another American analyst called it, the Soviets had to try it "on the cheap." That too was a consequence of Nicholas II's supreme obstinacy, which opened the way to revolution's immense devastation—and the Soviet drawbacks that followed. For all the dictatorship's scientific and industrial achievements, it probably *retarded* Russia's all-around economic development compared with what it would have been under the old regime. Agriculture returned to the level of 1913, the last year before World War I, only in the early 1960s! Industry did better, but even its sometimes soaring gains failed to lift to it where it would have matched the old economy if it had been left to do its lopsided yet slowly balancing thing. The evolution for which all right-minded Russians yearned would have paid off more handsomely than the revolution Lenin imposed, never suspecting how much destruction it would cause.

But now it's 1961. President John Kennedy—unknowingly using words that echoed Korolev's five years earlier—makes his famous speech about landing a man on the moon "within this decade." Congress approves, and the race is on.

America runs it as it has come to fight its wars, by pouring in resources, as it pours in tanks, ordnance, and bombs against military enemies. Although few of us were aware of it, our space effort, from the beginning, would cost *trillions*: a huge slice of federal government spending. But that strains out national economy far less than the Soviet effort strains its much smaller one, which can't afford to properly fund both immense military projects (ballistic missiles and submarines to launch thermonuclear weapons) and the superbly engineered but still dauntingly expensive N-1 rocket. Although Korolev tries to sell it to the Politburo as military hardware, priority is given to design groups working directly for the armed forces, so that authorization to test the N-1 is delayed until 1964—just when patron Khrushchev is ousted from power. Meanwhile, military leaders continue opposing the "pointless adventures" in space and vow never to "sacrifice our nuclear missiles for a moon program."

In short, Russia's human and scientific/technological excellence isn't enough to compete with far richer NASA. The Russians have won startling races so far, but the odds are now overwhelming—far greater than those faced by American missile "tsars," including Wernher von Braun. Soviet sources will say, when work on the N-1 has ceased in 1974, that the U.S. has spent almost seven times as much on its first manned moon flight. American sources will make it "only" two or three times as much, but the point is the same: The eventual Soviet defeat was much more caused by the sharp imbalance of resources contributed than by any inferiority in science or personnel.

ACADEMIC KOROLEV, AS HE WAS BY NOW, DIDN'T admit the game was up, perhaps even to himself. In 1965, the twice Hero of Socialist Labor gave himself about ten more years to live, which was all the more reason to press even harder. "I want to send humans to the nearest planet," he said toward the end of that year, meaning Mars rather than the moon. Maybe he was trying to explain something to himself because the American space effort, driven by the full might of the military-industrial complex, was rapidly catching up. Moving toward its employment apogee of over four hundred thousand people, the Apollo program was well on its way. Fatally restricted Korolev—who, for example, was forced to test his rockets in pieces because his budget didn't allow him to fire up the whole—sensed the futility of trying to keep ahead of it.

But maybe "ten years" was his way of willing more life to a deteriorating body. Although he still looked husky and strong, he was plagued by ailments, most worryingly of the heart. An incident there the previous year had forced him to spend ten days in a Kremlin hospital. Now he was again complaining to intimates about an aching heart, which he associated with the bureaucratic and technological obstacles to his program. He was, he admitted, "unusually deeply tired," and close friends registered that he didn't look well.

In January 1966, he put aside his huge burdens to reenter the elite hospital for what his surgeon, the minister of health in the new Brezhnev-Kosygin government, believed would be a relatively simple operation. Thinking the same, Korolev called his wife just after being sedated to remind her of their plans for after the operation. But complications developed. A large tumor was found in his intestine. Whether or not his gulag spell had indeed weakened his heart, his broken jaw ruled out use of a breathing tube because his mouth couldn't be opened wide enough—a common problem among the multitudes imprisoned under Stalin. Korolev died on January 14, two days after his fifty-ninth birthday. Two days after that, the press announced his name. He lay in state in Moscow's Hall of Columns, the traditional place for deceased heroes, before being given a solemn state funeral, attended by great crowds despite winter's cold. His daughter, Natalya, thought that "very touching," and also "an ironic twist that he received the recognition he'd craved only after his death."

Although the obelisk promised by Khrushchev hasn't been built, a large bust of Korolev, crowned by a titanium statue of a stylized rocket shooting into space, stands in Moscow's Alley of Space Heroes. A statue of Tsiolkovsky sits at its base. Another statue stands very tall outside the old artillery factory that became his Experimental Design Bureau, in a little town now called "Korolev." Plaques to his memory are affixed to several Moscow buildings, including one in which he lived for many years—and one of the moon's craters bears his name. There is also a prominent street named for Academic Korolev. And there is reverence. That came—as with other great achievers who somehow survived and flourished, despite everything—soon after his death. In the West, however, he remains scarcely known, and that probably won't change. The great Cold War battle for advantage and position in space is old news. Our nostalgia is for our American winners, with very little left over for our obscure enemies, especially one whose name was unknown to begin with. And although the Soviet successes are on the record, the nervy underdogs' obstacles, sacrifices, hardships, and triumphs are also likely to remain unknown to non-Russians.

By default, therefore, the last word must go to his coworkers and admirers—such as a close colleague who remembered the launchings before the teams had computers to guide them, let alone a center for flight control:

> At the most crucial moments of the flight, it became clear that there was a single person who had the best command of the arsenal of knowledge necessary for implementing command of the flight. That was Sergei Pavlovich Korolev. He knew how to orient himself instantaneously in complex situa-

tions, to involve the necessary people...to unify all efforts....And he did that not only because he bore the greatest responsibility for the flight. He really did see, feel, know, guess and predict better than any one else.

And this from the eulogy delivered by Yuri Gagarin (who would die in a plane crash two years later):

> The name of Sergei Pavlovich is linked with a whole epoch in mankind's history: the first flights of artificial earth satellites, the first flights to the Moon and to the planets, the first flights by human beings in space, and the first emergence of a human being into free space.

Although the moon's first visitors, during the summer of 1969, were American, likable Gagarin was right. Korolev's achievement, and that of the Soviet space program as a whole, displayed the remarkable feats of which Russia was capable, even under hamstringing dictatorship. De Tocqueville would have felt three-quarters validated and Nikita Khrushchev's prediction may yet become true. "It is like Christopher Columbus who discovered the Americas and opened the New World to everybody," the Soviet leader said in 1959. "And even when Spain declined, it was still *the* achievement. We know Christopher Columbus much more than any Spanish Kings, so I think Korolov will be in the memory of the world as Christopher Columbus of Space."

TOP Konstantin Tsiolkovsky (1857-1935), the "father of Soviet Rocketry and Space Travel," in Kaluga, 1932. His scientific works and his 1897 novella, "On the Moon" were prescient.

MIDDLE Sergei Pavlovich Korolov (standing left) with a brigade of the "Group for Study of Cosmic Travel" (GIRD). Young Korolev launched the first successful Soviet liquid-fuel rocket, the "09," in 1933.

BOTTOM Alexei Leonov, the first man to walk in space, in 1966.

ABOVE   Korolev and his design team, 1930s.

RIGHT   Korolev's design team before the NKVD sent him to the gulag, delaying progress in Soviet space science for years.

BELOW   Korolev and his rocket team at the Kasputin Yar launch site in the Astrakhan area of southern Russia. After World War II, they tested reworked Nazi rockets there on Stalin's explicit orders.

TOP   Korolev at the controls of the glider Kotobel in 1929. He and a fellow student designed the craft for a nationwide competition.

MIDDLE   Sergei Pavlovich Korolev in the early 1930s.

BOTTOM   Korolev at the Baikonur rocket test site in Soviet Central Asia (now Kazakhstan), 1960.

55

56

57

RIGHT Belka and Strelka, the first dogs to enter space and return safely, are displayed at a press conference. July 22, 1960.

BELOW After Sputnik, the Korolev team scrambled to fulfill Khrushchev's orders for more. In November 1957, as a tribute to the Bolshevik revolution, they rocketed the first living creature into space: soon-to-be-famous Laika.

58

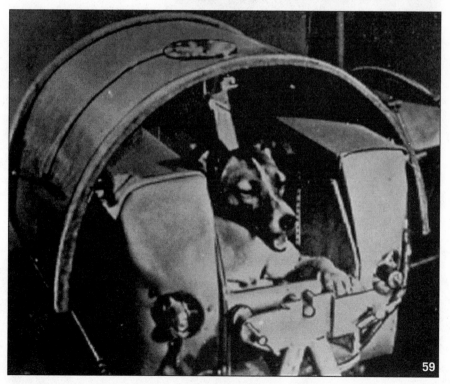

59

RIGHT Khrushchev hosts a Kremlin reception for Yuri Gagarin and his wife. Khrushchev's wife Nina Petrovna is on the right. Korolev attended such ceremonies only if they were closed to the press and the public.

LEFT Gagarin, the first man in space, is mobbed on his return to Moscow in 1961.

BELOW Khrushchev greets Gagarin atop the Lenin Mausoleum in Red Square, 1961. The adoring crowd had no inkling of the Chief Designer's identity.

LEFT Another Soviet first engineered by Korolev, celebrated by Khrushchev: the first woman in space, Valentina Tereshkova. Her capsule flew past Valeri Bykovsky's similar vehicle dozens of times in June 1963.

RIGHT Muscovites celebrated the first anniversary of Gagarin's flight as a national holiday. Rocket scientist, Vasily Mishkin: "Yuri Gagarin-the whole world would know him. But without Korolev, there would be no Gagarin."

BELOW More young Moscovites celebrate Soviet space triumphs in Red Square in 1962. The Chief Designer helped a new generation share Communism's optimism that "the future is ours, comrades!"

LEFT A model of Sputnik, the first artificial earth satellite, October 4, 1957. Its launch sparked a great crisis of confidence in America.

66

67

MIDDLE Soviet space capsules had to be rugged to survive hard landings. Gagarin's Vostok ship landed in a collective farm's field close to the Volga River town Engels in April 1961.

68

RIGHT Preparations to launch Voskhod-2 and Alexei Leonov, who walked out into space. The world's first EVA, "extra vehicle activity" took place in March 1965.

RIGHT Valentina Tereshkova, the first woman in space, later became a prominent propaganda figure and token politician. 1963.

Валентина Владимиров
Терешкова в скафандре.

MIDDLE One of the first pictures of the earth taken by a cosmonaut floating in space alongside Voskhod-2, in March 1965

BELOW Cosmonaut Alexei Leonov explains his historic EVA to a press conference at Moscow State University. He flew with Pavel Belyaev in 1965.

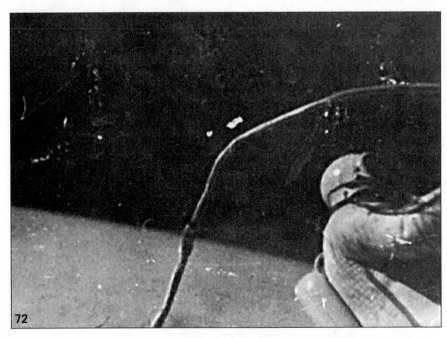

ABOVE Belyaev took the first pictures of his comrade Leonov walking in space in 1965.

BELOW After the EVA flight, Korolev worked on Luna lander so Leonov would be the first man to walk on the moon. But Korolev soon died. "We could have gone to the moon," Leonov recalled, "...but we let our chance slip away."

V
SOVIET PROPAGANDA MACHINE

"How's it going with you these days?" a weary man asks an old classmate when they meet in a line for milk.

"Really great!"

"Got any time to read the papers?"

"Sure! How else would I know?"

"Comrades!" a Party boss addresses the workers. "For the sake of your radiant Communist tomorrow, the Party suggests cutting your wages in half. Anyone against? No one? Unanimously approved."

One week later: "Comrades, to reach the Communist future even faster, the Party recommends cutting your wages entirely. No one against? Unanimously approved!"

Two weeks after that: "Dear Comrades, for the sake of international Communist happiness, the Party proposes you all hang yourselves tomorrow. Everyone agreed? Any questions?"

From the crowd: "Yes, should we scrounge for rope or will the powers supply it?"

IN 1898, A TWENTY-EIGHT-YEAR-OLD native of a provincial town on the Volga named Simbirsk was in Siberian exile for inciting workers to demand greater rights. The scarcely known would-be revolutionary used his time there—and his remarkable luxury compared to what was coming for the Soviet gulag's millions—to plan the goals of a socialist party he'd soon capture. It's cardinal tasks would include

conducting *propaganda* [his italics] in favor of the doctrines of scientific Socialism, in spreading among the workers a proper understanding of the present social and economic system... of the various *classes* in Russian society... of the struggle between those classes, of the role of the working class in that struggle... of the historical task of international Social-Democracy and of the Russian working class. Inseparably connected with propaganda is *agitation* among the workers.

The fervent exile was Vladimir Ilyich Lenin, né Ulyanov. (Simbirsk would be renamed "Ulyanovsk" after his death.) Two years later, while further refining the fundamentals of his soon-to-be Bolshevik Party, he scolded that "belittling socialist ideology *in any way, turning away from it in the slightest degree means to strengthen bourgeois ideology.*" Actually, Soviet jokes belittled persistently, although most seem less witty now than when they were told in the trenches of daily life, where the pleasure of mocking absurdities and official misrepresentations spiked the laughter and buoyed the spirits of almost every private gathering, at least in the major cities. George Orwell's "Every joke is a tiny revolution" probably exaggerates, but the Soviet ones gave a dimension to native society that was hard to see from abroad. Those about propaganda, which swelled the treasury more than any other subject, prompted the quickest mirth, aroused the sharpest derision, and provided some of the strongest insight into real attitudes. Many posed questions to a mythical "Radio Armenia," whose origins are obscure.

Question: "Is there a way to insure your refrigerator will always be full?"
Radio Armenia: "Yes! Plug it into Radio Moscow."

Three years after Lenin warned about belittling, he formed the party that would seize power in St. Petersburg fourteen years later, after many splits and twists in between. By the time the Bolsheviks consolidated their control of all of Russia, propaganda was so central to their thinking that imagining Soviet rule without it would be like baking bread without yeast—or perhaps flour; that's how essential it became to state designs and how ubiquitous in daily life.

From the very start of Soviet rule, when domestic enemies made its future precarious, the leaders placed great faith in propaganda. Even before the Red Army was founded, rolling stock that might have been used to supply hard-pressed Bolshevik detachments on various civil war fronts was assembled into propaganda trains. Stirred by Lenin's designation of propaganda as the revolution's main weapon, the mostly young enthusiasts distributed "Red" pamphlets by the millions. Their teams of agitators roused support among the workers and peasants by expounding about the White evil and the Bolshevik promise. None of that would have been done, of course—nor would the speeches have been made, the meetings held, the faith placed in the importance of the Party's newspapers—without profound conviction that it would do the vital job of broadcasting the socialist message. White military forces were clearly more powerful than Red. The dire circumstances made getting the Bolsheviks' truth *(pravda)* to the masses seem utterly essential.

What truth did they mean? None that would fit a Western definition. Sixty years later, near the end of Soviet rule, their successors were churning out even more of their curious version of it, revved by a sense that now the system was seriously ailing. In the early 1980s, the love-thy-Party outpouring—"The People and the Party Are One!" "Merge Yourself Even More Tightly With the Party of Your Roots!" "Communism: The Shining Future of All Mankind!"— approached the limit of frequency and volume. Films and videos; printed and broadcast materials; posters, banners and paintings festooning the streets, skies and barns.... My favorites were the swollen editions of Party leaders' tortuously boring speeches—by the slurring, shambling Leonid Brezhnev, for example, who had trouble reading a paragraph without mistakes. The groans of bookshop shelves under their weight echoed those of the old, exploited Volga boatmen, and neighboring sections spilled over with accounts of the leaders' lives that made American campaign biographies a model of political honesty by comparison. (The huge printings were ordered while books people yearned to buy were unobtainable because the land of unimaginable timber resources had a perpetual shortage of paper.) By that time, the fat volumes of exhausted clichés wouldn't sell to anyone even if they'd come with an alcoholic gift. The hackneyed message now spawned more jokes—yes, *even* more—than interest in, let alone respect for, Party explications.

A bent old granny with a collapsible "just in case" bag [just in case she finds something to buy] joins the line outside a butcher shop. Ninety minutes later, she reaches the counter, which is manned by two butchers, both beefy on their illegal private sales of government meat.

"Do you have any liver?" Granny asks the nearest of the two in a sweetly timid voice.

"No."

"Have you any cutlets?"

"No."

"Boiled beef, then? Or kidneys? Maybe sweetbreads?"

"No."

Veal, no; tongue, no; lamb no, stewing beef, no...ham, pork loin, pork shoulder, sausage, ox tail...*No.*

"Any minced meat? Good soup bones maybe?"

"No!"

The bag remains empty when the woman finally shuffles back to the street and the butcher turns to his partner. "What a pain in the ass that old crone is!"

"Yeah, but what a memory!"

Soviet propaganda's best feature was as fodder for humor. You ate and drank more in that deprived country (which therefore celebrated those activities) than anywhere else. You also laughed harder. During my initial visits, most Russians still believed Communism would eventually be reached. Their chortles at the follies of the wobbly march there implied no wish for the other side to win, any more than among bitching soldiers of virtually every country. But people also believed their eyes, and the proliferation of sarcastic quips and gripes spotlighted the contrast between what was and what was supposed to be.

It may take Russian residence to appreciate my choice of the propaganda's second-best feature. Party billboards, like ten thousand brightly colored toys scattered in winter's gloom, cheered your way, or were intended to, everywhere you went. On some bleak days when the sun and the future seemed to have disappeared forever, I'd find myself standing before one of those four-color proofs of mankind's shining tomorrow, registering its graph of inspiringly steep production rises. By that time, I could have composed the supremely predictable and repetitive messages myself. And I long knew the old saw that *"Pravda* has no news *(izvestiya)* and *Izvestiya* has no *pravda."* Still, the dumb optimism somehow warmed me. The demonstrations of the amazing progress of the Soviet economy and social services actually uplifted, even though I also suspected the figures were heavily padded. Double output of milk and meat? Great idea! Become a consumer paradise tomorrow? Why on earth not? Join the glorious effort that will make everyone happy in the end? *Yes!*—and I felt a little less sad and frozen already.

But those occasions were much less frequent than the shudders caused by the propaganda's other attributes. The worst was hard to choose. One candidate was Lenin's swift banning of non-Communist newspapers as he raced to manipulate minds *his* way as soon as his band took over in 1917. The young Soviet regime quickly installed an immense bureaucracy and machinery of censorship, without whose (literal) stamp of approval not a bus ticket could be printed. Without signed approval by Glavlit, the Chief Literature Department better known as the censor's office, "you couldn't publish a bottle, or a label," as a former Soviet journalist named Leonid Vladimirov put it. "You couldn't publish a wrapper of a sweet, an invitation card, nothing until you got the stamp of the Glavlit."

The army of censors numbered tens of thousands in their various units. And its orders to cut every mention of one thing and another weren't limited to possible associations with inconvenient facts and circumstances. Former censors now reveal that the prohibitions they applied against the use of this or that word or phrase in this or that context could make you weep. A journalist named Alfred Porter, whom the KGB banned from appearance in print, remembered that nothing negative could be written about the Soviet system, Communist Party, or the big bosses, "about anything that was [the] essence of Soviet system at all. So everyone had a censor in his own head."

A colleague named Victor Listov, who wrote for *Izvestiya*, helped fill in the curious picture.

> There existed a very strange rule saying that since both Lenin and Stalin were earthly gods, their names had to be written on the same line. Under no circumstances could one name be on a line below the other. Also, their names could not be mentioned in a paragraph which had a negative context. For instance, you couldn't say that work in the Stalin collective farm was not going well; that would have been insulting God.

That was but the beginning. The fortune spent on jamming shortwave radio stations may have exceeded the costs of the transmissions themselves. For the visual "aids," photographs were shamelessly doctored to make innocent "enemies of the people" disappear from the prints as they had from life. The West got glimpses of some of that "editing," but knew less about the cutting out of book pages and slipping in new ones when the leadership changed its mind about something or someone. All that and more, as they say, accompanied the incessant, inescapable blare of a Party line that was highly tendentious at best and nauseatingly servile at worst, from "Lenin Is More Alive Than the Living" to depressingly skewered history texts that were continually rewritten to conform to the latest dogma.

Naturally, the aspects that hit hardest were those with which I had some personal connection. The American National Exhibition on which I worked in 1959 featured the famous Nixon-Khrushchev "kitchen debate," never destined to achieve the place in Soviet mythology that nervous Nixon's self-promotion would give it in America. Although no such confrontation took place in the summer's counterpart Soviet exhibition in New York, it of course prompted the inevitable Soviet jokes, including one that managed to ridicule both the native habit of boasting about stirring plans as if they'd already been achieved and the reflex counterattack against "socialism's enemies" who actually questioned any of that:

> A visitor to that Soviet show for Americans approaches one of its guides (who, every Russian listener takes for granted, has been carefully trained by the KGB).
>
> "Hey, pal, that's a pretty fancy car you've got there, what's it called?"
>
> "Well, I can reveal it's called Chaika," responds the guide—without mentioning that the car is for Politburo VIPs only, or that the model displayed is a mock-up, still far from production.
>
> "Chaika, huh? Well it sure is big. Can I take a look at her engine?"
>
> "Hold it right there, you devious capitalist. As if you Americans don't lynch Negroes!"

It would be years before the guides, myself included, would realize how much the FBI had been involved in *our* training and supervision. At the time, we of the evangelical 1950s patriotism surged with excitement about our mission: nothing less than helping spread enlightenment and freedom to the truth-starved Russians who visited the exhibition grounds. And the kitchen debate itself that dropped the jaws of us onlookers hardly dented our convictions. Of course Khrushchev won, no matter how triumphant Richard Nixon declared himself after returning to Washington and his usual tricks. He won because the contest was on Soviet home grounds ideologically as well as geographically; like nothing else, Politburo politicians were trained to attack capitalism's flaws and failings.

Still, the Vice President's speech at the opening ceremonies inspired us. After a week of listening to Moscow radio and reading *Pravda,* he seemed nothing less than a modern Demosthenes, which was one way of registering just how awful the standard Soviet drone and bombast seemed at a first encounter, before one knew about the ritualism and jokes. It took comparison to something pretty bad to make Tricky Dick sound thrillingly civilized, wise, and liberal, even to an old Nixon-hater like myself.

Several years later, I was among a group of foreigners steered to the much-visited grave of a Young Communist hero named Pavel Morozov, immortalized in a million busts, portraits, and badges. Our Pavlik, as the patriotic fourteen-year old was lovingly called, was among the nation's great civilian idols and martyrs. Relatives murdered him in 1932 for having denounced his father for hoarding grain and helping farmers who were being banished from their native villages. Retelling the legend to busloads of rapt Young Pioneers at the kitschy monument, guides implored them to follow the example of Pavlik's supreme devotion to Communism. Raining tears on the snow, the scrubbed children in their proud red kerchiefs and utter ignorance of the real story clenched their fists in determination. We foreigners gagged, and not only on repugnance of a child's betrayal of his father for a political cause. On top of that, the banished farmers had suffered grievously for their "crime" of opposing Stalin's collectivization of agriculture, or seeming that they *might* oppose it, or provoking a neighbor's envy by working hard enough to own two cows instead of one. Utterly unequipped for survival in the wastelands to which they were exiled, the dispossessed families, the innocent together with the "guilty," lived like animals during the first winter. The large proportion who died terribly were never mentioned.

WHEN THE CUBAN MISSILE CRISIS UNFOLDED during 1962, Muscovites sensed something tense was brewing somewhere, but had very little idea what. Nor did I, living in their midst, until I happened to bump into an American diplomat on a downtown street. The following days of media silence demonstrated the power of state control more loudly than the usual harangues. A country kept ignorant of all substance of the Kennedy-Khrushchev clash, with its threat of national devastation, was an eerie place to be.

Another major Soviet campaign six years later got to me because I'd personally witnessed what it distorted. Now the setting was the Czechoslovakia

Poetic Pavel, the Denouncer

"**A** Poem about Hate," published in *Pioneer's Pravda* in 1933, conveys the flavor of the Morozov cult. (The Pioneers were the Soviet equivalent of Boy and Girl Scouts, but with much more ideological teaching and patriotic trapping.)

Pavlushka* won't be going

* "Pavlushka," "Pavlik," and "Pasha" are diminutives of "Pavel."

To the Pioneers anymore
Joyful and curly,
He won't come to school.
But his great glory
Will outlive everything.
"Pavlik is with us,
Pasha the Communist!"
Out in front, like a banner
Friendly and merry.
(That's how
Everyone should live).
How much
Every schoolchild
Resembles him.
Somehow.
All of their shirts.
Are abloom with red ties:
"Pashka! Pashka! Paska!
Here! There! Everywhere!

Soon after a show trial of the boy's uncles in 1932, a cult was created to infuse the Young Pioneer movement with another role model (young Lenin being the first, of course). Portraits, statues, and badges of Pavlik proliferated, and a kind of denunciation psychosis took hold of Stalinist society.

The cult was spun from a base of distortions and lies. Recent research shows that Pavlik was never a Pioneer. More than that, he denounced his father not because he hated the thought of hoarding grain; what upset him was that his father had abandoned the quarreling family. His son wanted to get back at him.

Almost no one knew that until the fall of the Soviet Union. Generations venerated the false hero, including a Soviet housewife named Tatiana Vorontsova, who experienced the complete political indoctrination that the Soviet system imposed on all its citizens from early childhood via the Little Octoberists, the Pioneers, and the Komsomol. She learned the Morozov lesson when she was in the fourth grade, in the 1950s. "So he died like a hero. We, of course, would also have liked to be heroes and at that time if I had been in the same situation, and my father had done something against the Soviet state, of course, I would simply have gone and reported him, just like that."

of the "Prague Spring" and "Socialism with a Human Face." The country that was an admirable democracy before the Soviet Union sucked it into its orbit had begun liberating itself from some of Moscow's controls and absurdities—until the Soviet invasion snuffed out the overwhelmingly popular reforms. Czech youths disliked speaking Russian, even though, or just because, they had a dozen obligatory years of it in school. But now they used their smattering of the sister language to plead with uncomprehending Russian soldiers manning their menacing tanks. "What are you doing here? Why have you invaded us? We were trying to make Socialism work—and for your sake too."

The boldest threw rocks. But back in Moscow several days later, I saw something else leave Czech hands and land much more gently on the same or identical tanks. *Flowers!* That lyrical rewriting, lacking only slow motion, was shown in a newsreel glorifying what it called the Czechoslovak people's profound gratitude for fraternal Soviet aid in suppressing "fascist counterrevolution." The narrator affected the required blend of solemnity and Communist radiance to describe the natives' imagined love for the Soviet soldiers who had helped frustrate the "mortal threat" by "Western imperialism."

My fellow movie-goers bought every word of it. Like the vast majority of Russians, they took pride in a noble job well done, having no idea that their forces actually mounted a naked assault on a supposedly sovereign people.

Later, when Mikhail Gorbachev's *glasnost* and *perestroika* would attempt to implement something similar to "Socialism with a Human Face," the invasion of Czechoslovakia would be recognized as one of the gravest of the supposed Soviet victories that was actually the opposite. (Question: "What's the difference between the Prague Spring and perestroika?" Radio Armenia: "Nineteen years.") But even in 1968, the spectacle of the Motherland of Socialism's tanks crushing the last grasp for a Socialism that might be made workable for its time was a study in fatal stupidity and irony as well as agitprop technique.

IF NOTHING CAN BE SAID IN DEFENSE OF ALL that, something *can* be explained. The country's prerevolutionary social and spiritual background can be taken into account, saving us from attributing too many Russian national qualities to the Soviet system. The place to begin a review of that background is the Russian Orthodox Church.

To cite Russian religion as a chief source of the ways of Soviet propaganda might seem perverse if not for its absolutely central place in Russian history and in forming habits and attitudes that of course persisted after the revolution. The Russian Orthodox Church—which, just like its sisters in other countries, reflected as well as shaped the national culture—placed distinctly more emphasis on dogma and less on theology than Western churches. Prizing faith over mere reason, it appealed more to the emotions than to the mind. (Many Russians, by instinct seekers of emotional and physical satisfactions in a "natural" community, still ridicule "artificial" Western rationality, legality, and preoccupation with the fine points of contracts and codes, as opposed to the promptings of hearts and spirits.)

That distinctly Russian priority was a direct antecedent of Soviet propaganda's reliance on relentless repetition of sermons, promises, and feel-good incantation. And although the propaganda machine's engineers and operators abhorred the laughter sparked by the contrast between the official expressions of faith and the reality of daily life, they felt no shame about the contrast itself. It can take some doing to accept that they never sought to depict domestic reality as it was, but as it *ought to be* and soon would—thus their "corrections" of temporary inconveniences, such as shortages and restrictions. They were convinced that the attractions of *will be* encouraged a people much in need of such hope because they were fulfilling the extremely difficult task of building Socialism in the teeth of its enemies' fierce opposition. ("How great it'll be when we reach Communism and enjoy its bounties as described! Let's go for it!") Well before Communism, Russian social thinkers had argued that the country couldn't afford the luxury of art for art's sake because it was too backward and unjust. Art's sacred duty, the pre-revolutionary social activists preached, was to serve the betterment of the shamefully oppressed peasantry. The Bolsheviks felt more or less the same about the idle indulgence of publishing truth for truth's sake. With the happiness of the poor—and the world!—at stake, *Communist* truth was needed. It was called "socialist realism" instead of just plain realism partly because the important "reality" was the shining future, rather than today's little mistakes and flaws.

That ideology raises a range of still-relevant questions about the ultimate responsibility of those who create and distribute any country's reading, listening, and viewing material. The first interest of media owners in nonsocialist countries isn't always truth for truth's sake either. The early Soviet leaders also prompt interesting personal questions, especially about how far they were willing to go for their noble cause. Still, it was their argument that mattered most, and that argument was essentially simple.

Its cornerstone was that there's no such thing as objective truth, only differing views of it perceived from various standpoints. That premise prompts memory of a true story (if the previous sentence doesn't invalidate "true") of a Soviet diplomat who was traveling to Washington after the United States finally recognized the Soviet Union in 1934. The eager man took a train to England, where he boarded a great new liner for its maiden voyage. Although the pier was bursting with bands, bunting, and celebrants dressed to the nines, the diplomat only knew what he saw, but only saw what he knew, to paraphrase the old saying. From a railing of an upper deck, his eye skipped past the evidence of prosperity and pleasure to land on a bedraggled, obviously homeless man on the fringe of the cheering crowd. That's how he'd tell *his* story of the festive sailing during the coming thirty years: as proof of capitalism's oppression of the poor.

Of the various competing perceptions of reality, the Bolsheviks "knew" that the most important by far reflected class interests. With objective truth even less possible in politics than elsewhere, their vision turned on the "fact" that there were only *socialist* and *capitalist* concepts, the immoral latter sometimes also called "bourgeois." Since civilization's fate, together with most human happiness and suffering, hung on victory for one side or the other, the war between the two versions was *it* for the world. And since capitalism, sometimes also equated with "the West," used its distortions and insidious pseudotruths as weapons, Socialism had to counter them with the *real* truth, which largely derived from the great benefits the new system would soon deliver. That truth was real because History and humanity's upgrading depended on it, and had bestowed the ultimate political wisdom on the working class. That's why Lenin proudly called for making maximum use of propaganda, which often had a *good* connotation in his Russia, at least until faith in it began dwindling in the 1950s and 1960s.

MARXIST-LENINIST EXPLANATIONS OF WHY socialist truth served as *the* beacon for the fractured world (even though there was supposedly no such thing as objective truth at all) rested on the assumption that it had been revealed to the Bolsheviks, and them alone. That, in turn, grew from their equally arrogant presumption that a "scientific" understanding of social laws and forces, drawn from Marx but updated with Russian brow-beating single-mindedness, had given them the keys to human nature and society, once and for all.

Of course that view contained some validity, especially about "bourgeois" truth. As our own society develops, more and more is revealed about how much upbringing and selfish interest shape perceptions—how differently a Wall Street broker and an unemployed worker are likely to think. In particular, it's now better appreciated how much Western media indeed reflects a capitalist worldview, if only in its assumptions and terms of reference: the arrangements are taken for granted, as if ordained. Many Western scholars, having studied Soviet propaganda and learning its tricks cold, write about the

Drawing Nontruths for *Pravda*

Boris Efimov drew political cartoons for *Pravda,* the Communist Party newspaper for six decades, even after his brother was arrested in the same offices and shot as an "enemy of the people." "I realized what was going on and prepared myself for my own arrest, since I was as guilty as he." But he was spared and continued drawing grim ideological caricatures that reflected the often fast-changing Party line. "I could have just said, 'You killed my brother, no, I'm not going to work.' But they would have sent me to the same place."

He survived by following orders. "My job as a political cartoonist was also to expose or make fun of or brand as a disgrace whichever of our enemies the occasion demanded." That included Winston Churchill, whom he personally admired. "I really liked him. But then suddenly it was announced that he was our enemy." Among other things, Efimov sketched the British Prime Minister as a drunken, rapacious pig.

---

fierce Marxist-Leninist bias that battered the world into unrecognizable shapes. I can't remember a single one, however, who didn't feel that such insight also opened up him or her to recognition of the immense influence of money and power on his or her own earlier perceptions.

Still, that does little to justify the far greater misrepresentation by Socialism's believers, particularly because they, for the most part, weren't working-class at all but Party warriors who arrogated to themselves the duty to speak for it. Moreover, their notion of the war of the systems included a need to censor and ban, to ruthlessly suppress information they considered possibly distracting from their program, if not actually helpful to its enemies.

In other words, the Marxist-Leninist approach might have better recommended itself if it hadn't instinctively obliterated competing views, with or without physical elimination of the people who held them. The Soviet rulers' need to do so suggests they knew all along that their propaganda was based not on society's "scientific laws" but on dishonesty. What did the "real" truth have to fear from the "false" and "doomed" bourgeois one? Well, they explained in superior tones that masked their insecurity, it had people's political immaturity to fear, their vulnerability to scheming capitalism's insidiously clever bunk. The worldview of the masses needed time to mature, especially since they were *Russian* masses rather than those of the more advanced Western countries where Socialism was supposed to have had its start.

Never mind that the same Russian masses were forever lauded as brilliantly forward-thinking as well as superbly courageous, that their innate perceptions and feelings were supposed to have made them *the* font of wisdom in the first place. That contradiction didn't bother the ideologues either. Now they explained that The People had to acquire class-consciousness—and the dirty brainwashing by Socialism's spare-no-resource domestic and foreign foes had to be refuted. So what could be wrong with *constructive* propaganda, especially since the lovely pictures of the future would soon materialize, just as painted? Like all closed philosophical systems, this one had an answer to everything. If you objected, that proved you were an enemy of Socialism.

IT CAN'T BE SAID TOO OFTEN THAT MANY OF THE early Party propagandists truly considered the revolution a "leap from the kingdom of Evil to the kingdom of Good," as a Soviet scholar put it forty years ago. "Nothing had value or made any sense except in relation to the revolution." I've been trying to suggest that that conviction remained more or less solid during the Stalinist period's huge strivings, despite the widespread fear that accompanied the reverence for the monster himself. My surprise at the range of Russian types I saw in 1959 doubled when almost all professed a socialist faith. My first reaction was that people were mouthing the Party line to an American—which was surely untrue except, perhaps, for one or two courageous young men who talked differently in private. Then came my Moscow University year, when even the dormitory wiseacres who always mocked everything truly believed that fundamentally good Socialism would replace fundamentally bad capitalism.

That confidence diminished during the 1960s and even more during the following decades, when ever shallower propagandists had ever less genuine conviction about Socialism fulfilling its promise. Now they chanted the old come-ons because doing so paid well in Soviet currencies. One winter night in the 1970s, a Russian friend of mine brought along a visiting Englishman to a typically hedonistic party of Moscow's non-Party jet set (which actually never set foot abroad, except in socialist-bloc countries). Charmed by the uninhibited drinking, dancing, and carousing in an artist's studio, the earnest Londoner attributed the lusty good feeling to the virtues of the Marxism his London smart set embraced. His statement to that effect dropped the Russian jaws in astonishment. So there *were* Marxists left in the world! But not among anyone with a brain in Moscow. Have a drink, friend, you'll get over it.

From Lenin to Gorbachev

The Communist Party of the Soviet Union's ultimate goal was a total transformation of society, economy, government—and human nature. To achieve it, the state required overwhelming control, down to the work of painters and musicians. Mass indoctrination in the virtues of Communism began immediately after the revolution, when the Bolsheviks disbanded all opposition parties, shut down non-Communist newspapers, and stamped out "decadent bourgeois" forms of culture. Only a new "proletarian" literature was deemed suitable, one that glorified workers and Communists and pointed the way toward a brighter future.

The propaganda efforts reached new heights after Lenin died in 1924 and became the first Soviet saint. Factories and cities were renamed for him, including the former Russian capital, St. Petersburg, which became Leningrad. Among the masses of adulatory books that commemorated his death was a five hundred–page volume with nothing but photographs of every wreath sent to his funeral. A bust of him stood at the entrance to every major institution. His corpse, which had been lying in state throughout the cold winter, began decomposing in the spring. The Politburo had it embalmed and put it on permanent display in a specially built mausoleum on Red Square.

When Stalin, after a vicious power struggle, managed to make himself Lenin's heir in the late 1920s, he founded a cult of personality for himself that far exceeded the previous one. The supreme dictator was called "the father of all peoples," even "the greatest genius of mankind." History books were rewritten to exaggerate his role in the revolution and his accomplishments afterward. Doctored photographs showed him standing beside Lenin, while his eliminated or soon-to-be eliminated rivals were airbrushed out.The heroic aura built up around one of the century's most brutal leaders caused millions of Soviet citizens to weep in desolation when he died in 1953.

His successors, unable or unwilling to exert the same domination, scaled down the cult of personality. After Khrushchev admitted in his 1956 "secret speech" that Stalin had committed crimes, the use of terror declined markedly. Celebrated political dissidents like Solzhenitsyn and Andrei Sakharov were harassed, sometimes painfully, but not dispatched to labor camps.

The ideological fervor that had gripped so many Soviet citizens under Stalin also diminished. Many still ardently believed in Communism's future, but others began to see the slogans, rallies, and parades as empty rituals, to be followed only because they were obligatory. Apathy and cynicism grew apace. The Party found it ever harder to seal the country from contact with the outside world, including elements of Western popular culture with much appeal to Soviet teenagers who formed underground rock bands and sported jeans bought from visiting foreigners.

After becoming general secretary in 1985, Mikail Gorbachev initiated his *glasnost*, or "openness," in order to help revitalize a stagnating economy. A flood of formerly unthinkable publications was unleashed. Suddenly people could speak more or less freely. At first tentatively, then more forcefully, the public criticized, which had the effect all previous leaders had feared: it chipped away at the credibility of the system as a whole. Gorbachev had hoped *glasnost* would spur reform. What it actually did was to speed the collapse of Communism, which was probably inevitable, if not expected to be so quick.

How could Soviet propagandists lend themselves to their chants of hoary slogans and sordid half-truths during Soviet rule's final, morally empty decades? The answer shouldn't surprise most Americans. How often do we too stick to ignoble work, even convince ourselves of its importance? No comparison to advertisers functioning in a democratic society's very different context is fair except in some of the personal motives. I know Madison Avenue veterans who wouldn't consider leaving their beautifully paying jobs, even when they'd rather not let their children know what they're pushing. Soviet propagandists had much more than good salaries to lose, partly because the general scarcity of living comforts increased the value of their every perk and privilege. Few cadre members were now directly punished for leaving a Party job, but quitting was more like giving up a whole way of privileged life.

By the mid-1970s, those who enjoyed propaganda tended to be, well, third-rate. People joined the Party for a variety of reasons, often to advance their careers and, especially, their chances of being permitted to go abroad. But full-time Party service now attracted the hacks—and propaganda, the worst of them. Those who gravitated to the tacky work tended to be not only cynical but also reactionary and, not to put too fine a point on it, dense. That's why so much of their babble was water off the population's back—except when it quenched a thirst.

Nevertheless, the babble helped make political discussions with many Russians impossible, even in the post-Stalin decades when broaching any political topic at all, let alone with a foreigner, was no longer foolhardy. This is not to suggest discussions were impossible with everyone. The high Moscow and St. Petersburg intelligentsia stayed surprisingly well informed, and often bitterly critical of Soviet rule, by reading "anti-Soviet" literature and listening to foreign shortwave broadcasts—whose audience numbered forty to fifty million in a former high propagandist's estimate. Many would have felt politically at home at a Western dinner party (even if it would have seemed to them too stiff socially). But attempts to talk politics with the general public were often maddening. The gap between most ordinary Russians and most Western visitors was too great for anything but both sides' confirmation that the brainwashed other simply refused to see *the obvious truth*.

"Incessant" is insufficient for describing Soviet propaganda, especially if you lived in one of the older apartments with a Radio Moscow speaker wired into the wall—or in a dormitory room, like mine. A new word needs coining to convey the sheer repetitiveness of the tedious oversimplifications. It should be noted, however, that the savage mocking of capitalism and capitalist governments did not usually extend to recognizable individuals. Much of it was like Boy Scout moralizing, its messages of "Don't Steal" and "Honor Your Parents" closely resembling the Ten Commandments. But the new adjective is needed more than anything to describe the homage to Lenin that hogged every day's media time and space, sometimes without an hour's break.

The paeans made Lenin the single greatest gift to the world for his work in shifting it, in the teeth of the mighty West's fury, to a socialist foundation. They also made him a paragon of truth, foresight, and creativity, a secular saint. (And God forbid a foreigner criticize him in public, as I was once accused of doing!) That sanctification too was generously fed by traditional habits. The parallels between the "New Soviet Man" and the old Russian ones were remarkable only if you'd fallen for the notion that revolutionary governments change ancient patterns of behavior together with state arrangements. Delegations of peasants bearing Lenin's portrait on high reminded me of, well, the obvious: the same peasants, or their parents, holding aloft religious icons and *believing*, or at least hoping, that they'd be blessed with the good life. Dear Lord, give us a break!

The constant preaching revealed that the achievers of the country's every accomplishment—from fishermen who landed a good catch to theoretical physicists who won international prizes—had been inspired by the glorious ideals and impeccable life of the uniquely brilliant, sublimely courageous, and touchingly modest Vladimir Ilyich. Special campaigns periodically supplemented the permanent torrent of selected truths and half-truths in honor of the "Teacher of All Mankind." One such campaign in 1970 marked the

Cultivating the Cult of Lenin: Childs' Play

Many former Soviet citizens whom the series producers asked about propaganda quoted an old Russian saying that you can influence a child only when he or she is small enough to fit across a bed (a variation of the Western belief that formative influences must come before the age of six). Alfred Porter, a retired journalist, was among the interviewees who recalled his early childhood indoctrination.

> The moment you arrive in kindergarten you are Little Octobrists [a kind of Red Pre-Cub Scout]. They put on you [a] badge with some little face, supposedly Lenin when he was [a] little one and they start to indoctrinate you. Grandad Lenin, kindest of all people, Grandad Stalin kindest and wisest of all people.... By the age of four, I could already read by heart some poem called "The Death of Ilyich," Ilyich of course being Vladimir Ilyich Lenin. I was singing songs something like 'I am a little boy, I dance and sing, I never saw grandad Lenin, but I love him.'

hundredth anniversary of his birth. As directed, all newspapers ran article after article about his insights and achievements, often several on the front page. It was as if the Politburo had some revolutionary new hose for pumping out the streams of stuff about his youth, his revolutionary wisdom, his answers to all problems.

The only escape was to not see or hear the eternal buzz—a defense used by almost everyone, including the majority who genuinely saw benevolent Father Lenin as their teacher and friend. Russian umbrellas against the rain of tedium automatically unfolded when their owners went out into the world from their sanctuary of family and friends. What, then, did those owners actually think? Now we're headed beneath our own inclination to see things in black and white, because the propaganda itself was one thing and its reception another. It often worked and often didn't.

Russians told a hundred bathroom jokes about the ubiquitous "Lenin Is Always With Us" slogan. Why did the newlyweds most likely to succeed buy king-sized beds for their new households? "So that Lenin can always be With You." (Not that I ever saw a king-size bed for sale in Russia.) As for the campaign to commemorate the hundredth anniversary of his birth, a new word *was* coined. A variation of a colloquial verb for to "plague" or "bore to death," the new verb, "to hundredth-anniversary," was used as a superlative form of the old one, as when someone would complain that a tedious old movie on television "hundredth-anniversaried me."

At the time, I thought nothing could be more Soviet than the massive anniversary overkill, but it turns out that's not entirely true now, any more than before the red flags were raised over the Kremlin. As I write in the eighth year of post-Communism, some of the same excess threatens to submerge the celebration of the two-hundredth anniversary of Alexander Pushkin's birth in similarly deadly idolatry.

Incidentally, it's a mystery why Americans know so little about the limpid, resplendent humanitarian and poet, recently translated into lively English at last. For Russians, Pushkin is an eternal joy, and not just because they had to memorize some of his passages in school—a relatively easy task, thanks to the exceptional clarity and simplicity of his language. Both dissidents and their KGB oppressors who fought about everything else loved him as Russian culture's crystalline backbone. So when it was time to commemorate the 150th anniversary of Pushkin's birth—eleven years before the 1970 campaign to do the same for the 100th anniversary of Lenin's—the country willingly leapt overboard. The depressing city of Ivanovo, northeast of Moscow, was among those that chose to express their devotion with a new statue of the poet in Lenin Square, just where the main street, Lenin Prospect, entered. As usual, architects, painters, and designers as well as sculptors were invited to submit proposals for the statue's anniversary motif. Together, they entered by the hundreds, and then waited tensely, with the entire citizenry, for the judges to announce their picks.

> When the great day finally comes, Third Prize is awarded to a drawing of a statue called "Lenin Reading Pushkin." Second Prize [which prompts belly laughter because *all* Russians know Pushkin died thirty-three years before Lenin's birth] is for "Pushkin Reading Lenin." And First Prize, the winning entry that will now be built, is entitled simply "Lenin."

Second place in the nationwide propaganda output itself probably went to the eternally vigilant, ever-stalwart yet merciful KGB, which manned the front lines of the Motherland's defense against perfidious capitalist agents and insidious internal enemies. The portrayal of the valiant, gloriously resourceful champions who shouldered the "Highest Duty" was even more swollen with clichés about the good guys defeating spy/saboteur scoundrels than sim-

ilar stuff about the FBI in 1950s America. However, another category of jokes
revealed quite different thoughts about those supposedly incomparable heroes. One of the largest collections was about the "typical" KGB operative, of
whom a whole crew was needed to screw in a lightbulb, and so on. His name
was Vassily Ivanovich.

So now it's International Geographical Year, and the Soviet Union, as always
acting on its peaceful intentions, sends a fitting man—none other than Vassily
Ivanovich in a pith helmet—to join well-known English and American explorers on the Dark Continent. Things go reasonably well in one of Africa's last un-
explored pockets until natives capture the trio and take them to their leader,
who happens to be an Oxford-educated sophisticate. Still, laws are laws, including the one that mandates execution for trespassing on sacred tribal grounds.

"So very sorry, old chaps. But I can offer a choice of how you'll go—by firing
squad or as the pioneers for our brand-new electric chair. *You*," he continues, pointing to the American, "since our chair came from you, you can
choose first." Reluctant to disappoint his host, the American indeed chooses
the chair. As he's strapped in, he exchanges some final words with the leader,
who himself will pull the switch on this inaugural occasion. Pull he does,
and proudly, and...nothing happens! No juice! Whereupon the leader as-
sures the condemned that his people certainly aren't barbarous enough to
subject anyone to a second go.

Passing the Englishman, the shaky but freed American whispers news of
the happy failure. Now the Chief's fellow alumnus, having made the obvious
choice of methods, exchanges clever banter with him as he submits to the
straps. Then the Chief again pulls the switch—to a second reprieve. Whereupon the Englishman whispers to the Russian as they pass. "The electricity's
down. *Choose the chair, man!*"

But intrepid Vassily Ivanovich never makes choices without thinking
everything through about trickery against the Motherland. Having done that
for several hard moments, he thrusts his chin forward, its unshakable Soviet
patriotism further angled by triumph for outsmarting the enemy.

"Well, I was going to pick the chair but I found out your electricity's
kaput, so you might as well shoot me."

The pith helmet also figured in commentary on KGB methods, which
propaganda undeviatingly described as uncompromising but scrupulously

correct. Now the setting is Egypt, where a team of Italian archaeologists have uncovered a new tomb deep below the desert. It's amazing, the find of the century; but the Italians, stumped by the hieroglyphics on the sarcophagus, have no idea of who was buried there so magnificently. Nursing their pride, they finally beckon a British team working nearby. But the Brits fail too, as do specialists hastily summoned from Athens, Hamburg, and Boston. With no more good old college tries to make, the assembly of the world's best archaeological minds mopes about in despair—until one member has an inspiration. Why not call in the Russians? Why not indeed? After all, they read the same scholarly literature, and decoding's a Soviet specialty. So out goes a cable to Moscow, and back comes a trio of Academy of Science professors—accompanied, of course, by the same number of KGB watchdogs in their helmets:

> All business, the Russians shake hands and descend into the tomb on the very morning of their arrival. They remain there all day and night, then a second 24 hours. It's late on the third afternoon when they finally emerge—very weary, in need of shaves; but triumphant.
>
> "That stiff down there," announces the chief watchdog. "He's Ramses III!"
>
> The other scientists are awed. The popping of a cork sounds over their elated applause. "But tell us," asks a Brit as he pours Champagne for his dazzling Russian colleagues. "Tell us how on earth you figured it out?"
>
> Now the KGB captain steps valiantly forward. "He confessed, the bastard."

The millions of Russians who traded such stories mocked the official portrayal of the KGB's socialist rectitude more than the agency's purpose, just as they were sick not of Lenin himself but of the dear-Ilyich-forever litany. In other matters, however, they essentially rejected the substance of their lessons. The constant reportage about America's horrific treatment of blacks got nowhere because most Russians were deeply prejudiced against dark skin in any location. (That upped their resentment of Moscow's much-ballyhooed foreign aid to Africa.) Similar anti-Chinese prejudice—reinforced by a longing for Russia to look West, not East—nourished sour feelings even when the People's Republic was supposedly the Soviet Union's closest, most beloved ally. While the media churned out steady glorification of their Chinese "brothers," Russians now found another reason to dislike them: their "antlike" devotion to building Socialism. Yes, Russians wanted that too, but in their own less conformist way. Most of my university dormitory was contemptuous of the furiously diligent Chinese exchange students who were all work and no play, who leapt to attention from their beds when Radio Moscow signed off with a rousing rendition of "The Internationale."

Of course there were exceptions to those outlooks. Like every large country, Russia had many, and it would take forever to summarize the full population's diverse attitudes. It's almost as misleading to speak of "Russians" or "the Russian" as to do the same for Americans, with their gaping differences in views between, say, Bible Belt and Beverly Hills. Inasmuch as popular attitudes did exist, however, they were solid evidence that some Soviet propaganda encountered stiff opposition.

Yugoslavia provided an example of resistance drawing on *positive* gut feelings about some foreigners. Fierce anti-Tito propaganda during the years when the Yugoslav ruler pursued an independent foreign policy was ineffective because Russians had—and still have—a soft spot for their fellow Serbs, whose language and religion are related to their own. As for other "fraternal" East Europeans in the satellite countries Moscow controlled, however, Russians tended to envy them for living standards distinctly higher than their own, especially "after all we've done for them." In particular, East Germans were never liked more than West Germans, possibly even less—and no amount of print or broadcast time changed that.

In short, many propaganda lessons were indeed drilled home—but home was often where it shouldn't have been on the indoctrinational map.

The United States, although always a special case, followed the same pattern. Not a day passed without at least one major exposé of America's evils and troubles. Wall Street tumbles got headlines; the gains were never mentioned. (Although it didn't take much perspicacity to figure out that no stock market could only fall, the propagandists kept going their own dumb way.) Every plane crash was elaborately described as evidence of the grim life under brutal capitalism, while none of the far more frequent Soviet ones were ever reported. (The news about them, and reports about which Russian planes were riskiest, circulated only as rumors—which, however, were surprisingly accurate.) Those were two of the least objectionable features of an immense effort to blacken the stronghold and armory of imperialism.

Despite the propaganda, however, Russians' admiration and affection for Americans remained powerful, more so than in any of our fellow NATO countries that I visited. There was a strong sense that Russians and Americans instinctively understood each other because they had more in common than either did with the more polished, pretentious West Europeans. It was true that a telling proportion of Russians drew back from me when we were introduced, and they remembered the possible consequences of making the acquaintance of an American, the most dangerous of all foreigners with whom to be seen. But their first instinct, before such calculations kicked in, was to beam and embrace. (The rapidly swelling popular dislike of Americans in today's "free" Russia makes that even more ironic.)

Actually, the anti-American propaganda often had a reverse effect because Soviet eyes were trained to read between the lines, where they often found more interesting information than in the proffered story. When viewing American movies, those eyes leapt to the cars, clothes, and houses of capitalism's "oppressed," whose living standards far surpassed their own. Despite the very careful selection of films that portrayed the country as deeply flawed along the lines of Soviet dogma, the overall presentation of American workers often prompted that kind of flip-side reaction. Among a portion of the intelligentsia—those most disgusted by Soviet ways after, say, 1970—it even generated a glorification of America. Convinced that their propaganda always dished out the opposite of the truth, those crypto-dissidents assured visiting Americans who criticized one thing or another that they were mistaken.

AND WHAT WAS ACTUALLY HAPPENING IN AMERICA at the time? Who recently declared that during the Cuban Missile Crisis we were told the "nonsense" that the Soviets might challenge us to a nuclear exchange? That, in reality, Moscow would "never contemplate that" because it knew "they were outgunned twenty to one"? And that the West "never understood" that the Soviets, with their "stone-age missiles...believed from the outset that they were no match for the West in direct military terms"?

That critic of our willful overestimation of the Communist menace is no former American Communist, revisionist historian, or even hangover of old-Left causes. On the contrary, he's none other than General Alexander Haig, Jr., supreme commander of NATO, Republican presidential adviser, and secretary of state. The fighting foe of Communism recently explained that our government had, in effect, pumped fear into the American people by deepening a sense of danger in which the government itself didn't believe.

That pumping hardly equaled Moscow's. Apart from calculated lying by officials such as the secretaries of state and defense—on whom the media relied and in whom the public implicitly believed—and the secret plantings of doctored reports, especially by the CIA, Washington wasn't directly involved in most of what we learned about Russia. Oh yes, the CIA also secretly financed the Congress of Cultural Freedom (more irony), which helped publish and broadcast powerfully anti-Communist materials. Still, we had no ministry of information, let alone an establishment one-tenth the size of the Soviet Union's. Strictly speaking therefore, it may be wrong to speak of "American propaganda"—but a steady rain of distortion served the same purpose. A whole mini-industry produced and distributed feature and television films about Commies invading and enslaving us, along the lines of *Red Dawn*. Those entertainments, and the skillful manipulation of information for the mainstream, probably stuck to our popular culture's bones better than the cruder Party stuff did over there, all the more because most of us knew less about real Russians than they did about us.

I used to lecture about Russia to college audiences. Although I claim nothing scientific here, shows of hands by Americans who'd read Mark Twain convinced me they were fewer than their Russian counterparts. Although the Soviet selection of American books to translate and publish was sharply slanted, considerably larger numbers of young Russians, and older ones too, read some American classics than the other way around. Chinese parents of the time admonished their youngsters to clean their plates because American children were starving. That was the kind of bunk that wouldn't have washed in Russia.

On that lecture circuit, I learned of a Texas experiment that analyzed children's drawings of other countries' children. They invariably drew happy little Belgians, Italians, Swedes, and so on—while they represented Russian boys and girls as glum figures in barren landscapes. I have to say that Russia's serious flaws didn't include many unhappy children. Where did *ours* get that idea? How far did it extend, and what did it imply for their other attitudes toward our adversaries? During the question-and-answer period following one of my talks, a woman in the audience rose to say that her nine-year-old son had begged her not to attend that evening. "But why?" she asked him. "Because, Mommy, you said it's going to be about Russians. I'm afraid. Something might happen to you."

That was an extreme case, but not a misleading one. One way and another, we countered the Soviet propaganda machine with *our* disinformation, which was no less effective—probably more so—because it was much more subtle and sophisticated. At the time, many thought that was necessary and good, but others knew it was destructive. It degraded the very things for which we were fighting the good fight. It clouded our judgment by confusing us about our adversaries. It pictured every Soviet dissident and malcontent as a fighter for democracy, when—as more of us are now learning—many hadn't the vaguest idea of what democracy was. We're still paying for that.

IT WASN'T CENSORSHIP BUT INFORMATION selection that warped our image of Soviet reality. With the Cold War in full swing, we began hearing more about the Red Army's raping and looting when it pushed into German territory in 1945 than about the incomparably worse atrocities, including the intentional burning of thousands of Russian villages, by German invaders during the previous four years. And if the thirty-odd percent of German prisoners of war who died in Soviet captivity seemed shocking evidence of Bolshevik cruelty, that was partly because few of us knew the toll of Soviet soldiers captured by the Germans was roughly double, or *60* percent! Although the most recent books about the eastern front, including Richard Overy's *Russia's War: Blood Upon the Snow* (1998) and Antony Beevon's *Stalingrad: The Fateful Seige* (1997), offer far better balance, the general public was little interested in that during the East-West struggle, and hardly more now.

As for the Soviets, perhaps the only aspect of Communist propaganda that fully gripped the entire population was glorification of the Red Army's defeat of Nazism during World War II itself. No day passed, and certainly not an evening, without television showing a new or old movie about the victory of victories—regarding which, however, I never heard a complaint about "tedium" or exaggeration. Far more than in America's current craze of World War II nostalgia, Russia's terrible struggle of many decades ago was fresh as yesterday's soccer match because it enabled the country to swell with pride over something entirely real and admirable. Richard Overy reports a veteran's comment that Victory Day, May 9, was "celebrated in a much more spiritual way" than the anniversary of the Bolshevik Revolution. And whatever the politics of Russians as I write, from westernizing liberal to unregenerate Communist, all agree that the defeat of Nazism—which surely saved Europe from decades of hell—was the Soviet Union's finest feat.

Did the Russians, in their poverty and social backwardness, really crush Germany, that most advanced, most militarized nation that had rapidly, easily flattened all the other European armies? Yes, they did—with their blood. German generals had assured their soldiers that the Soviets were "unsuited for modern warfare." They rode to war, Overy continues, "confident that victory was a matter of weeks" (eight to ten at most) against the "ill-educated, half-Asiatic" Russians, led by Soviet commanders of matching incompetence. (The American joint chiefs of staff predicted Soviet defeat in one to three months.) Yet it was largely the remarkable quality of Soviet military leaders—and of Soviet weapons, and even the seemingly destroyed Soviet economy—that began turning the tide well before Western forces were committed on land. Without those huge contributions, "Germany could not have been defeated," Overy concludes.

Disappointed American correspondents are right to report that the Russian people, having been starved of truth by Soviet propaganda, know little of the Western contribution to that achievement. But most Americans know equally little about the vastly greater Soviet contribution, which resulted in four in five Wehrmacht casualties—*80 percent*—coming on the eastern front. America's widespread ignorance of what really defeated Nazism, and at what cost, surely derives more from a tendency to trumpet one's own triumphs, even when they're secondary, than from anything that can properly be called state propaganda. But since the two tend to have much the same effect, it's important to assess Soviet propaganda's effect on Soviet minds in its larger context.

So what, in the end, did Russians actually believe? It would take forever to answer that about a people of 150-odd million individuals. To the extent that generalizations may help, however, it now seems clear that they, like the rest of humanity, believed what their history and circumstances conditioned them to believe. That is, they believed what they wanted to believe—which comes to roughly the same thing. And although most people do the same, Russians' capacity to believe despite the evidence of their eyes was surely greater than that of people elsewhere in Europe, thanks to the Orthodox Church and other cultural factors that shaped them to prize faith over thought, doctrine over analysis. Living among some Russians as closely as a foreigner could, I always sensed that all the propaganda in the world wouldn't have worked on them if it hadn't been rooted in the pre-Communist notions and visions that lay in their temperamental and cogitative bones.

It's hard to be too pessimistic about present-day Russia which is stuck in its political and economic swamps, wallowing in disarray and disgust. The only silver lining is its new, unprecedented links to the outside world. Throughout the millennia from the nation's national origins until quite recently, foreigners had scant knowledge of what was really happening in its deeply isolated vastness, and only a sprinkling of privileged Russians had a better understanding of how other societies functioned. Now, however, every Russian can get satellite-relayed information of every kind, from British parliamentary debates to pitches for Riviera real estate, together with CNN and BBC-TV.

But how many want that? How quickly can information change perceptions formed over centuries? If Soviet propaganda had been decisive in forming popular attitudes, you'd think its cessation in 1991 would have led to radical change. So far, however, the persistence of fundamental attitudes is much more striking than the relatively minor adjustments in secondary matters. My son, who lives in Moscow and studies the Russian media, finds that few Russians still have any real idea of what's going on in the world, so biased is their media. That makes the most interesting questions about the Soviet propaganda machine those that probe its connection to the traditional national attitudes, which can no longer be dismissed as solely its creation.

This takes me back to the American National Exhibition in 1959. None of the guides, myself included, were aware of just how many Russians blessed it as "a ray of sun," "a real blockbuster," as "Red Files" interviewees described it. But it's now clear that the Soviet leaders' decision to tolerate the exhibition signaled how they would resolve one of their most difficult dilemmas: whether to continue to protect the country's ideological purity by playing ostrich or to seek economic advantage by making at least some real links to the West—thereby risking the undermining of its own propaganda, since one link tends to lead to another.

At the densely thronged exhibition, a scattering of visitors with hard faces asked the same questions again and again, hour after hour: Why did the United States surround the peace-loving Soviet Union with military bases? Why did Americans lynch Negroes? Why was supposedly prosperous America disfigured by millions of wretched poor and other grievous faults of class warfare? Although we guides never thought to draw a conclusion about those middle-aged questioners with their nearly identical wording, many "ordinary" Russian visitors recognized them as paid Party agitators. The brave among the visitors risked notice, usually shouting from the relative safety of the surrounding crowds, by telling the professional questioners to shut up. "Are *you* American, Comrade? Have you visited America? [Not one Soviet citizen in ten

Peasant Wisdom

Russians' attitude toward the ownership of natural resources, especially land, resembled that of native Americans. A Congress of Peasants expressed it in 1905, twelve years before the Bolshevik Revolution.

Land is like air, no one should own it.
Everyone needs it.
Each must use what he needs to live.

million ever had.] If not, let *him* speak." And that was in 1959, only six years after Stalin's death—because, as I said, the public wouldn't swallow the line about America whole.

When answering questions at my stand, on the other hand, I learned not to mention that my father was a (very small) manufacturer. When I did, listeners' expressions revealed that whatever I, the boss's son, would say next, or had just finished saying, had to be taken with a heavy grain of salt. Just as Russians *knew* the vaunted freedoms of the Western press were trappings because it naturally served the capitalists who owned it, I of the capitalist father couldn't be counted on to give them a true picture.

What that suggested, although I didn't realize it then, was that Russians had long wanted some form of collectivist economy, and still do. It didn't take the Bolshevik Revolution to convince them that Western capitalism was nasty and cruel. The American politicians who predicted that the good Russian people would race to a free-market economy as soon as they broke their bad Soviet regime's chains demonstrated woeful ignorance of the country's history.

John Hazard, my adviser during my graduate studies, was among a handful of Americans who'd studied in the Soviet Union. He survived, even prospered intellectually, through the 1936–37 purge years as a student of the Moscow Judicial Institute, where Stalin's show-trial prosecutor, Andrei Vyshinsky, was among his professors. Professor Hazard's years living in Moscow made him a natural exception to the general rule that academic analysis deals with theory and models much more than memories and attitudes. When he wrote his respected *The Soviet System of Government*, he took pains to point out that even émigrés, whose dislike of the Soviet Union was strong enough to prompt them to risk everything in order to be free, remained convinced that only nationally owned industry, natural resources, and transportation could maximize the general welfare. "Private enterprise as a way of life has been rejected even by those who hated the Stalin regime. The key to long-range prosperity has come to be for most Soviet citizens, whatever their political persuasion, state ownership of the means of production."

Although that conclusion was written decades ago, little has changed for the majority. Don't they *see*, even after the dismal Soviet failure, that capitalism far more benefits the general welfare? No, they see the opposite, even while ogling the Western merchandise on their shopping streets. Actually, the primitive Russian and foreign grabbing of national resources practiced in the 1990s, the tearing off by the rich and unscrupulous of chucks of wealth from the carcass of the old socialist enterprises, is doing more to confirm the majority's traditional suspicions of capitalism than to refute them. Now, after digesting the evidence of their own eyes and wallets, they can say for certain that they understand the capitalist system, which they define as:

- Snatching the biggest profit as fast as you can, or
- The way the rich and powerful squeeze the poor even more, and cut down their safety net, or
- Any clever way to screw the customer.

Besides, generations of families had labored, sometimes sacrificially, under the conviction that the country belonged to them and its other citizens—only to see its wealth grabbed by tiny cliques (even smaller in number than Communist Party apparatchiks) of the best-connected and most ruthless thieves. How would *we* react to that? Although real Soviet life was very rarely the "all for one and one for all" of the slogan, that slogan was at least emotionally comforting, unlike its rough opposite now. Vague as it always was, the notion of common ownership of the entire economy was much more consoling than knowledge that *your* old factory, where you and your father before you put in your years if not your diligence, is now the property of criminal robber barons.

This isn't to suggest that collective ownership of anything is ipso facto morally superior. In practical terms, it has serious disadvantages, especially in our era, which demands increasingly fast reaction to market needs. Nor does it mean that Russians are totally hopeless in private commercial pursuits. During the short periods of the tsarist and Soviet governments when private enterprise was encouraged, the national economy spurted ahead. Still, the Russian instinct is much less for "rugged individualism" than for security. Where we see opportunity, Russians are much more likely to see threat. We tend to think of what can be gained, they of what can be lost.

That dichotomy is among the contradictions of the conventional wisdom about the powerful Russian-American similarity. Actually, we resemble each other only in selected traits—one of which, however, is fundamental. Maybe because we live on great, once scarcely inhabited landmasses, we both tend to think in cosmic terms about great movements that will make us free, prosperous, and happy forever. In that sense—in the conviction that we can build a far better New World—both societies, despite all the secularization, are deeply religious. That can't be said of the English people, for example, or the French, or the Dutch. But Russians are deeply unhappy without a dream that includes a sense of national redemption and fulfillment.

The already weakened Communist version atomized in 1991, together with the regime. Hunger for a new one is swelling in the national gut. That's not necessarily a good thing because some of the previous dreams came with an equally deep conviction that the country is a special one, with a special mission—despite or even because of its suffering—to guide the world toward higher spiritual achievements. (In that way, among others, the prophet Solzhenitsyn resembles the prophet Lenin, for all the former's loathing of the Marxism he once championed.) No one in the muddle of current political and economic life now knows what the new clarion call might be, but the odds are strong that another one *will* sound, sooner or later. Russian history has been one of long slumbers broken by periodic outbursts of anger and violence—which is a good reason for taking smoldering Russian pride into consideration.

American statesmen have taken to using "hurt Russian pride" as a patronizing dismissal of Moscow's supposedly juvenile or irrelevant opposition to this or that proposal or decision of theirs. Russians see things very differently, just as they did when their pride in the Soviet Union was, generally speaking, very great. They complain that although they surrendered the "evil empire" without a shot (a substantial truth) and Moscow gave up huge strategic advantages in Europe, the West—again, particularly America—responded with empty promises of compensation. More than that, it thrust NATO, that feared alliance founded in hatred of Russia, straight to the Motherland's borders, when it no longer had any business there at all! What better proof of the West's essential enmity toward Russia?

The thirst for respect is nowhere so great as for a fair evaluation of World War II. Although the old Soviet figures are surely inflated, the destruction in Russia probably included something in the region of the official ones: seventeen thousand towns, seventy thousand villages, thirty-one thousand factories, eighty-four thousand schools and forty thousand miles of railway track—in addition to fifteen, twenty, or twenty-five million dead, depending on whose figures you accept. It was like a thousand Bosnias and Kosovos, and Russians still yearn for recognition of that. The lack of it so far feeds an abiding sense of injustice—as, for example, in the elaborate fiftieth-anniversary commemoration of the Normandy invasion of 1944. That valorous landing by American and British forces would have been unthinkable without the massive Soviet victories that had torn the guts from the German armed forces during the previous two years, with vastly greater casualties than the Western Allies ever suffered. Russians may have been oversensitive in seeing the failure to invite their representatives to the ceremonies as yet more evidence of the West's essential lack of concern for their dead or their memories. But it would have cost us little to soften that feeling.

Their resentment, sharpened by the privations of their increasingly disorganized economy, often curdles even their gratitude for Western aid. Russians are no better than others, and too often worse, at containing feelings of inferiority or obligation. Besides, they're tired of doing so; they're up to the gills with the financial prudence they must acquire in order to keep attracting Western loans and investments—and increasingly furious that they can't do without them, increasingly anxious that foreigners are taking over their economy, snapping up everything for a song, while pretending to rebuild it. Alas, nothing can change that for the foreseeable future, and perhaps nothing can fully assuage their increasingly ugly seething about the West. But a fairer recognition that the old Soviet society wasn't *only* horrid might deflate some of their wounded pride.

Few of them, however, will soon accept that the Soviet Union ever threatened Europe in any real way. The majority continue to see their Cold War military posture as purely defensive, especially as a need for defense lays in their bones. That applies particularly to the satellite countries of eastern Europe. Most Russians—unless they had a good friend in one of them—still believe they were East Europe's benefactors from 1945 to 1990—yet more evidence that the propaganda that worked on them was rooted in pre-Communist perceptions. An old Russian saying (which rhymes nicely in the original) has it that "a chicken's not a bird, Poland's not abroad." In other words, "naturally" Russia should hold sway over Poland—and also, they feel, over other smaller neighbors and the former minority Soviet republics such as Ukraine, Georgia, and Kazakhstan.

"We let them go in 1990 with hardly a drop of blood," goes the average person's thinking, "but they belong in our orbit." That attitude (which has something in common with ours about South and Central America) shames the intelligentsia. But the Russian "masses," their nationalism fired by impotence and humiliation, are convinced they deserve at least a right of consultation even about the far more developed Baltic countries that suffered much under the old Soviet dominion.

But wait, that reminds me of the human tendency to forget such offenses when recollecting the past, instead remembering only the good. To check on myself, to see whether these pages have been too kind to Russia, I just glanced at some notes I kept during my Soviet stays, and remembered how often the din of the Party campaigns had me in shudders. But maybe thought about what prompted the then permanent propaganda flood can help avoid more in the future, by not needlessly pushing the wrong buttons, opening the sluice gates to a rush of troubled Russian notions and memories.

74

ABOVE Propaganda trains were brightly painted in styles derived from traditional, vividly-colored woodcuts that illustrated simple stories. May 1919.

75

LEFT Bolsheviks embraced the latest technology. Trains brought films and gramophones. Note the movie camera and the reel painted on the left side of the "Lenin" propaganda train. 1919.

ABOVE The propaganda train named for Lenin carried a library and a printing press for "enlightenment" of the countryside. Peasants associated literacy with liberty.

BELOW "Lenin" train staff. The slogan reads: "From the gloom and oppression of capitalism, the Dictatorship of the Proletariat will bring us to a radiant future!"

LEFT Anti-religion campaigns. The banner reads: "Pioneers be on alert if your parents pray to god," which was always spelled with a small "g." Moscow, 1929.

BELOW To build a new society, Soviet utopianists tore down much of the old. A church bell is rolled towards meltdown at the Moscow Brake Factory. 1925.

ABOVE Pioneers and Young Communists mobilized to help the spring sowing after Stalin's ruthless collectivization of agriculture. Ukraine, 1930.

LEFT Young Communists getting the vote out in Moscow, 1934. "Hail to the Soviet. Long Live the Bolshevik Party."

RIGHT Pioneers during flag lowering in Artek, the showplace summer camp in Crimea. 1934.

ABOVE Diligent older children inculcated Soviet values to their juniors. At a school in the Latvian capital of Riga, 1946.

RIGHT Pioneers ceremonies, a daily part of school life, reinforced obedience and order. At a Moscow girls' school in October 1949.

LEFT Post-war Soviet life featured mass displays of ritualized allegiance. Here chosen youth from the Karelo-Finnish Republic salute Stalin at Moscow's Dynamo Stadium. July 1947.

RIGHT The Moscow Garrison parades during the May Day celebration of 1950.

86

BELOW Pioneers prepare for the honor and thrill of marching on Red Square during the 1950 May Day Parade.

87

RIGHT Pioneer induction ceremonies were often staged at Communist shrines such as this museum dedicated to Old Bolshevik Mikhail Kalinin. 1956.

LEFT Marshall Aleksandr Vasilevksy (1895–1977), Minister of the Armed Forces, leads Red Square's military parade on May Day 1950.

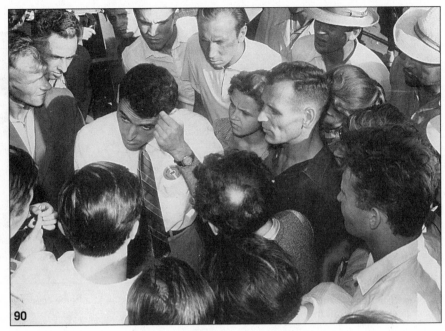

90

ABOVE   A guide ponders a question at the American National Exhibition, a blessed "ray of sunshine" and an "eye-opening blockbuster." Moscow, 1959.

BELOW   American portraits at the 1959 exhibit which Khrushchev used to signal change. He wanted a more open country than under Stalin and with better American exchange.

91

ABOVE Nikita and Nina Khrushchev observe a housekeeping lesson at a home econom-ics class at Iowa's Eileen University. September 23, 1959.

BELOW Khrushchev inspects the sorghum crop at Roswell Garst's Idaho farm in 1959. Garst sparked a mania for planting corn in Khrushchev.

VI
AFTER THE FALL

The present generation of Soviet people will live under Communism!
—Ubiquitous slogan of the 1960s

Question: Can you find a job that will protect you from unemployment *forever*?
Radio Armenia: Certainly. Become a lookout for the approach of Communism.

THE SOVIET SPACE EFFORT, ALTHOUGH publicly relegated to second place after Americans landed on the moon, continued producing superb scientists and ingenious equipment. The sports effort remained internationally powerful with Soviet teams competing in more and more events. (Of the ten Olympic Games in which the USSR participated, Soviet athletes won the most medals eight times.) The propaganda effort, although it was becoming distinctly less strident and crude, showed no signs of being abandoned, any more than did KGB espionage, although now the agency could offer only money to Western traitors instead of the old, almost entirely discredited idealism. Those four aspects of Soviet life illustrate convincingly, I think, that Cold War Russia, for all the weaknesses of its institutions and undemocratic ways, was a viable society during the Brezhnev years of 1966–82.

Gradually—of course many Russians felt much *too* gradually—more and more popular expectations were being satisfied. Opportunities to express individuality—as long as it wasn't seen as a threat to the regime—were also growing; no space program could be run without that, nor a successful sports program either. Society's burgeoning complexity was engendering increasing sophistication and subtlety, and although both were still very far behind the Western norm, that was not always painful.

Then what caused the Kremlin's red flags to be lowered in December 1991? One would like to think that it was an irresistible urge to be free, that Olga Korbut's cry in the "Red Files" documentary about sport—"I was in [a] big prison. You can't live without freedom!"—was true for the population as a whole. Alas, that was but a small part of the answer, no matter how important to her and other luminaries. The major part was less stirring: the drying up of the means to fund the KGB, the space probes, the athletic triumphs, and the propaganda extravaganza. As if to demonstrate Marxism's validity, the Communist regime collapsed because its economic foundation crumbled. The Kremlin had always chanted the Marxist dogma about the primacy of every society's economic substructure. Now it failed to recognize the irony that it doomed its own rule by working day and night to keep out the "bourgeois influences" that might have achieved enough reform to save it. Just like its massive spending on arms, its inordinate preoccupation with security hastened the collapse of the system it was intended to protect.

No major economy could survive in isolation from the global one's inventiveness and discipline. Given the number of Russian mouths to feed, niche merchandise like caviar and papier-mâché boxes couldn't do the trick. Without international stimulus, the Soviet economy remained woefully noncompetitive in most other areas, despite much excellence in pure science and in designing prototypes never put into fruitful production. It could not go on remorselessly milking natural resources, producing furiously but inefficiently, polluting heedlessly... and still not satisfying a people increasingly weary of sacrifices.

We've seen success as well as failure in the institutional doings of the people involved in sport, propaganda, espionage, and space exploration. But what was happening beneath the programs, as it were? The *bardak* ("unholy Russian mess") was swelling just when order—the creative, not the authoritarian variety—was needed to keep up with the non-Communist world.

Socialist waste was indescribable. Armies of part-time informants watched their neighbors and coworkers, although the decent souls among them tried to see nothing worth reporting. Various categories of cops—some five hundred thousand in the KGB alone, according to an estimate for "Red Files" by David Major, an American counterintelligence officer—watched the watchers. Bureaucratic infighting on a scale intolerable in open societies further bled the economy. The squander would have been staggering even without a payment system that rewarded quantity and weight rather than quality or appeal. One look at the mounds of raw materials rotting outside Soviet factories was enough to suggest the problem's scope. The horde of equipment rusting in the mud sometimes included precious Western machinery that had never been installed because plant managers benefited themselves more by preserving the swindles perfected for their current procedures. The anomalies were legion, starting with charging for commodities like natural gas by the month rather than the amount used. Therefore, lucky *dacha* owners—including, incidentally, Kim Philby and George Blake—kept their central heating at high when they left for Moscow after a weekend; that way, they'd be cozy warm the minute they returned on Friday. Such was the mad extravagance throughout the country—and the government didn't know how much it was paying for it because the real value of the economy's inputs, from kilowatt-hours to iron ore to chicken feed, were unknown and unconsidered.

The mess and disillusionment swelled as the global economy raced to stimulate and satisfy new needs, invent and produce new technologies, increase efficiency, beat the competition. While world market pressures were shaping sleek miniaturization, an insecure authoritarian state used obsolete goals and dictates to try to manage its nonmarket morass. Antiquated central planning desperately tried to keep feeding the elephantine (since I've already used "dinosaur" in this connection) ponderousness, but its extinction was inevitable.

Among the contributing factors, America's plan to build the "Star Wars" antimissile shield threatened the Politburo, already strained by its space and military allocations, with bankruptcy if it tried to match the effort. (President Reagan pitched the massive missile shield as purely defensive; First Secretary Gorbachev saw it as menacingly offensive.) The 1980s plunge in the price of oil, by far the country's largest earner of foreign currency, hurt even more. And the witless venture into Afghanistan weakened Soviet morale and state power more than our Vietnamese mistake weakened ours. Those superpower thrusts at foreign enemies were similar in that both diverted attention from domestic problems that posed a greater danger to national well-being. However, the sounder American society better withstood the damage.

Since the belief is widespread that what did the trick was President Reagan's Star Wars defense, it may bear repeating that the central Soviet drawback was isolation from the global economy's massive exchange of information, technology, incentive, insight, and creativity. As we've seen, the highest-priority projects such as space and military manufacture had long operated under special arrangements that avoided some of the ordinary economy's gigantic inefficiency. But now not even they could compete.

Might it have gone differently? Of course. Might the Soviets have woken up and *made* the global connection before it became too late? Maybe. Would the end result have been better for both East and West? Clearly, if only because it would take little to beat today's unhappiness and latent instability.

However impoverishing Soviet life was, many who lived it look back on the 1970s and 1980s as golden years. The current wretchedness is hard to credit unless you see it for yourself. The poverty! The despair and degradation! They are reflected by polls revealing that teenage Russian girls admire prostitution as a highly respected profession. If that misfortune seems of little interest to foreigners, remember the small army of Russian hookers now hawking themselves in Europe and the Middle East. Norway's sense of being invaded is another irony after it managed to maintain its border with the Soviet Union in relative civility throughout the Cold War. The menace of atomic weapons may fit the same pattern: the selling and smuggling of the extant seven thousand may pose a greater real danger than their use actually did under Soviet rule.

Such ironies riddle post-Communist Russia. Impotent resentment of their predicament has turned Russians' old, instinctive liking for Americans, despite the Soviet anticapitalist propaganda, to unprecedented anti-Americanism. Great numbers believe we're responsible for reducing them to their current condition; for robbing their dignity; for tricking them with *our* capitalism that milks *them*. (A substantial poll on the eve of the new millenium established that 41 percent of Russians believed the West—always led by the U.S.—was attempting to turn Russia into a Third World country, as opposed to less than 4 percent who believed the West was helping.) Can that view be taken seriously as more than evidence of their tendency to blame others for their troubles? Perhaps it can, since their current plight has left them liking themselves little more.

The scramble to survive, and in very rare cases succeed, has drained the camaraderie from the intimate evenings in the overcrowded kitchens and denuded the country of values. Success in their new, fractured society is thought to be attained by grabbing and deceiving—well practiced under Socialism, but now seen as capitalism's very canons of behavior. The warm feeling that juiced life despite everything—or because of everything—is giving way to a dog-eat-dog ethic, more cynical and crass than Western varieties, and with less interest in the common good.

That Russians are as likely as anyone else to prettify their past shouldn't keep us from reflecting about their pining for the supposed good old days. Communism could not survive. Foreigners may consider nostalgia for it as perverted nationalism, but great numbers of Russians themselves are convinced the rigid old society better served them, despite all its shortcomings. They have a point. For the vast majority, present life during the much-heralded, little-accomplished transition to democracy and a free-market economy is even *more* dismal. Our victory became their new misery, and they can see no end to it. Maybe the present chaos is good for foreigners who are seeking their fortune in the new "Wild East," but it's disastrous for the natives.

Was there a chance to avoid that? Were there any alternatives? A few years ago, Anatoli Dobrynin, the Soviet ambassador to Washington during twenty-five of the Cold War's forty-five years, regretted that his service had come during the time of Soviet-American hostility: "If only it had been possible then to build a sensible foundation of trust between our two nations, how much more could have been done and could still be done by both sides to bring our nations closer together." That noble wish is a little like one for Communism to have been born without its zeal to consign its opponents to history's dustbin. There were very good reasons for the lack of trust the good Dobrynin regrets, the first of which was the Russian revolutionaries' tunnel vision at the turn of the twentieth century.

They convinced themselves they'd attained the supreme wisdom, uncovered the answers to everything important, held the keys to human history and happiness. They founded their Party in provocative challenge not only to Western capitalism but also to the increasingly liberal democracy in which it functioned. They taunted and derided "bourgeois" governments from day one—and resumed quickly after World War II, when the Party official in charge of ideological affairs used the pages of *Pravda* to remind its readers, for the millionth time, that socialist society "is on a higher plane" than the bourgeois-democratic one, and that Soviet culture "is obviously superior" to the bourgeois variety. "Therefore it hardly needs saying that [we] have the right to teach others the new, universal morals."

It wasn't that the ideologues didn't know or care that their assumptions frightened the West; they positively delighted in that, because they knew what was good for everyone. "We'll do you a favor by helping tear down your rotten, doomed institutions."

That was in pursuit of the better world they'd taken upon themselves to design. Some of the seers were educated and humane. Many meant well. However, their understanding and reasoning—derived from a long line of Russian prophets who ordained "The Way" in virtually everything—were juvenile.

But lack of trust is necessarily two-sided. America shares some of the blame for its reaction—myopic in its own ways—to Moscow's arrogant bragging and threats. And that reaction too started from the first days of Soviet rule. Few Americans remember that our freedom-loving country joined the predominantly European intervention against the Bolsheviks in 1918, essentially in order to help the Whites rout the Reds. That was something Soviets never *forgot* because their schools, books, and media wouldn't let them. The intervention seemed to confirm Marxism-Leninism's catechism about capitalism's fundamental antagonism toward the Soviet republic. And although the American fumblings on Russian soil were actually half-hearted and feeble, Soviet propaganda made a field day of the "mortal threat to Socialism."

(The argument surprised me when I first heard it at the American National Exhibition in 1959. "What have you got to fear from us?" visitors asked. "After all, *we* never invaded *you*, did we? Like you invaded us!" It was hard to fashion an answer to that. "Well, look what you're doing *now* to Poland, Hungary, and Czechoslovakia!" didn't work. On the contrary, that only further persuaded most Russians of our deviousness and/or brainwashing, since they were convinced they weren't dominating but generously benefiting the eastern Europe they'd liberated from Nazi occupation.)

Our ill-considered, ill-fated intervention in 1918 was never what Soviet propaganda made of it. It had been provoked by the Bolshevik catcalls just mentioned, proclaiming the ideologues' ambitions for world Socialism. It was also a response to the strain of World War I, which the revolutionary new regime made harder for the other Allies by dropping out. Besides, all that was well in the past.

Alas, however, we continued losing opportunities to soften Soviet attitudes.

The best chances came during the regime's later decades, when those attitudes had begun easing by themselves. The difficulty was that our official and popular resolve had been formed during the early Cold War years, when Moscow made it very easy to be seen as an implacable, basically unreformable enemy. Within a year or two of the start of the Cold War, our leaders were telling us that Nazi Germany and Soviet Russia were essentially alike because they were both totalitarian. That largely accounted for the failure to react *enough* to the Soviet changes after Stalin's death, and especially after the 1960s, when it was palpably stupid, and damaging, to compare the USSR to the Third Reich.

We gave scant praise to commendable Soviet efforts to dismantle the dictatorship's worst features. We almost never publicly assured a traumatized people that we respected and admired them, let alone thought hard about what might have helped their society loosen further. What would that have cost? Why did our leaders avoid mention of the regime's positive aspects and our friendly intentions? Was the carrot forgotten because so much effort went into making our stick?

Yes, the Communist regime still made menacing noises and moves, but less of both as time went on. Nevertheless, our reactions, often formed by hit-'em-hard intelligence warriors rather than statesmen, came to resemble nothing as combative as the primitive Soviet ones. More might have been expected of a richer, stronger, luckier, far-better-protected people, of a country that was much more politically developed and much less ravaged by a difficult past. A less alarmed, longer-sighted view, a calmer reaction to challenge, and a greater commitment to encouraging further Soviet reform would surely have worked better. The Russian history I knew didn't support the model of an unchangeable totalitarianism adopted by many American political scientists and politicians.

DOES THAT MATTER NOW? MAYBE IT DOES, even knowing how easy it is to exaggerate our influence abroad—as the rueful Ambassador Dobrynin does, perhaps just because he spent so much time in Washington. Once the Soviet mess collapsed into the deeper post-Soviet one—with its orgy of grabbing and thieving that far surpasses the Communists'—neither Washington nor any other foreign capital could have provided truly significant help, apart from tiding-over loans during the transition period. (The sums involved represent less than a crumb of our old and even new military appropriations. On the other hand, much of the cash ends in the new robber barons' Swiss bank accounts.) But before that happened—that is, during the course of Soviet rule itself—there might have been better options than the one we chose.

American thoughts about the Soviet Union divided into two basic schools. The conservative conviction (more accurately, the belief of most conservatives) was that a totalitarian dictatorship could not evolve into something better because the top leaders' determination to cling to their power overrode their every other concern and consideration. Since evolution invariably wound its way toward greater freedom to think and act, it was a grave threat to the hierarchy of Marxist-Leninist overseers and medicine men, who responded by squelching all attempts at meaningful reform. The opposing view was that forward movement could indeed take place, even though the state apparats sometimes stopped it cold. Measuring the ground covered over the long haul, however, "stalled" was more accurate than "stopped." For although there were regular steps back toward greater repression, two shuffles more or less forward usually followed.

My own view was closer to the more optimistic one—but not always. The maddening, monumentally sloppy, deceitful, and sometimes brutal system that operated as if it had been programmed to ignore all reality periodically pushed me and my despair into the other camp. Still, the Soviet Union *was* evolving for the better, as measured by our standards as well as theirs.

You had to be blind not to see that, or else not know the troubles *before* (or so dislike the place at the time of your visit to not care what had been before). During the thirty-odd years of my own visits, the aggregate growth of openness, sophistication, knowledge of the outside world, availability of foreign news and materials, respect for differing opinions and willingness to compromise—in short, the maturing—was indisputable. Publishing something controversial still required pushing it past the various censorship obstacles with the "locomotive" of an introductory tribute to Lenin's inspiration; but those pages were growing more and more pro forma. Direct opposition to the system was still quashed, but increasingly substantive, even provocative, criticism was tolerated, some by economists and sociologists warning that Socialism actually *wasn't* going beautifully at all. The budding movement toward reality rarely included middle-class ambition for individual success, as opposed to desire for its rewards. But Kremlin leaders were actually visiting the West, and not even disguising their appreciation there—unlike the lucky mathematician who was permitted to attend a conference in Paris:

"How was it?" his friends press in to ask the upright man upon his return.

"It was just terrible!"

"You mean the homeless hordes?"

"No, everybody seemed to have these terrific apartments."

"The exploitation then? Seeing the workers mercilessly squeezed?"

"Actually, I didn't see any ravages of capitalism, and the food was indescribable—and also the fantastic streets. The Lido, wow! I never imagined such fabulous living."

"Then what was so terrible?"

"Of course it was *morally* terrible."

To appreciate that the maddeningly closed Soviet society was actually becoming more open, you had to remember how tight it had been before. The good things came in proportion to the subsiding of the ideological fervor and the loosening of the controls, however repulsive they seemed on any given visit. When the Kremlin zagged back toward harder lines and harsher retribution, I think I was as sad, and sometimes as frightened, as any foreigner. But those retreats were temporary. The overall trend toward European norms seemed to me undeniable. (One example: the reversal about Pavlik Morozov, the fourteen-year-old who was murdered after reporting his parents for helping feed banished farmers in 1932. That once-idolized act was publically recognized as a betrayal of the family foundation of all societies.) Anxiety about meeting foreigners didn't disappear, but the increasing numbers of tourists and businesspeople inescapably eased it.

This is not to say the trend would inevitably have led to the liberal democracy that most Americans assume to be the natural order of such things. However, formative factors in the *Russian* national consciousness, fundamental developments in *its* history, seemed to indicate that for all Russians'

difficulty in reaching that liberal democracy, the country was vaguely lurching toward that destination through all its wobbles and detours. Recognition
of that might have enabled us to pay less attention to its fist-shaking at real
and imagined enemies as it stumbled and staggered.

Tsarist Russia had long been disadvantaged because its upper layer of best-
educated, most promising people—mingled with, but not necessarily members of, the aristocracy—was very thin. The monarchy's collapse and ensuing
upheavals pruned that layer still more. Many of the enlightened and progressive West-looking thinkers and doers who survived the revolution of 1917 fled
during and just after it. More droves left during the civil war; still more were
silenced or eliminated during Stalin's purges. Then World War II ravaged the
educated together with the cannon fodder. (I forgot to mention how many
veterans among the scientists, technicians, and workers in the atomic and
space programs mourned slain friends and colleagues.) The combined losses
in the kinds of people needed to sustain a liberal democracy impoverished the
country as much as the huge material damage caused by natural and Soviet-
made disasters.

However, the number of replacements who filled the ranks of the depleted
intelligentsia was also remarkable, as I hope the story of the space program
has shown. Yes, most were young recruits to the new *Soviet* intelligentsia, politically educated not in the Western spirit (at its best) that no one view is
"correct" but in the homegrown conviction—well watered by the legacy of
Orthodox faith—that a single truth indeed explains all others, and Marxist-
Leninism had revealed all the important ones. But that was changing—again
slowly, often tortuously, but unmistakably. Scientists often led the way because the single-truth cast of mind impaired their work. The Soviet Union's
hordes of good scientists—more every year—had much to do with the greater
acceptance of complexity by society as a whole. No one who observed Russia
over the years could have much doubt about who was winning the internal
fight for the uses of the mind: the thinking people or the propaganda hacks.

By the 1960s, Sergei Korolev's patriotic personnel felt no commitment to
crude ideology or desire to convert the world. Predictably, there was more of
that among the propagandists and the KGB staff, and among sports leaders
too. But many of the latter were beginning to relax a bit as teams went abroad
more and more regularly. Even the humanities textbooks and lectures—not
to mention the media's popular renditions—were less likely to make you ill
than in the old days.

I hope I'm not overstating the improvement or minimizing the obstacles,
if for no other reason than respect for my memory of how the restrictions ap-

palled me. While the Politburo equivocated or thundered, millions of will-ingly benighted civil and military servants did its bidding, suffocating much of the land. Please don't believe there was any lack of ugliness among the Rus-sian people, or of louts who'd self-righteously squash you when not blubber-ing stinking-drunk love for you, their brother. They welcomed ideas grown on other than home soil as much as Bull Conner, Birmingham's notorious police chief, welcomed the civil rights demonstrations there.

More important, toleration among the equivalent of the middle class re-mained far too narrow. I could cite persuasive evidence that it might never widen to Western dimensions. I could argue—and have, elsewhere—that Russians would be an eon in attaining genuinely parliamentary freedoms be-cause they didn't *fight* for them like Westerners but merely accepted whatever little liberties were handed down from on high. But if what counts is which way a society is moving, Russian toleration and understanding of genuine democracy, as opposed to the regime's forked-tongue version, were clearly growing over the years. New communications technologies and the increas-ing numbers of travelers from both sides were piercing the isolation in which Russian despotism did its offensive things (starting well before the Soviet pe-riod). Openness and enlightenment were coming, as George Kennan, the State Department's wise Russia expert, had predicted.

IS THERE SUCH A THING AS A TAKEOFF POINT for liberal-democratic society? Must a critical mass of people with the necessary instincts and education be attained in order for it to work? I don't know—nor do I know when late Soviet society would have achieved that mass or reached the takeoff point, if ever. Still, since we know that evolution almost always benefits the majority more than se-verely radical change does, it's clear that progression into something freer and more wholesome would have been better than the collapse into the pres-ent near chaos and miserable despair. Better for us too.

But collapse was the American goal. It was an objective set with no real consideration of what might follow it. It was sustained by CIA reports that ig-nored signs of the Soviet system's coming apart at some of its seams.

For decades, defeating Communism—not helping it improve itself—was the lodestar of our national purpose (to the great detriment of our social needs, especially tackling our critical problems of race and the economic un-derclass). The goal wasn't simply containing Soviet expansionism, or what we took as such. Soon after that sound and necessary policy was in place, its ar-chitect, the same George Kennan, expressed dismay at what was accompany-ing it: a religiouslike crusade to destroy, fed by fear and contempt of the "evil" that was taken for the system's sum and substance. That probably prolonged the struggle by undermining the Soviet progressives, if that's what they should be called. We took too little account of the Soviet fear, and of the help our hard-liners gave to theirs.

The crusading mentality prompted a similar appeal from a once staunch anti-Communist warrior named John Kennedy, who helped make himself president with talk of an invented missile gap that was the opposite of the real one of huge American superiority. Once in the White House, Kennedy was severely tested by the building of the Berlin Wall, the possibly cataclysmic Cuban Missile Crisis, and other confrontations of Soviet fomenting. Still, he sought reexamination of our Cold War attitudes because they, over time, seemed to him as responsible as Soviet ones for the hostility. "Every thoughtful citizen who despairs of war and wishes to bring peace," he appealed five months before his assassination, "should begin by looking inward—by examining his own attitude toward the course of the Cold War." In the American attitudes, the president saw "ignorance too often abound[ing]" and truth "too rarely perceived."

That concept was a shock after seventeen years during which, as David Halberstam put it, "the American government had espoused the line that it was Soviet attitudes and only Soviet attitudes and actions which had brought on the Cold War, that the United States had been an innocent auxiliary to it all." Moreover, the attitudes Kennedy asked us to reexamine were formed in suspicion and loathing not just of Communism but also of Russians—whereas, the president's appeal continued, we and they had common interests despite the great differences between the two systems. And if those differences couldn't now be ended,

> at least we can help make the world safe for diversity. For in the final analysis, our most basic common link is that we all inhabit this small planet. We all breathe the same air. We all cherish our children's future. And we are all mortal.

The resort to such truisms from a man who ordinarily disdained them further signaled how thoroughly a war spirit had captured the national mind. The speech itself prompted new yelps. Large numbers of Americans weren't at all happy that the Commies breathed the same air as we did because the only good one was a dead one. They didn't *want* a world safe for diversity that included Communism. Anything less than a call to destroy it was "selling out" by "traitors." Therefore, invade and finish Communist Cuba. Impeach the chief justice of the Supreme Court, that "nest of Communists." Terminate recognition of the Soviet Union, ban Picasso's "Communist" art, prohibit foreign pinkos from entering the country, expose reformist legislation as a plot by the Communist brain trust, bare Dwight Eisenhower as an active agent of the Communist conspiracy, boycott the duped Kennedy.

Although some of those convictions came from fringe groups, the mainstream press was the chief booster of the fighting spirit. It constantly cast the Soviet Union as our immutable enemy in an irreconcilable struggle—which again reflected more a Marxist-Leninist view than the evolution-minded Western one. To pretend otherwise, raged Kennedy's critics, wasn't just wrong but also deceitful. It was perfidious to speak of Soviet losses in World War II, as the hoodwinked president had, when Moscow *now* tyrannized eastern Europe. It was soft-on-Communism drivel to praise people for cherishing children they were turning into state robots. It was blasphemous to pretend there were mutual interests, villainous to ask that Americans examine *their* attitudes, when the Soviet masses were submerged in foul lies about America. It was criminal to imagine that so-called historical vision suggested the present antagonism would ever be resolved.

No, their stark truth was that Communism was fundamentally incompatible with freedom and happiness. Preventing its unalterable drive for world domination was the most important task on earth. Or, as a biplane streamer would put it more succinctly in Houston, the day before the assassination, "Coexistence Is Surrender."

That's the way it was, although we tend to forget it just as Russians forget the dark sides of Soviet rule. Our thinking about Russia and its future came pretty much to *Rub Out Communism!*

DID MORE POTENTIALLY REFORMIST GORBACHEVS lurk in the Politburo we visualized as a block of oak? We became skilled at playing on differences between Russian and Chinese Communists, but gave less thought, as far as I'm aware, to attempting the same within the Soviet leadership. Not that success would have been anything like ensured; but it wasn't necessary to *reduce* its chances—to strengthen the die-hard Soviet reactionaries—in so much of what we said and did. One of the saddest incidents came when bubbly, blustery Nikita Khrushchev was in power. The prime mover of de-Stalinization may have been the last leader to truly believe in Socialism's preached advantages, a belief that opened him to reform precisely because he remained convinced the Soviet system would win in peaceful competition. And reform he did, his lurching from one experiment to the next having a liberalizing net effect. In those years of 1956–64, there may possibly have still been time, just barely, to save the Soviet economy by giving managers more scope for their own initiative and judgment—but that threat to central control angered the hard-liners. Still, the wily politician held to his generally progressive course until his opponents amassed enough power to oust him—with our help.

When Krushchev's 1960 summit with Dwight Eisenhower was impending, the president, although also no stranger to Communist harassment, believed peaceful progress was possible; therefore, he declined to authorize more flights over Soviet territory in the supposedly invulnerable U-2 spy plane. But Eisenhower gave in to a CIA that much preferred direct action to "softer" tactics. Angry as he was at the agency when the plane piloted by Francis Gary Powers was downed, he felt unable to give Khrushchev the apology for which the Soviet leader pleaded to help deflect his Politburo enemies' attacks on him for being soft on capitalism. Khrushchev then took another protective tack: he turned more hard-line himself. Those kinds of tactical blows caused more harm than good, and we were devoted to them.

What would follow Communism when we licked it? Well, that wasn't our business, was it? But since a healthy Europe depends on a healthy Russia, maybe it *is* our business to autopsy the old dictatorship that no longer need be feared.

Perhaps a new light cast by the recent massacres in Yugoslavia will show its post-Stalin years to have been *relatively* bearable. Surely that's true in contrast to the far greater current horrors for which Marxism-Leninism can't reasonably be blamed. Compared to them, the behavior of the late Soviet leaders might almost be called civilized. Although profoundly authoritarian, they very rarely resorted to barbarity, let alone the mass atrocities of Yugoslavia and our Latin American allies. For all their narrowness and resolve to maintain their power, the Soviet leaders were bullies, not monsters; hacks, not killers. Their Politburo meetings were less like war councils than gatherings of oligarchs nervously determined to keep down everything—including making controversial decisions of their own—that might disturb the corporate ladder they'd climbed. "The people put us in charge, get that? So don't rock *anything!*"

Of course, worldwide trends far beyond their control *did* rock them, upping their fear. To borrow a recent observation by Václav Havel, they substituted "megalomania, or self-regard, for a natural self-confidence." But although the country brimmed with unpleasant and even abhorrent features, the Soviet Union wasn't hell except to its scattering of Western-leaning dissidents—and to the Western public.

For we forgot, no less than the politically crude Soviets did, that conflicts in the past had also been seen as *the* test of civilization, and wrongly so. As a French philosopher put it in 1999, the French Revolution too was once considered "the turning point of world history, the culmination of all earlier struggles for human freedom and the messianic promise of a final emancipation to come." Now we embraced that huge hyperbole almost as tightly as the Communists did, and it helped us to demonize what we saw as the mother of historical enemies. During World War II, some effort had been made to humanize ally Uncle Joe, much as the advancing Nazi artillery had caused Stalin to relent a little about capitalism's wickedness. Throughout the Cold War, however, public officials and the media fashioned our conception of Soviet life by concentrating overwhelmingly on its repressive aspects. They said very little about the ambiguity, let alone about Russians' partial admiration for our system.

It's not clear whether that practice carries a lesson for our relationship with Slobodan Milosevic's Yugoslavia ("South Slavia"). However, the relevance to present-day Russia, where Communism's demise gladdens far fewer hearts than here, should be apparent. New jokes are being minted, some about the economic debacle.

"I'd like to open an account," says a man who enters the State Bank. "Who do I have to talk to?" "To a shrink," answers the clerk. But now ditties better express the popular mood:

> What embarrassment!
> Now all Europe knows we're simpletons.
> Because the ass we licked for generations
> Turned out to be the wrong one.

> We Russians have always had our own path,
> Which will take us to Happiness very soon.
> We'll pray and Merciful God
> Will find us the right one.

Maybe that cynicism can help outsiders appreciate the depth of liberated Russia's disgust and despair. The great majority's fact of facts is that their present life is worse than life under Communism: much poorer, less promising, more degrading, bereft of all ideals. Not even a broken dream now sustains a people whose need for one makes them susceptible to new, nationalistic demagoguery. Meanwhile, many seek solutions in self-deluding myths about a supposedly glorious Russian past.

That gives a good ring to Anatoli Dobrynin's "how much more . . . could still be done [now] by both sides to bring our nations closer together." However dreamy the ambassador's own view of the past may be, the present cries out for the kind of understanding that the Cold War served to preclude. Can we try again, now that there's nothing to fear from Communist deception?

A clearer view of Russian attitudes that preceded and now follow the seventy years of Communist rule would profit both peoples. As before, however, the major initiative must come from happier, less traumatized and isolated, more advanced and successful *us*—not in charity but in recognition of the fact that the growth of a maturing, liberalizing Russia that can respect itself is essential to the West's well-being. So far, contemporary Russia has found no such respect, only nationalistic snarls heightened by failure and humiliation.

This is not an appeal for revisionist judgment about responsibility for the Cold War. Too many Soviet tanks operating on too much foreign soil rules out a reassessment, as does too much oppression under their guns, especially in eastern Europe and the Baltic countries. Far and away the largest share of the blame for Russia's current misery must go to its own offensive behavior during those seventy hard years—including the suppression of the East German workers' protests in 1953 (although the initiative for that came chiefly from the local bosses, not Moscow), the crushing of the Hungarian rebellion in 1956, and the appalling "fraternal help" to Czechoslovakia that I witnessed in 1968. (It's a depressing sign that few Russians themselves are so far willing to accept that blame; that they express so little concern for the millions of victims of Soviet crimes and all the lesser mistakes that so dearly cost their socialist "brothers" together with themselves.) If Western fear was exaggerated because we failed to appreciate the extent to which the Kremlin operated on *its* fear, those bullies who knew no better than to bellow when they were scared did what they could to make themselves be seen in the worst light.

Despite our Cold War preoccupation, we better remembered our need to advance our social well-being than did those where virtually *everything* was considered for use as ammunition. Too much of Soviet society—permanently mobilized, stuck in its class-war ideology—was afflicted by a confrontational virus. (That too had Russian roots, expressed by *Kto kovo*, an old us-against-them saying dear to the Politburo warhorses: "Who'll get the better of whom?")

The West scarcely noticed the large Soviet step toward joining Europe taken by Mikhail Gorbachev when he finally renounced the class struggle and granted that we all live in one world with one truth and one aspiration, not the "diametrically opposed" bourgeois and socialist ones. Rejecting the old dogma that what's bad for capitalism is good for Socialism, the Soviet premier virtually stood Marxism on its head. But that reversal came in 1988, when it was too late. Until then, Soviet politicians could not, dared not, drop the rhetoric, empty as it had become. To quote Lenin again, almost a century earlier, when he was plotting his then seemingly impossible revolution, the proletariat had a "great historical mission." The "broad-shouldered" Russian working class would lead the way toward creating a social order "in which the exploitation of man by man will have no place." The exalted mission gave the nation the right to establish the famous "dictatorship of the proletariat"—which was actually a dictatorship of the Party in the name of the proletariat, and then of the Party bosses in the name of the Party. It also gave it the duty to criticize, challenge, and threaten the countries of despised capitalism—which it shrilly and relentlessly did.

Although few Soviet citizens now actually heard the hoary refrains, the combativeness in the national bloodstream impeded all kinds of progress. Having achieved stunning results of some kinds, especially in the 1930s and 1940s, the stoic Russian people long tolerated the strain, but it was eventually too great. Although they still believed Khrushchev's 1962 predication that Communism would bury capitalism (peacefully, his words suggested), rising expectations of *our* kind began shoveling soil on the coffin of hope.

I'VE ARGUED THAT THE CRITICAL TIME CAME when the economy that had shown much promise into the 1970s was unable to react to the challenges and opportunities of the postindustrial computer age. When worldwide communications and freedom to make quick individual decisions became decisive, capitalism began winning even more handily in the design and production of goods and services—and the same technological leap made information from around the world much more accessible to Russians. Soon they began suspecting they'd not only *never* "catch up and surpass" but only fall further behind. In most societies, public opinion is a key factor, even when not openly expressed. The momentum the Russians sensed—the backward slide—was as important as their competitors' actual positions at any given moment.

As in other countries, perceptions affected public morale more than facts. For example, food shortages were nothing new. Under Stalin, terrible famines, some manmade to force the peasants into collective farms, had stomped the land, but faith in Socialism endured nonetheless. Then why did the relatively mild shortages of the mid-1970s wreak so much damage on the national spirit, even though the government took measures to alleviate it? The answer lay less with the West's long-standing superiority in agriculture than with the Russians' new *recognition* of that superiority, a *perception* that the good cause was lost—because the information-technology revolution had made it impossible for the regime to keep the people so deeply in the dark. The great majority who once *did* believe their aspirations and life were the best in the world learned more daily about the fruits of incomparably more efficient, resourceful capitalism. The fables were wearing thin. Some were abandoned, as in the old effort to pass off Alexander Pushkin as a pre-Bolshevik revolutionary.

Ordinary Russians began admitting to themselves that Communism really *wasn't* going to be reached, not even by their grandchildren—a disappointment that the accumulation of jokes about it served to express more than to dismiss. In the broadest terms, what won in the long run was the Russians' acceptance of the superiority of Western society. Never mind that they saw that superiority in material terms—the production of alluring cars, clothes, computers, and the like—and didn't grasp the social, political, and economic arrangements that made it possible. (They still don't.) The main factors remained dwindling patience and their confrontation by evidence—no longer nearly so easy to suppress, as I said—that they'd never match the better, richer systems elsewhere. And although no polls were published about that, and no Politburo decision is known to have turned directly on public opinion, it underlay everything that led to the Soviet collapse.

That too might contain a lesson. Democracies challenged by dictatorships are very hard-pressed not to adopt the other side's dirty tricks.(While more and more ex-officers expose the KGB's criminal activities, declassified American documents reveal the extent to which the CIA engaged in some of the same crimes, down to ghoulish experiments with the brains of people it did not inform about what was happening to them.) But the more those democracies are able to hold to their own values, the better their chances of prevailing. A free society's methods are usually more effective—because more attractive—in the long run, no matter how tempting the adversary's repugnant ones can seem during the cold sweat of battle. So although many Russians had but the dimmest view of what accounted for American superiority, they did accept the fact itself—and *we* now know which factors made the critical contributions. Our superiority was diminished when we stopped playing our own game and switched to the Soviet one of one truth and one-track beat-the-enemy vision. Our fight for hearts and minds took uppercuts to the jaw when we conceived the invasion of Cuba's Bay of Pigs and our massively misplaced intervention in Vietnam, called "Godsends" to Soviet propaganda even by its haters.

Those assessments don't come entirely from hindsight's wisdom and safety. Thoughtful people, including the best Russian specialists, said the same things then, but were drowned out by the battle drums.

WAS IT ALL FOR NOTHING, THE WHOLE, HUGE Soviet "experiment?" I still wonder. Is Communism's only surviving component what it sought to destroy, as a distinguished French historian concluded in 1999? Will our grandchildren see *nothing* worthwhile in the Soviet legacy?

It's hard to predict what benefit Russians themselves might one day make of it. As for us, maybe the only value will be recognition that deeply troubled Russia will continue to be a difficult and possibly dangerous presence in the world. As Anatoly Kolessor, the high sports official who wrestled in the Olympics, told "Red Files" in another connection, "Talented people are always difficult, that's why they're talented."

That's reason enough to consider Russian attitudes, especially about national security. Soviet propaganda succeeded in portraying NATO as a dangerous threat because the depiction played on historic Russian anxiety about the West. Although many Americans saw NATO's recent inclusion of East European countries as no more than the iron curtain's final lifting, Russians feel the expansion of the Western military alliance smack to their borders not only betrayed earlier promises and defied geopolitical sense but also proved the West's anti-Russian bent. Western statesmen appear to believe that it's enough to deny that. But serious consideration of Russian sensibilities, especially their traditional insecurity, would have resulted in better ways to guarantee East Europe's independence, probably through bilateral treaties.

More and more, Russia feels America treats it like a defeated client state, dismissing its interests, ignoring its historical memory and its attitudes, assuring it that deeply felt concerns don't really matter, denouncing it for brutality in Chechnya, as if we did no such thing in Vietnam or Cambodia. Wrong about so much else, the resentful losers may be right about that. This inwardness is hardly unique to the American outlook, but the world's only remaining superpower would do better with a little less of it.

Although Russia inched westward before and after Soviet rule—even during some parts of that rule itself—it is still far from joining us. The East in Russia continues manifesting itself in the leading politicians' scant interest in building civil society. Boris Yeltsin, like his tsarist and Soviet predecessors, was insecure—"dreadfully" so, in the newest reading of a distinguished observer of Russian politics. In that and other respects, the present government, especially the secrecy in which it operates, bears strong similarities to the last Soviet ones. But our treatment of the profoundly troubled country can be more enlightened than it was during our Cold War crouch, when most of us assumed you could sum it all up by saying a hateful government was deceiving and dominating an essentially captive people. We can be better informed than when most of us took it on faith that a free-market economy, once established, would quickly deliver the country to health and prosperity—another resemblance to Marxist-Leninist thinking, in this case its opposite but similarly simplistic conviction that overthrowing capitalism was all the magic it would take to attain human happiness, to ascend to paradise. We now have an opportunity to contemplate what Russians really thought and wanted *then*, and to what degree it remains unchanged today. "If," wrote Barry Gewen recently, "we could snap our fingers and magically transform Russia into a country with a respected constitution of checks and balances, a stabilized and noncorrupt free market, a widespread regard for individual rights and an internalized ethos of tolerance, everyone—in the East and the West—would be better off. But the problem is how to get there from here."

Since that's been the problem for at least several centuries, the Cold War's end ought to encourage us to try again to imagine the perspective from over there—still *far* over in distance and thought. In the short run, Russia counts for less than they did under Communism. In the long, its importance in a shrinking world may be no less great.

Bibliography

Secret Victories of the KGB

For all the fascination of spy stories, their fact and fiction are difficult to separate. That is especially true about the torrent of information released after the end of the Cold War. One of the best non-fiction accounts of atomic espionage is *Bombshell: The Secret Story of America's Unknown Atomic Spy Conspiracy* by Joseph Albright and Marcia Kunstel (New York: Times Books, 1997). A somewhat outdated standard study of the earliest confirmed atomic spy, Robert C. Williams' *Klaus Fuchs, Atomic Spy* (Cambridge: Harvard University Press, 1988), still reads well. The FBI's Freedom of Information Act public documents website has recently posted some interesting documents about British citizens spying for the Soviets. See "Burgess, Maclean and Philby," at foia.fbi.gov/.

Norman Polmar and Thomas Allen, *The Encyclopedia of Espionage* (New York: Random House, 1998) is a handy guide for making one's way through the wilderness of mirrors. Another is: Harry T. Mahoney and Marjorie Locke Mahoney, *Biographic Dictionary of Espionage* (New York: Austin & Winfield, 1998). Still another good general resource is Jeffrey T. Richelson, *A Century of Spies: Intelligence in the Twentieth Century* (New York: Oxford University Press, 1995). A less-reliable defector's perspective, although filled with telling insights, is Oleg Gordievsky and Christopher Andrew, *KGB: The Inside Story of its Foreign Operations from Lenin to Gorbachev* (New York: HarperCollins, 1990). Those interested in the Anglo-American-Moscow connection will want to read Genrikh Borovik and Phillip Knightley, *The Philby Files: The Secret Life of Master Spy Kim Philby* (New York: Little, Brown and Company, 1994). Phillip Knightley is among the most careful and well-informed European writers about Soviet spying. His books on Kim Philby are notable, especially *The Master Spy: The Story of Kim Philby* (New York: Vintage Books, 1990). His earlier *The Second Oldest Profession: The Spy as Bureaucrat, Patriot, Fantasist, and Whore* (London: A. Deutsch, 1986) also holds up well.

British writers, predictably, continue to add to their vast literature about Philby's Cambridge circle of communists turned upper-crust spies. Important facts are put in perspective by a KGB officer turned democratic politician and business consultant: Oleg Kalugin with Fen Montaigne, *The First Directorate: My 32 Years in Intelligence and Espionage Against the West* (New York: St. Martin's Press, 1994). Pavel Sudaplatov and Anatoly Sudaplatov, *Special Tasks: The Mem-*

oirs of an Unwanted Witness: A Soviet Spymaster (Boston: Little, Brown, 1994), is a contentious work full of information as well as unsubstantiated accusations. Kim Philby himself published *My Silent War* (London: Granada, 1973), a classic ghosted Cold War spy memoir, billed by Graham Greene as "far more gripping than any novel of espionage I can remember."

Reliable histories of the secret police are: George Leggett, *The Cheka: Lenin's Political Police* (Oxford: Clarendon Press, 1981); Amy Knight, *The KGB: Police and Politics in the Soviet Union* (Boston: Unwin/Hyman, 1990); *Beria: Stalin's First Lieutenant* (Princeton: Princeton University Press, 1993); *Spies Without Cloaks: The KGB's Successors* (Princeton: Princeton University Press, 1998). Also useful is Robert Conquest, *Inside Stalin's Secret Police: NKVD Politics:1936–39* (Stanford: Hoover Institution Press, 1985). Contrarian views are assembled in a provocative volume, J. Arch Getty and Roberta T. Manning (eds), *Stalinist Terror: New Perspectives* (Cambridge: Cambridge University Press, 1993). A sometime breathless warning of evil runs through Herbert Romerstein and Stanislav Levchenko, *The KGB against the Main Enemy: How the Soviet Intelligence Service Operates against the United States* (Lexington: Lexington Books, 1989).

Robert C. Tucker's *Stalin as a Revolutionary 1879–1929: A Study in History and Personality* (New York: W.W. Norton, 1973) and *Stalin in Power: The Revolution from Above, 1928–1941* (New York: W.W. Norton, 1990) offer some of the best insights into Stalin. Stephen F. Cohen's *Bukharin and the Bolshevik Revolution: A Political Biography, 1888–1938* (New York: Alfred A. Knopf, 1973) is also very valuable, as is David Holloway's *Stalin and the Bomb: The Soviet Union and Atomic Energy 1939–1956* (New Haven: Yale University Press, 1994). Richard Rhodes' *The Making of the Atomic Bomb* (New York: Touchstone Books, 1995) is a kind of parallel account of the American effort.

As for general histories of Soviet and post-Soviet affairs, Ronald G. Suny's fine *The Soviet Experiment: Russia, The USSR and The Successor States* (New York: Oxford University Press, 1998) takes into account the most recent Western scholarship. Norman Naimark's *The Russians in Germany: A History of the Soviet Zone of Occupation, 1945–1949* (Cambridge: Harvard University Press, 1995) is a pioneering examination of the Soviet's role in a satellite state, including how the hunt for uranium shaped Soviet policy in prostrate Eastern Germany. A good general work on the relationship between science and Communist politics is Stephen Fortescue, *The Communist Party and Soviet Science* (London: Macmillian, 1987). Peter Kneen treats the same material in his *Soviet Scientists and the State* (Albany: State University of New York Press, 1984) and Paul Josephson, *Physics and Politics in Revolutionary Russia* (Berkeley: The University of California Press, 1991) throws strong light on the exceptional world of physics. Roald Z. Sagdeev's

The Making of a Soviet Scientist: My Adventures in Nuclear Fusion and Space from Stalin to Star Wars, edited by Susan Eisenhower (New York: John Wiley & Son, 1994), is a more personal account that includes telling observations about Igor Kurchatov, the man in scientific charge of espionage yields in the making of the Soviet bombs.

    Science in Russia and the Soviet Union: A Short History (New York: Cambridge University Press, 1993) is by Loren R. Graham, America's premier historian of Soviet science. His book about the impact of science and technology on Soviet society—*Science and the Soviet Social Order* (Cambridge: Harvard University Press, 1990)—is equally useful. Those interested in Marxism's influence on Soviet science will want to read Graham's *Science, Philosophy, and Human Behavior in the Soviet Union* (New York: Columbia University Press, 1987). Harley D. Balzer's *Soviet Science on the Edge of Reform* (Boulder, Colorado: Westview, 1989) concentrates on scientists' problems in recent decades. Balzer is working on a long-anticipated study of the history of engineers in Russian and Soviet society. Zhores Medvedev, the well-connected former dissident, wrote the interesting *Soviet Science* (New York: W.W. Norton, 1978); his twin brother Roy wrote one of the strongest books about the sins of Stalinism: *Let History Judge* (New York: Columbia University Press, 1989). The full body of literature about repression under Stalin is enormous. Other key works include: Robert Conquest, *The Great Terror: Stalin's Purges of the Thirties* (London: Penguin Books, 1968); Alexander I. Solzhenitsyn, *The Gulag Archipelago*, 3 vols. (New York: Harper & Row, 1974-78); Moshe Lewin, *The Making of the Soviet System: Essays in the Social History of Interwar Russia* (New York: Pantheon Books, 1994); and Moshe Lewin, *Russia/USSR/Russia: The Drive and Drift of a Superstate* (New York: The New Press, 1995). Recent Western revisionist views are well represented by J. Arch Getty, *The Origins of the Great Purges: The Soviet Communist Party Reconsidered, 1933–1938* (New York: Cambridge University Press, 1985). Although revisionists raise stimulating questions, the thrust of their writing can puzzle those who have lived in the Soviet Union. A more reliable work that traces the fate of some who survived the Gulag is Nancy Adler's *Victims of Soviet Terror: The Story of the Memorial Movement* (London: Praeger, 1993).

    Much new information about espionage is just now appearing. The Cold War International History Project (cwihp.si.edu/default.htm) presents cutting-edge research in a sober fashion. As its title indicates, people from throughout the world contribute. See, for example, "Stalin's Secret Order: Build the Bomb on a Russian Scale" at

    cwihp.si.edu/cwihplib.nsf/16c6b2fc83775317852564a400054b28/9357c372f
9a91723852564bf006b73eb?OpenDocument

and an important admonition about sifting the literature emerging from the former Soviet Union, Vladislav Zubok, "Atomic Espionage and Its Soviet Witnesses," cwihp.si.edu/cwihplib.nsf/16c6b2fc83775317852564a400054b28/de600620 6b9780c4852564bf006991ee?OpenDocument.

With Constantine Pleshakov, Zubok has written one of the more important books of the Glasnost Era, with vital new knowledge and thoughtful new perspectives: *Inside the Kremlin's Cold War: From Stalin to Khrushchev* (Cambridge: Harvard University Press, 1996).

The Venona Project provides rich primary source materials. Robert L. Benson, *Introductory History of Venona and Guide to the Translation* (Venona Historical Monograph #1) (Fort Meade: National Security Agency, July 1995); *The 1942–43 New York–Moscow KGB Messages* (Venona Historical Monograph #2) (Fort Meade: National Security Agency, October 1995); and Robert L. Benson and Michael Warner (eds), *Venona: Soviet Espionage and the American Response, 1939–1957* (Washington: National Security Agency and the Central Intelligence Agency, 1996). Digital reproductions of declassified Venona documents can be obtained on line at www.nsa.gov:8080/docs/venona/). But by John E. Hayne and Harvey Klehr, *Venona: Decoding Soviet Espionage in America* (New Haven: Yale University Press, 1999) reverberates with right-wing righteousness.

Some passions about Julius and Ethel Rosenberg remain heated. A discussion at www.theelectricchair.com/rosenbrg.htm conveys that and also the even greater heat generated by their execution. Since the new information from the archives and the memories of ex-NKVD, KGB agents such as Alexander Feklisov, who ran Julius Rosenberg, haven't yet been incorporated in books, the most useful starting point is

www.law.umkc.edu/faculty/projects/ftrials/rosenb/ROSENB.HTM.

Important earlier books about the Rosenberg case include: Michael Meeropool (ed.), *The Rosenberg Letters* (New York: Garland Publishing, 1994) and Alvin Goldstein, *The Unquiet Death of Julius and Ethel Rosenberg* (New York: Lawrence Hill, 1975). Louis Nizer, the prominent lawyer, wrote *The Conspiracy Implosion* (New York: Doubleday & Co., 1973). Oliver Pilat's *The Atom Spies* (New York: Putnam's, 1952) is an "instant history" time capsule. The standard indictment of the Rosenbergs remains Ronald Radosh and Joyce Milton, *The Rosenberg File* (New York: Holt, Rinehart, & Winston, 1983). The classic defense is Walter and Miriam Schneir, *Invitation to an Inquest* (New York: Pantheon Books, 1983). (They acknowledged their mistakes in "Cryptic Answers. The Case of Julius and Ethel Rosenberg," *The Nation*, August 14, 1995, p. 152.) A first-person account by the Rosenbergs's co-defendant, Morton Sobel's *On Doing Time* (New York: Scribner & Sons, 1974), is very emotional. The limits of FBI competency in controlling spies is evident in the "FBI Documents Regarding Julius and Ethel Rosenberg," foia.fbi.gov/.

Soviet Sports Wars

The outstanding book about Soviet sports is Robert Edelman's *Serious Fun: A History of Spectator Sports in the USSR* (New York: Oxford University Press, 1993). Edelman builds on some earlier works, including: Henry Morton, *Soviet Sports: Mirror of Soviet Society* (New York: Columbia University Press, 1963); James Riordan, *Sports in Soviet Society* (Cambridge: Cambridge University Press, 1977); James Riordan, *Soviet Sport Background to the Olympics* (New York: Washington Mews Books, 1980); and Victor Peppard and James Riordan, *Playing Politics: Soviet Sports Diplomacy to 1992* (London: JAI Press, 1993).

For more about the famous Spartak soccer team go to www.geocities.com/Colosseum/7326/index.html.

A more general site, www.football.ru/, is largely in Russian. Some basic information on Russian gymnastics can be found at:

www.geocities.com/Colosseum/1264/

and a site for promoting gymnastics in Russia and the Ukraine (www.olympic-eurogym.demon.nl/) also contains interesting current and background information. Information about daily sports matches can often be found in the sports section of www.russiatoday.com/ or through the guides on www.glasnet.ru.

Other popular works vary in quality. They include: Yuri Brokhin, *The Big Red Machine: The Rise and Fall of Soviet Olympic Champions* (New York: Random House, 1978); Victor and Jennifer Louis, *Sport in the Soviet Union* (New York: Pergamon Press, 1980); Baruch Hazan, *Olympic Sports and Propaganda Games: Moscow 1980* (New Brunswick: Transaction Books, 1982); Grigori Raiport with Monique Raphael High, *Red Gold: Peak Performance Techniques of Russian and East German Olympic Victors* (Los Angeles: J.P. Tarcher Inc., 1988); Simon Freeman and Roger Boyes, *Sport Behind the Iron Curtain* (New York: Lippincott & Crowell, 1980); and Yuri G. Khromov and Russell W. Ramsey, *Ten Soviet Sports Stars* (Boston: Branden, 1990).

Specialized works include: Lawrence Martin, *The Red Machine: The Soviet Quest to Dominate Canada's Game* (Toronto: Doubleday, 1990); Paavo Seppanen, *The Role of Sport in the Soviet Type Society* (Helsinki: University of Helsinki Department of Sociology, 1984); N. Norman Shneidman, *The Soviet Road to Olympus: Theory and Practice of Soviet Physiculture and Sport* (Toronto: Ontario

Institute for Studies in Education, 1978); David J. Foley and Bill Evans, *Physical Training of the Soviet Soldier* [Prepared for the Soviet/Warsaw Pact Division, Directorate for Foreign Intelligence] (Washington: Defense Intelligence Agency, 1978); Michael Yessis with Richard Trubo, *Secrets of Soviet Sports Fitness and Training* (New York: Arbor House, 1987); Norman MacLean and Barry Wilner with Earl Hoener, *Soviet Sports Exercise Program: The Gold Medal Guide to Physical Fitness* (New York: Drake Publishers, 1977); and Olga Korbut with Ellen Emerson-White, *My Story: The Autobiography of Olga Korbut* (London: Century Publishers, 1992). Information from a local-level women's sports club in the Russian city of Barnaul can be found at tbs.dcn-asu.ru/commu/.

Handy guides to the Olympics include: *Chronicle of the Olympics, 1896–2000* (New York: DK Publishers, 1998); David Wallechinsky, *The Complete Book of the Olympics* (London: Aurum Press, 1996); David C. Young, *The Modern Olympics: A Struggle for Revival* (Baltimore: John Hopkins University Press, 1996); and Bob Fulton, *The Summer Olympics: A Treasury of Legend and Lore* (South Bend, Indiana: Diamond Communications, 1996).

Secret Soviet Moon Mission

The best book in English about the space race is William E. Burrows' *This New Ocean: The Story of the First Space Age* (New York: Random House, 1998). Well-written, judicious, and balanced, it is a model of science writing.

Bill Keller's "Eclipsed," in *The New York Times Magazine* of June 27, 1999, is a recent provocative interpretation of the failures of the Korolev and Soviet systems, emphasizing the irony of Soviets behaving more like their capitalist competitors and Americans following something in the pattern of a centrally planned economy approach to reaching the moon.

The Encyclopedia of Astronautica (solar.rtd.utk.edu/~mwade/) is an extremely useful online resource, complete with an excellent index, timeline, and hard-to-find in English technical drawings.

James Harford's *Korolev: How One Man Masterminded the Soviet Drive to Beat America to the Moon* (New York: John Wiley & Sons, 1997) provides the fruits of long, dogged research. Iu.P. Semenov's *S.P. Korolev Space Corporation Energia* (Moscow: RKK, 1994) is a bi-lingual history of the design and production bureau begun by Korolev, with unique photographs.

James E. Oberg is the dean of American experts on Soviet space efforts. His early book are very good, his latter ones take advantage of the opening of Soviet secrets during the late *glasnost* [candor, openness] era. See his *Red Star in Orbit: The Inside Story of Soviet Failures and Triumphs in Space* (New York: Random House, 1981), and *Uncovering Soviet Disasters: Exploring the Limits of Glasnost* (New York: Random House, 1988).

Although dated, Leonid Vladimirov's *The Russian Space Bluff: Inside the Soviet Drive to the Moon* (New York: Dial Press, 1973) is an interesting account by a Russian. Walter A. McDougall's *The Heavens and the Earth: A Political History of the Space Age* (New York: Basic Books, 1985) is better on the American side than the Soviet. A good counterbalance is a crisply written account by journalist Nicholas Daniloff, *The Kremlin and the Cosmos* (New York: Alfred A. Knopf, 1972). A more stilted one is Evgeny Riabchikov's *Russians in Space* (Garden City, NY: Doubleday, 1971). Both Phillip Clark's *The Soviet Manned Spaced Program* (New York: Orion Books, 1988) and Brian Harvey's *Race into Space: The Soviet Space Program* (New York: John Wiley & Sons, 1988) provide good summaries of salient events. John Rhea's (ed.) *Roads to Space: An Oral History of the Soviet Space Program* (Aviation Week Group, 1995) is strongest on post-Korolev developments. Nicholas Johnson published a handy annual volume entitled *The Soviet Year in Space* during the 1980s. His *Handbook of Soviet Lunar and Planetary Exploration* (San Diego: American Astronomical Society, 1979) is limited but interesting.

The Space Program of the Soviet Union site (www.cs.umd.edu/~dekhtyar/space/) provides some good basic information and basic links. A new Russian site, www.space.hobby.ru, provides an examination of contemporary issues which can help in understanding the Soviet era. And Sven's Space Place in neutral Sweden (www.users.wineasy.se/svengrahn/) is free of all residue of the old East-West rivalry.

On the impact of Sputnik, the papers presented at a conference dedicated to its 40th anniversary are available at www.hq.nasa.gov/office/pao/History/sputnik/. The more synthesized Robert A. Devine, *The Sputnik Challenge* (New York: Oxford University Press, 1993) is also useful. Two good insiders' views on Sputnik's impact on the upper reaches of the U.S. Government are: James Killian, Jr., *Sputnik, Scientists, and Eisenhower* (Cambridge: MIT Press, 1982); and George B. Kistiakowsky, *A Scientist at the White House* (Cambridge: Harvard University Press, 1976). Rip Bulkeley's *The Sputnik Crisis and Early United States Space Policy* (Bloomington: Indiana University Press, 1991) offers a more specific perspective. And the shock waves Sputnik generated can be felt at:

www.nytimes.com/partners/aol/special/sputnik/main.html.

The above-mentioned Vladislav Zubok and Constantine Pleshakov's *Inside the Kremlin's Cold War: From Stalin to Khrushchev* (Cambridge: Harvard University Press, 1996) helps readers peer over the Kremlin walls. Nikita

Khrushchev's *Khrushchev Remembers: The Last Testament,* (New York: Little, Brown and Company, 1974) touches on Korolev in true course of its self-justifying, always fascinating bombast. To see the Kremlin from above and to get a picture of the capabilities of spy satellites, visit the National Security Archives at www.seas.gwu.edu/nsarchive/NSAEBB/NSAEBB13/index.html.

Frank H. Winter's *Prelude to the Space Age: The Rocket Societies, 1924–1940* (Washington, D.C.: Smithsonian Institution Press, 1983) is a good account of the early days of rocket building and dreaming. Richard Stites' *Revolutionary Dreams: Utopian Vision and Experimental Life in the Russian Revolution* (New York: Oxford University Press, 1989) makes exciting reading of Russia's revolutionary visions, including science fiction and utopian writing about flying and space.

A very uncritical English biography of Tsiolkovsky appeared just before Sputnik compelled the West to recognize Russian space expertise: A.A. Kosmodemianskii, *Konstantin Tsiolkovsky, His Life and Works* (Moscow: Foreign Language Publishing House, 1956). Growing interest in him prompted NASA to translate his works: B.N. Iur'ev and A.A. Blagonravov (eds.), *The Collected Works of K.E. Tsiolkovskiy* (Washington, D.C.: NASA, 1965) TT F–236, 237, 238.

Soviet Propaganda Machine

The history of Soviet propaganda is intimately tied to the history of its communist party. The best overview is in the superior general history of Soviet and post-Soviet Russia mentioned above, Ronald G. Suny's *The Soviet Experiment: Russia, The USSR and The Successor States* (New York: Oxford University Press, 1998). Martin E. Malia's *The Soviet Tragedy: A History of Socialism in Russia* (New York: Free Press, 1994) is less fair-minded, grinding its ideological axe hard. A worthy survey that pays special attention to propaganda issues is Peter Kenez, *A History of the Soviet Union from the Beginning to the End* (New York: Cambridge University Press, 1999). Kenez also wrote one of the most insightful books on the mass cultural education mission rooted in the Bolsheviks' ideological outlook: *The Birth of the Propaganda State: Soviet Methods of Mass Mobilization* (Cambridge: Cambridge University Press, 1985). Victoria E. Bonnell's *The Iconography of Power: Soviet Political Posters under Lenin and Stalin* (Berkeley: University of California Press, 1997) thoughtfully tackles the thorny problem of Bolshevik visual culture.

For many years, the standard history of the CPSU was Leonard B. Schapiro's *The Communist Party of the Soviet Union* (New York: Random House, 1971).

Revelations from the Kremlin archives have dated this book, but many still base their understanding on its conclusions. As for the experience of the general population, Sheila Fitzpatrick's recent *Everyday Stalinism: Ordinary Life in Extraordinary Times: Soviet Russia in the 1930s* (New York: Oxford University Press, 1999) is especially valuable and insightful. Fitzpatrick began writing (under the above-mentioned Schapiro and E. H. Carr, a pioneer of Soviet history) about culture-making in the early Soviet period, a subject closely linked to propagandizing. Her *The Commissariat of Enlightenment: Soviet Organization of Education and the Arts Under Lunacharsky, October 1917–1921* (Cambridge: Cambridge University Press, 1970) remains a good source for tracing the complex strands of early Bolshevik policy, and her essays, collected in *The Cultural Front: Power and Culture in Revolutionary Russia* (Ithaca: Cornell University Press, 1992), are interesting and provocative.

Although there are not many web-related materials about Soviet propaganda, a collection of political posters can be viewed on: www.ruhr-uni-bochum.de/lirsk/plakate.htm. A thoughtful guide to Stalinist poster art and political art is www.stanford.edu/~gfreidin/courses/147/propart/propart.htm. A general resource on political agitation can be found at: www.mcad.edu/classrooms/POLITPROP/politprop.html.

James von Geldern and Richard Stites (eds.), *Mass Culture in Soviet Russia* (Bloomington: Indiana University Press, 1995) is an important examination multiple strands in Soviet society and Soviet history. The collection, with material often difficult for non-Russian readers to find, provides good insight into Soviet attitudes and culture. It builds on Richard Stites' important *Revolutionary Dreams: Utopian Vision and Experimental Life in the Russian Revolution* (New York: Oxford University Press, 1989).

David King's exciting *The Commissar Vanishes: The Falsification of Photographs and Art in Stalin's Russia* (New York: Metropolitan Books, Henry Holt and Company, 1997) shows how Stalinist values distorted realities. A good introduction to generally underappreciated Soviet photography is Margarita Tupitsyn's *The Soviet Photograph 1924–1937* (New Haven: Yale University Press, 1996). For more on photography look at the ROCK project links at www.abamedia.com/rao.

Visual culture was very closely related to Soviet propaganda, especially during the first twenty-five years of Soviet rule when millions were largely illiterate. A good starting point together with the fine Bonnell book cited in the first paragraph of this section, above, is Stephen White's *The Bolshevik Poster* (New Haven: Yale University Press, 1988). His *Political Culture and Soviet Politics* (New York: St. Martin's Press, 1979) also remains important reading. Igor Golomstock's *Totalitarian Art in the Soviet Union, the Third Reich, Fascist Italy and the People's*

Republic of China (New York, 1990) makes intriguing comparisons. Another insightful book is Boris Groys' *The Total Art of Stalinism: Avant-Garde Aesthetics Dictatorship, and Beyond* (Princeton: Princeton University Press, 1992). Many museum exhibits were accompanied by excellent catalogues. Even the non-English language volumes, such as studies of the Moscow-Paris and Moscow-Berlin connections, are valuable for their visual materials, and the most handy collection is *The Great Utopia: The Russian and Soviet Avant-Garde, 1915–1932* (New York: Abrams, 1992).

Thomas F. Remington's *The Authority of Truth: Ideology and Communication in the Soviet Union* (Pittsburgh: Pittsburgh University Press, 1988) is a reliable political science study of the late Soviet propaganda apparatus. More readable and helpful for understanding Soviet citizens is Angus Roxburgh's *Pravda: Inside the Soviet News Machine* (New York: 1987). Some may find Vladimir Pozner's self-serving autobiography, *Parting with Illusions* (New York: Atlantic Monthly Press, 1988), a useful, if tangled, mirror of propaganda realities. Although dated, Martin Ebon's *The Soviet Propaganda Machine* (New York: McGraw-Hill, 1987) offers some insights.

Some may draw insight from Scott Shane's *Dismantling Utopia: How Information Ended the Soviet Union* (New York: Ivan R. Dee, 1994); Jack Matlock's *Autopsy of an Empire* (New York: Random House, 1995); and Archie Brown's *The Gorbachev Factor* (New York: Oxford University Press, 1996).

Much writing about the techniques of Soviet propaganda is outdated and extremely tendentious, since the writers were driven by obvious political agendas. Their books are now most useful as examples of Cold War culture, left and right. See, for example: Marian Leighton, *Soviet Propaganda as a Foreign Policy Tool* (New York: Freedom House, 1991); Lyman B. Kirpatrick, Jr. and Howland H. Sargeant, *Soviet Political Warfare Techniques; Espionage and Propaganda in the 1970s* (New York: National Strategy Information Center, 1972); Suzanne Labin, *The Techniques of Soviet Propaganda*, A Study presented by the Subcommittee to Investigate the Administration of the Internal Security Act. 90th Congress, 1st Session (Washington, D.C.: U.S. Government Printing Office, 1967); Jack Rosenblatt, *Soviet Propaganda and the Physician's Peace Movement* (Toronto: Mackenzie Institution, 1988); Clive Rose, *The Soviet Propaganda Network* (New York: St.Martin's Press, 1988); and Ladislav Bittman, *The New Image Maker: Soviet Propaganda and Disinformation Under Gorbachev* (Boston: Boston University Program on Disinformation, 1987).

Index

Acknowledgments

The television series "Red Files"—an international collaboration of scholars, film and visual researchers, Abamedia and its Archive Media Project (www.abamedia.com), producer/director William Cran's InVision Productions, PBS, and Devillier Donegan Enterprises—cast light into four corners of Soviet life. East-West cooperation now enables audiences everywhere to see long-hidden images and explanations. In particular, the Archive Media Project (AMP), a collaborative venture of Abamedia, Russian partners, and The Russian State Film and Photo Archive at Krasnogorsk (RGAKFD), is contributing to post–Cold War insight. AMP was created to help preserve the archive's unique media collections, make it systematically accessible by digitizing its catalog, and produce television documentaries, films, and new media forms that will use the rich holdings. Many of the visual images discovered for *Red Files*, both the television documentaries and the "Red Files" website (www.pbs.org/redfiles), were not previously available to the public of any country. Jonathan Sanders and Barbara Keys provided research assistance for both text and photos.

Photo Credits

The pictures in this book were provided courtesy of the following:

The Russian State Film and Photo Archive at Krasnogorsk (RGAKFD): 1, 2, 3, 4, 5, 15, 16, 17, 18, 19, 21, 22, 23, 24, 25, 26, 27, 29, 31, 32, 33, 34, 35, 36, 37, 38, 39, 46, 47, 58, 60, 61, 62, 63, 64, 65, 69, 71, 74, 75, 76, 77, 78, 79, 80, 81, 82, 83, 84, 85, 86, 87, 88, 89, 90, 91, 92, 93.

Russian State Archive of Scientific and Technical Documents: 52, 57, 59, 66, 67, 68, 70, 72, 73.

Igor Prelin: 6, 7.

PIX Features: 8, 9.

National Security Agency: 11.

Los Alamos National Laboratory: 13, 14.

Igor Ter-Ovanessian: 28.

Olga Korbut: 30.

Anatoly Firsov: 45.

N. Koroleva: 49, 50, 51, 53, 54, 55, 56.

William Cran: 10, 12, 20.

Anatoly Bochinane: 40, 41, 42, 43, 44.

Boris Smirnov: 48.

About the Author

George Feifer's first trip to Russia was in 1959, when he was a guide at the ground-breaking American Exhibition there. He was an exchange student at Moscow State University during 1961, after which he often visited as a journalist. His last look was in 1999, when he observed the December parliamentary elections for the Office of Security and Cooperation in Europe.

His previous books about the country are:

Justice in Moscow, 1964

Message from Moscow, 1969

The Girl from Petrovka, 1971 (the basis of the film starring Anthony Hopkins and Godly Hon)

Solzhenitzyn, 1972

Our Motherland, 1973

Moscow Farewell, 1976

To Dance (with Valery Panov), 1978

His translation of *The White Steamship,* a novel by Chingiz Aitmatov, appeared in 1976, and he has written scores of major articles about the country for, among other publications, *Harpers,* the *New Republic,* the *Saturday Review,* the *Reader's Digest,* the *New York Times Magazine,* the *Boston Globe,* the *Nation,* the *Saturday Evening Post*—and, in England, *The Times,* the *Daily Telegraph,* the *Sunday Times,* the *Sunday Times Magazine,* the *Sunday Telegraph,* the *Guardian,* and the *Observer Magazine.*